James Shepard Dennis

Foreign Missions after a Century

James Shepard Dennis

Foreign Missions after a Century

ISBN/EAN: 9783743334571

Manufactured in Europe, USA, Canada, Australia, Japa

Cover: Foto ©ninafisch / pixelio.de

Manufactured and distributed by brebook publishing software (www.brebook.com)

James Shepard Dennis

Foreign Missions after a Century

PREFACE.

These lectures were delivered in the spring of 1893, before the faculty and students of Princeton Theological Seminary, on the basis of the newly established Students' Lectureship on Missions, being the first course delivered on that foundation. The second lecture has been extended to double its original length, in order to give a fuller survey of the world's Macedonian appeal than was possible within the usual limits of a single lecture. Otherwise the course is printed substantially as prepared for delivery, except that some passages here and there which were omitted for the sake of brevity have been retained, and some later facts of interest have been inserted.

The establishment of lectureships on missions in our prominent theological seminaries is timely and in touch with the leadings of the Spirit of

God in our day. They serve a useful purpose in imparting fresh information and quickening an intelligent interest in a subject which stands easily at the present hour in the front rank of hopeful Christian effort. No student of the kingdom, no servant of Christ and His Church should fail to give serious and sympathetic attention to the marvelous development of missions as manifestly one of the foremost movements of Providence in the religious history of our century.

J. S. D.

NORFOLK, CONN., August, 1893.

TABLE OF CONTENTS.

LECTURE I.

                                                                                                  PAGE

THE PRESENT-DAY MESSAGE OF FOREIGN MISSIONS TO THE CHURCH 9

    Introductory survey of the general theme of the course—The inductive method applied to Foreign Missions—The range and limits of discussion indicated—Foreign Missions personified and their message voiced—Some reasons why this message should be received with special honor: (1) It speaks to us of world-wide reformation; (2) It voices to us a thought of God; (3) It teaches anew the great lesson of the universal meaning of redemption; (4) It announces God's purpose to train His Church for wider service and larger usefulness in the world—The message of Foreign Missions a clear and direct call of Providence to the Church—The message analyzed: (1) It summons the Church to contend for the spiritual dominion of the world; (2) It brings us tidings of abounding opportunity; (3) It is a personal, confidential revelation of special privilege; (4) It presses upon us the claims of duty; (5) It sounds a ringing note of encouragement—Foreign Missions vindicated by history, supported by a divine purpose, and indorsed by a divine blessing.

LECTURE II.

THE PRESENT-DAY MEANING OF THE MACEDONIAN VISION 53

    The Macedonian Vision a typical incident—It has its present-day counterpart in the claims of Foreign Missions

—The Macedonian Vision of to-day a vivid and picturesque reality—The verisimilitude of some of the Macedonian calls of the hour—A Macedonian Telegram from Japan—A Winged Message from Korea—A Weighty Call from China—An Appeal from the Waiting Isles—Other messages from Siam, Burma, India, Africa, the Turkish Empire, Persia, South America, Central America, and Mexico—The Macedonian Vision expanded and glorified—Its special urgency at the present time—The present condition of the heathen world would call for the sacrifice of Christ had it never been made—The Church has the privilege of coöperating with God in a service which is worth the sacrifice of the Son of God.

LECTURE III.

THE PRESENT-DAY CONFLICTS OF THE FOREIGN FIELD 149

Conflicts inevitable in aggressive efforts at reform—The conflicts of Foreign Missions: (1) With a self-centered Christianity in the Church at home; (2) With rival and intrusive missions; (3) With misrepresentations on the part of those who, through ignorance or prejudice, bear false testimony against the cause; (4) With dangerous climates and unhealthy environments; (5) With the political and commercial ambitions of European governments, and with vice and greed as exhibited in the lives of unworthy representatives of Western Civilization in foreign lands; (6) With the opposition of heathen governments and ecclesiastical hierarchies; (7) With the aroused and quickened antagonism of devout and loyal adherents of opposing religions; (8) With the prejudices, superstitions, jealousies, traditions, and conscientious convictions of the native mind; (9) With the Prince of Darkness and his immemorial ally, the fallen nature of man—These conflicts have a useful mission in the religious history of the world.

LECTURE IV.

THE PRESENT-DAY PROBLEMS OF THEORY AND METHOD IN MISSIONS 195

Problems distinguished from conflicts—God trains His Church in the school of problems—Some present problems of the foreign missionary enterprise: (1) The problem of theory—a true theory of missions involves correct ideas as to the motive, the object, the necessity, and the results of missions; (2) The problem of finance; (3) The problem of coöperation; (4) The problem of method; (5) The problem of native development.

LECTURE V.

THE PRESENT-DAY CONTROVERSIES OF CHRISTIANITY WITH OPPOSING RELIGIONS 243

Christianity the mother of Controversy—Religion and its mission in the world—The genesis of false religions—They are the corruptions and perversions of a primitive revelation, mingled with a large increment of rationalistic speculation and degrading superstition—Their practice always worse than their theory—Christianity as a missionary religion enters a preoccupied realm—It addresses itself, as Paul did among the Athenians, to a "very religious" as well as a very sinful people—The religious state of the heathen world—The struggle of the human mind to formulate and put into practice a saving religion has been sadly and completely in vain—The unconscious call of the heathen world to Christianity for light—The sublime message of Christianity to heathenism—The serious aspects of the controversies of Christianity with ethnic religions—The message of Christianity compared with the teachings of the prominent religions of the East—The difficulties which environ Christianity in her entrance among heathen religions—There is no cause for discouragement

—The triumph of Christianity assured—Another "fullness of time" is hastening on—The message of Christianity analyzed in its adaptation to the needs of the heathen world—Christianity enters the Eastern world after the failure of the ethnic religions has been fully demonstrated—Christianity has already rallied to her support a multitude of living witnesses among heathen nations—The beauty, sublimity, and worth of our simple Gospel.

LECTURE VI.

The Present-Day Summary of Success............ 295

What is meant by success in the mission enterprise—A true estimate of missionary success must take cognizance of many things besides mere visible results—A review of the successes of the century: (1) Success as indicated by the manifest tokens of God's favor, and the signs of His providential coöperation for the advancement of missions—He has opened the world to the entrance of the missionary—The era of colonization—Modern facilities—The coöperation of modern scholarship—The removal of hindrances; (2) Success as indicated in the rapid multiplication of missionary agencies; (3) The success implied in the establishment of the mission plant in foreign lands—evangelistic, educational, literary, medical, industrial; (4) The success involved in the introduction of the Gospel leaven throughout the heathen world; (5) The success implied in the growing coöperation of native agencies, and the development of spontaneity in the mission churches; (6) The success as revealed in actual conversions that have resulted from missionary work—Rapid transformations and large percentage of growth in missions—The indirect results of mission progress—The Church's heritage in the past century of missions.

LECTURE I.

PRESENT-DAY MESSAGE OF FOREIGN MISSIONS TO THE CHURCH.

"*No Church can live on its past; it must live by faith and duty in the present; no Church has any claim to be whose only right is historical. The only claim is present truth and life, love and service, making the Church a temple of the living God, a body for the living Spirit of Christ. Churches, then, everywhere live under the judicial and by the evangelical law. This makes it necessary that no Church or body of Churches lose for one moment their evangelical zeal. The Churches are bound to be vehicles of the grace of God, living centers of evangelical energy and force, changing ever the secret life that is in them into the lives that are to be, penetrating the present, preparing the future, being in all their parts as bodies of the living God.*"—DR. A. M. FAIRBAIRN.

"*The signs of the times, the lessons of the past, the indications of the future, the call of Providence, and the voices which come borne to us by every breeze, and from every nation under heaven, all alike bid us lay our plans upon a scale worthy of men who expect to conquer a world.*"—BISHOP J. M. THOBURN.

I.

THE PRESENT-DAY MESSAGE OF FOREIGN MISSIONS TO THE CHURCH.

I AM grateful for the privilege and deeply sensible of the honor of addressing this audience upon a theme so important, so timely, so vital to the highest interests of the Church, so worthy of the attention of theological students, and so charged with the freshest energies and the largest hopes of modern Christianity. It has given an added interest and incitement to the pleasant task of preparing these lectures, that I have been invited to meet you as the " Students' Lecturer on Missions."

Were a veritable prophet of God commissioned in our day to deliver a divine message to the Church, I think the " burden " of missions would occupy a prominent place, if not the leading one, in his discourse. I am not a prophet, nor the son of a prophet, but, alas! I have a prophet's theme, and I can only pray that God will give me His special help, and give to you a large measure of kindly charity, while I invite your attention to what might be called a Columbian Brief on Foreign Missions. Since this is a year of exhibits in connection with the World's Exposition, I might give a graphic touch to my theme by calling it A Centennial Exhibit of Mission Progress. I am afraid, however, that the fragmentary and painfully inadequate make-up of the exhibit would fail to justify the title, and so I am inclined to announce it as simply "Foreign Missions after a Century."

As we review the past history of the Church, we can find many unmistakable signs of God's presence and power, but I am sure that present history is also full of God, and, if I mistake not, this missionary movement of the Church is as much a divine inspiration as any great event in sacred records. Let us try to realize this, and it will make us stronger and braver for the special work which God will give us to do in this our day of unparalleled opportunity and promise.

Your kind invitation to lecture upon the subject of Foreign Missions led me to ask myself this question: "If you were yourself a student in a theological seminary, and a lecturer on missions should present himself, what would be the aspect of the theme which you would particularly desire him to bring before you? What would you like to hear about? What would you especially welcome in the line of information, or instruction, or practical contribution to your working capital as a minister?" The answer came almost instinctively to my mind, and gave instant shape to the subject as I now propose to bring it before you. I replied to my own question that I should like to know about the present status of Foreign Missions; I should like to have a realistic picture of the actual state of things in our foreign fields; I should like to know the true inwardness and the unclothed outwardness of the whole subject; I should like to feel, after I had heard such a course of lectures, that I had been to the front and knew from personal observation the top and bottom facts of the whole situation.

If we wished to know something about Westminster Abbey, or St. Peter's at Rome, we could adopt no plan which would result in such satisfactory knowledge and give us such clarified and vivified impressions, as that of an actual visit and a personal inspection. I invite you, therefore, in these lectures to accompany me upon a voyage of discovery, a tour of personal observation, to those regions of thought and service and practical experience which are occupied by this great enterprise. I would like to organize an exploring expedition into those realms of Christian labor and conflict and heroism which have come into view during our present century, like one of those vast continental upheavals in old geological times, when out of the mists and vapors and submerging waters a new world was slowly lifted into sight. This whole continent of modern missionary effort invites to exploration. If I mistake not, it is veritably a new realm, of continental proportions, which has come to stay, and is to be the scene of the noblest triumphs and the most convincing vindication of historic Christianity.

Our plan, then, is the application of the inductive method to this subject of Foreign Missions. Induction may be broadly defined as entering in, finding out, and giving a report. Deduction may be described as accepting premises and assuming that certain facts follow. The result of the former is a systematic statement of facts and the truths indicated by these facts; it is a simple statement of the case. The result of the latter is a theoretical generalization of inferences, involving supposed laws and causes; it is a statement of what lies back of visible facts. It is difficult to base an appeal upon theory; we must bring forward facts, and state actual conditions. The theory that there was a famine in Russia would never have sent ships of food there, but the fact was all-persuasive; the actual condition of starvation was irresistible. In connection with the ministry of Philip, the multitude gave heed when they " heard and saw the signs which he did"; so facts are the " signs " to which men will " give heed " in the consideration of the subject now before us. I shall endeavor to be brief, and must often be abrupt. I shall have no time for Gothic architecture in words, or for landscape gardening in rhetoric. I must generally take the short cut, and I cannot avoid the sharp angles. My object will be to give as full a treatment to the theme as limits of time and space allow, and my effort will be to give information in a condensed form, which it is to be hoped that you yourselves will elaborate in future study and treatment of this theme.

I have divided the course into six lectures, the subjects of which will be presented in succession, as follows:

1. The Present-Day Message of Foreign Missions to the Church.

2. The Present-Day Meaning of the Macedonian Vision.

3. The Present-Day Conflicts of the Foreign Field.

4. The Present-Day Problems of Theory and Method in Missions.

5. The Present-Day Controversies of Christianity with Opposing Religions.

6. The Present-Day Summary of Success.

It will be seen at once that my plan is panoramic, but that there are many important aspects and discussions of the subject which are ruled out of court at once, and however interesting and pertinent they might be in some other scheme of treatment, yet here they would only embarrass and encumber us. I must, for example, leave out of our view any extended consideration of the proper basis of foreign missionary service, its scriptural warrant, its inspiring motives, and its high obligations. I must give scant attention to its history, its heroes, and the magnificent story of its early toils and sacrifices. I must omit any elaborate discussion of the theory or philosophy of missions, and all attempts at any exhaustive treatment of the peculiarities of the great non-Christian religions of the world, or the social and moral condition of the countries outside of Christendom and the characteristics of the peoples inhabiting them. I must forego all mention of the direct and indirect benefits that have come to the world through missions, of their discoveries and achievements in adding to the sum of human knowledge. We must move swiftly through present scenes, and only glance hastily into these vistas of delightful research that radiate in different directions from our present standpoint.

The subject of my lecture to-day is The Present-Day Message of Foreign Missions to the Church. If we should personify the cause of Foreign Missions, and give it a message to the Church of Christ at the present hour, what would be the spirit and the tenor of that communication? Let me bespeak, however, in advance, a special welcome for the message it would bring, for several reasons, of which I will name four:

1. It is a message which presents to us the inspiring conception of a world-wide reformation; or perhaps regeneration is the more proper term to use. We have had local reformations in religious history; we had them in Hebrew history, before the coming of Christ. The result of early Christian labors was the conversion of the Roman Empire, and in the sixteenth century came the great historic Reformation of Europe. Now, for the first time in the history of our earth, this great movement in the direction of regeneration or reformation is beginning to shape itself into a world-wide enterprise. If the Reformation of the sixteenth century, which was, strictly speaking, only European in its influence, has broadened and deepened into such glorious streams of Christian progress, may we not expect that a reformation so extended as that contemplated in modern missions will produce world-wide fruit, especially since it has all the advantages afforded by modern inventions, and facilities, and methods of communication, and international relations, and the almost magical expedients for disseminating knowledge?

2. It is a message which speaks to us of the realization of God's own thoughts; it suggests to us the practical evolution of divine ideals. The special thought or purpose of God concerning any age of the world is the peculiar glory of that age; it differentiates it forever from every other; it is the "white stone" with a new name written upon it, which God alone knows, which He gives to that special generation in the world's history. We have illustrations of this all through history; it will be sufficient for my purpose to call your attention to that "white stone" which God gave to that age which was forever immortalized as the Era of the Incarnation, and upon which was written, in God's own hand, the words "fullness of time," and to remind you that the "white stone" of this age of Christian history seems to bear upon its face the legend of "world-wide missions."

3. It is a message which must be interpreted as a significant and impressive evidence of a new effort on the part of the Spirit of God to introduce into the religious experience of God's people a recognition of the universal meaning of redemption. There has appeared with unusual vividness

at intervals in the history of revelation what might be called a world-embracing consciousness in the experience of prophets and teachers who have spoken for God, and there has been manifest at times in God's messages to His Church an unmistakable purpose to develop in the spiritual experience of His people a sense of the universal meaning of His redemptive purpose. This religious world-consciousness is one of the higher moods of feeling in the Word of God, and in the Christian experience of the Church; it is a sign in our day of the ripening plans of God; it is a later and fuller unfolding in the realm of practical experience of the deep meaning of many of the Old Testament prophecies and of the New Testament teachings. Among the prophets of the Old Testament the most conspicuous exponent of this world-consciousness was Isaiah; his prophecies throb with universal terms. When Christ came He brought into divine revelation and into human history the fullest expression of the all-embracing purpose of God which the world has received. His personality became for all time the radiating center not only of universal truth but of universal love and world-embracing purpose. This noble conception has been sadly forgotten and ignored as centuries have passed. The world-consciousness seemed to die out in the experience of the Church, and it is only in our present century that it is reviving, in connection with the missionary enterprise of our age. It is a consciousness which has been identified with all the great movements of history in different spheres of activity. Great military leaders have aspired for more worlds to conquer; Mohammed seems to have been a man of world-wide aspirations; Rome had her dreams of universal sway; the thought which was embodied in the scheme of the Holy Roman Empire reached out after world-wide dominion. Our Lord Christ has given this thought to His Church in some of the most memorable sentences that fell from His lips: "Go ye into all the world, and preach the Gospel to every creature" is a text which reaches out into all time and all space, and there is no true exegesis of that verse except the world-wide missionary interpretation of it. It voices the eternal, ever-vivid world-consciousness of Christ; it is addressed to the corresponding capacity for largeness of vision in the Church, and this message of Foreign Missions to the Church of to-day is the latest and clearest and sweetest echo of Christ's voice which the history of Christianity gives us.

4. It is a message which indicates God's purpose to lead His Church to a higher stage of spiritual training and discipline in these latter days. The Church seems to have had special experiences of training at various stages of her history. In the early centuries she walked through fires of persecution. She has had special periods of intellectual and spiritual schooling in the great doctrinal controversies of history. Now it would seem that God is leading her into a realm of practical training and discipline in the school of unselfish love and loyal service. "Go work to-day in my vineyard" is the lesson of the age. He is opening up to her unprecedented opportunities for doing her work in the world in a spirit of practical philanthropy, and is making it possible for her to win the world by love. It is a school of training in the higher and finer and more Christlike graces of Christianity. It will bring her into sympathy with Christ in the breadth and depth of His love, in His willingness to serve without reward, and His readiness to die in sacrifice for

those who are separated from Him in a sense which no material measurements can indicate. God would seem to be alluring the Church to an experience of service in imitation of her divine Master, which will surely lead the world to take knowledge of her that she has been with Jesus. She is thus to fill up "that which is lacking of the afflictions of Christ" and so to hasten His triumphs, which are to come in the extension of His kingdom among the Gentiles. Let us be sure that He means to speak comfortably to her, and give her the tokens of His gracious favor, as never before, if she responds loyally to His leadings.

If this message of Foreign Missions is the exponent of the spirit of religious reformation in a world-wide sense; if it marks a distinct and significant advance in the evolution of redemptive purpose; if it is the sign of the Spirit speaking once more in the ears of the Church in the terms of those grand universal conceptions, which have been ever the finest and most sublime strains of prophetic song; if it indicates an effort on God's part to bring the Church into a sweeter and higher realm of spiritual training, where her discipline will be in an atmosphere of love and have to do with the deeper things of faith—then let us humbly pray that God would give us ears to hear "what the Spirit saith to the Churches."

Every age has its message to the world, and every generation has its call of Providence to the Church. In the days of John the Baptist came a message from God to the Church of that generation, and there was no mistaking its significance: "Prepare ye the way of the Lord; make His paths straight." The Church has heard these voices in every age, and there is one which at the present hour seems to come to her out of the wilderness of the heathen world, and it is the same startling and impressive call which John brought to the Church of his age from the wilderness of Judea: "Prepare ye the way of the Lord; make His paths straight." The Church is accustomed to take counsel and gather inspiration, courage, and cheer directly from her divine Lord and Redeemer, but she can also find much to arouse and direct her energies in the special message of the age in which she lives. One hundred years ago, and there was no call of Providence throughout this vast continent, summoning the Church to activity and service, if we except the special needs of that line of original settlements, not very old, extending along our eastern seaboard. There was a stillness like the silence of our primeval forests brooding over all the continent. Now, the voice of Providence sounds throughout a vast and populous nation, from the entering in of dawn upon our eastern borders, gathering might and volume as it advances, until it passes out of the golden gates of sunset upon our western shores. One hundred years ago, and so far as any general recognition of the need was concerned, or any apparent consciousness of the call, there was a silence like that of the grave resting like a pall over all the heathen world—a silence which, though eloquent as death, utterly failed to touch the sympathies or move the conscience of Christendom. To-day the whole world is ringing with voices "like the sound of many waters," calling the Church to an aggressive campaign of world-wide activity, and eventually of universal conquest and peaceful occupation.

I would like to speak to you in some detail of this Present-Day Message of Foreign Missions to the Church of Christ; I would like to attempt to give you in brief outline what seems to me some of the significant points of this wilderness call to the Church of our day; I would like to attempt, perhaps in a very fragmentary and imperfect way, to interpret this voice of Providence, which comes to us at the present hour so grandly enforced by our foreign missionary enterprise.

The first point to which I would call your attention in this message is that it is a summons to the Church to engage in a contest for the spiritual championship of the world. Now, we have no difficulty in understanding the significance and importance of a game for the championship in connection with any of our popular athletic sports. Any schoolboy can tell us why a game for the championship will arouse more interest and call forth more enthusiasm than any ordinary contest, and yet when we speak of a contest for the spiritual championship of the round earth, there are many who fail to catch the inspiration of the idea; it is altogether too unreal and too tame to touch the heart and stir the pulse. And yet, do we realize how thoroughly the Church of Christ is now committed to this struggle for the championship, and what importance and significance attaches to it? This conflict of the Church with her spiritual foes is rapidly assuming a world-wide magnitude. It is rapidly assuming the proportions of a final struggle for universal dominion. The Church must never fail, or even falter; she must gird herself for the final struggle, and, with God's help, she must and will win. Should she fail to do this, it would surely be the result only of carelessness or indifference or sloth on her part, and in that case we can hardly estimate what an immense loss of her prestige there would be, and what painful dishonor would come to the name of Christ. Every sceptic would see additional reason to doubt; every infidel would find another occasion to scoff; and do we realize how difficult it would be should the Church of Christ sound a retreat, or even proclaim a truce in this great conflict of missions, to convince the world that Christianity is not simply one of the various human religions which has now in its turn had its day, and failed in accomplishing the purpose for which it was professedly established? On the other hand, let us note well that the success of the missionary enterprise will be in itself the invincible apologetic argument of our age. This will be the weapon which can so easily subdue and silence scepticism. It will be the sign of the presence and activity of a supernatural force which Heaven vouchsafes in these latter days of Gospel conflict. There is no mightier antidote to infidelity than reality. The manifest power of the Gospel in its missionary triumphs will vindicate Christianity before the eyes of a wondering world. It will be the nearest possible counterpart of the revealed personality of Christ Himself, before which scepticism can never hold its ground.

The second point to which I would call your attention in this Present-Day Message of Foreign Missions to the Church is its inspiring tidings of abounding opportunity. Never in the history of the Christian Church has she received such impressive and wonderful tidings of brilliant opportunity as come to her to-day from all our foreign mission fields. When in the history of the Church has it been so easy to send our missionaries to the ends of the earth, and extend to them adequate protection and support and sympathy, as at the present hour? All the facilities of modern methods of travel, of postal arrangements, of international comity, of financial exchange, and of telegraphic communication are in the interest of foreign mission work. By means of the telegraph our government is enabled to extend its protection to missionary citizens living in distant lands. And when at any previous time in the history of the world has there been such an organized effort on the part of missionary societies and boards to attend properly to the vast and complicated details of the practical business of missions? The facilities of our age in this line of things are simply wonderful. An ordinary contribution-box has become an instrument by which the contributor as he sits in his pew can touch every continent, and do a work for Christ where his own footsteps can never tread. It is just as easy now to do missionary work in degraded Asia, or in darkest Africa, as it was a few years ago in the western regions of our own country.

And then what tidings come to us of beckoning opportunities in the foreign field which are at the same time so alluring and so burdensome to the missionaries! It is difficult for the Christian public at home to understand or appreciate the needs and emergencies of these distant fields. A few months ago and we all read in the papers of a terrible earthquake in Japan, in which 7000 human beings were reported killed and 10,000 wounded, and 80,000 houses destroyed, and yet it was all so vague, so unreal, so far away, that I will venture to say that not one of us lost a wink of sleep at night on that account. And it is just so with these tidings of the needs and emergencies and pressing opportunities which come to us from our foreign missionary fields: they are all so unreal, so vague, so apparently far away, that we fail to catch their significance; and yet the opportunities are there just the same, and they are such as any military commander would be cashiered for neglecting if he dared to ignore them in the midst of a military campaign. The Church needs a new, a larger outlook of faith; she needs more seeing of the unseen in the sphere of that kingdom which "cometh not with observation." There are traces of an invisible presence among the nations; we see in the unequaled opportunities which greet us on every hand, the evidences of a transcendent purpose moving rapidly toward its goal. Bishop Thoburn of India said, in a recent address, that since he went to the foreign field, the door of access, which had been heretofore closed, has been thrown open to more than 700,000,000 of the human race.

This message of unparalleled opportunity is in itself a call for generous support and enlarged activity on the part of the Church. Has God ever called so impressively for the facilities and the men needed to do His work? Has He ever summoned more directly, will He ever command more solemnly, the consecrated energies of His people in whole-hearted dedication to His service?

We are tempted sometimes to wish that God would perform miracles in the interest of His Church and for the progress of His kingdom, as He did in Old Testament times for His chosen people, the Jews; and yet it seems to me that here is what might be regarded as almost a miracle in our day, and one which will compare with some of the most conspicuous examples of the Old Testament. We read of how Moses stretched out his rod across the sea and made a pathway upon dry land for the hosts of Israel out of Egypt, and how Miriam, with her timbrel and other instruments of music, sang her song of triumph after the Israelites had safely marched across their pathway through the waters. Think now of that surging sea of prejudice and ignorance and heathen hostility and obstinate exclusiveness which separated, only a few years ago, the Church of Christ from the inaccessible heathen world; and now look to-day, and see the missionary hosts of the Church marching dry-shod into the very heart of heathendom. Is not this worthy of being called a miracle, or at least a special intervention of Providence in the interests of the advancement of the divine kingdom?

Then, again, we read in the Old Testament of how Elijah went to the top of Carmel and prayed for rain, and how God sent a little cloud, about the size of a man's hand, in the heavens, to indicate the coming of abundance of rain. And so within our memory the Elijahs of our Church have gone to their Mount Carmel of prayer, and prayed for access to the whole earth and for a blessing upon the heathen world, and to-day the Church has entered almost every foreign field, and we can hear the pattering of those great drops of divine grace which foretell the coming abundance of blessing, when God's time shall have fully come. Is not this also, if we have eyes to see, if not indeed a miracle, at least a special intervention of Providence, and a manifest answer to prayer?

A third point of singular beauty and winsomeness in the Present-Day Message of Foreign Missions to the Church is the new, fresh, almost confidential revelation of privilege it brings to us. Our Lord has never, at least for centuries, spoken to any generation of the Church in such terms of providential entreaty and with such a spirit of personal confidence concerning the privileges of His service. From all the foreign mission fields the Church has this same inspiring message of privilege. It is as if Christ sat down with His Church to tell her in the freedom of a personal interview what she can, if she will, do for Him at once. The word "privilege," if we consider its derivation, from *privus*, separate, and *lex*, law, means a separate law enacted for the advantage of some individual or community, and in common usage it has come to have a signification indicating some special benefit or favor or advantage belonging to kings and queens and ambassadors and princes, which separates them from other people. Now it seems to me that in just this meaning of the term missionary work is a privilege; it is a separate law enacted by the great Author of all law, for the benefit and advantage of Christ's followers, and gives them a position of privilege in the world which separates them from all others. It makes them kings and queens and princes and ambassadors in the royal realm of Christian service. All merely earthly distinctions, honors, and privileges will some day fade away, and perhaps be altogether forgotten, but this privilege of missionary service, if humbly received and rightly used, will shine as the stars for ever and ever.

May we not interpret the missionary providences of our day, and the present marvelous story of an opening world, as the voice of Christ speaking to His bride concerning His own personal desires, and indicating to her a noble service which she might well feel to be a privilege to do for Him with promptness and alacrity?

Now notice how this privilege of missions will bear analyzing in our day. Here is the Bible translated fully into 90 languages of the earth and partially into 230, making in all 320 languages through which enough Gospel truth is revealed to guide the soul to Christ. There are 280 missionary societies organized for work; there are 9000 missionaries in the fields; there are 44,532 native assistants associated with them; almost a round million of converts have been gathered into the Church; and there are fully 4,000,000 adherents, under the influence, directly and indirectly, of missionary instruction. There are 70,000 pupils gathered in higher educational institutions, and 608,000 children are gathered in village missionary schools. The Gospel leaven has penetrated every land; Christian instruction is disseminated in almost all the languages of the earth; medical missions with healing touch are allied with evangelistic agencies on every field. There are many and varied facilities waiting to do our bidding all throughout the earth.

Does this seem to you rather a cold and perfunctory way of looking at this matter of missionary privilege? Then let us see if we cannot look at it in a more practical way, and get, as it were, an inside view of what it means. Come with me across the seas to some of our foreign mission stations, and let us call at the home of some native convert, and try through a personal interview with him to learn more of what the privilege of missionary work really means. We will select some elderly, dignified, keen, intelligent, observant native gentleman of Japan, or China, or India, or Syria, and enter his home to have a friendly chat with him, and ask him what he has to say from his own experience, and out of his own memory, which runs back perhaps for fifty years, of the results of missionary work in his native country. He will tell you that blessings and benefits have come to his people, within his own memory, through the foreign missionary work, which were never dreamed of before. Ply him with questions: ask him who gave him his Bible; go to his library, and ask him whence he received his Christian literature; see who is the editor of his religious newspaper; ask him who established schools and trained his school-teachers and prepared his school-books. Ask him who established churches and trained his native pastors, and whence came those revivals of religion which we read of in these distant lands, those strange and marvelous exhibitions of the power of God's Spirit to win souls to the kingdom of Christ out of the surrounding darkness, and he will tell you that they had not so much as heard that there was a Holy Ghost until your missionaries came there, and God poured a blessing upon their labors, and these "dry bones lived." Ask him about Young Men's Christian Associations, and Young People's Societies of Christian Endeavor, and Missionary Societies in the native churches; ask him about Sabbath-schools, and International Lesson Papers, and Sabbath-school Libraries, and those songs set to music so familiar to you; ask him about Christian homes with their family altars and their prayerful training of the children; ask him about the new views of the position and dignity of woman in the home and in society; ask him about these changes so full of light and hope and inspiration and joy to so many around him, and whence came these new and bright experiences. A few years ago, and this native convert, and all around him, were living in the environment of about the tenth century of the Christian era, in the intellectual and spiritual ignorance of the Dark Ages. Whence came this great light so suddenly in his day? He will tell you that the missionaries you have sent there have been the apostles of light and knowledge and the messengers of Gospel instruction to his people. Ask him, if you will, about more secular matters: about changes in the government methods; about the adoption of modern facilities and the introduction of the economics of modern civilization; of the administration of law, and the expansion of commerce, and the education of the young. Ask him, as you could do, especially in such a land as Japan, about liberty, justice, and freedom of conscience; about cabinets and parliaments, and a whole list of brilliant changes in the interests of modern civilization; and if he tells you the real, though often unrecognized, secret of these latter days, he will say that the men and the women who have had more to do, humanly speaking, than all others, with this breaking of the day in those eastern lands, are the humble missionaries whom you have sent there with the key of knowledge in their hands, the love of Christ in their hearts, the message of the Gospel upon their lips, and the destiny of souls in their keeping. I am reminded of those lines of James Russell Lowell:

"O Truth! O Freedom! how are ye still born
 In the rude stable, in the manger nurst!
What humble hands unbar those gates of morn
 Through which the splendors of the New Day burst!"

Is it not a privilege to have a share in a work like this?—so far-reaching and so helpful in its influence to these degraded nations, and so full of hope and promise to these misguided souls.

A fourth point in the subject-matter of this message of Foreign Missions to the Church brings to our attention the claims of duty. Duty is always a vigorous and forcible word, and in this connection it burns and throbs with a living energy. It has the power of divine love and the weight of divine authority in it. It is a word after Christ's own heart, and He has spoken it out of the depths of His incarnate nature. He means it for our own sake, as well as for the good of the world. There are many who are inclined to doubt whether there is any obligation resting upon the Church of Christ to publish the Gospel to all nations. We cannot stop to discuss this question. If the command of Christ, so manifest and so explicit, does not make it clear to the mind of the Christian believer, then I despair of producing conviction by any arguments that may be brought forward. I can conceive of a profound and elaborate appeal carefully drawn up in behalf of Foreign Missions, based upon considerations of expediency, or upon the claims of humanity and universal brotherhood, or the duty of helpful service to others in a spirit of benevolence and philanthropic generosity, and I can conceive of that argument having due weight with cultured and sympathetic and unselfish natures; but I would not trust it to carry the day, even with the Church of Christ, if we did not have His own express commands and His glowing promises to glorify and enforce this duty. This we have, so that not only the claim of brotherhood, and the obligation of stewardship, and the debt of Christian love, all conspire to urge the Church to this world-wide ministry, but Christ's own command still holds its supreme place among His last words, and still exercises its powerful influence over the Christian heart. What the Church of Christ needs at the present hour is a higher and a tenderer consciousness of her duty to the unenlightened and the perishing. The great need of the Church is not a new theology, nor new ecclesiastical machinery, nor the advanced and revolutionary theories of the higher critics; nor even, in my judgment, is the present highest need of the Church a revision of the Confession of Faith, although I think that is a very proper thing to do, simply in the interests of a clearer and fuller expression of acknowledged truth, and for the removal of certain apparent infelicities of language from that venerable document. I am inclined to question very much also—perhaps I am mistaken—whether the Church is in very serious need just now of the ecclesiastical miseries and the doubtful advantages of trials for heresy, even though they may seem to many to be both justifiable and necessary. But, dear friends, what the Church of Christ does need is the blessing of an enlarged heart; a deeper, truer, tenderer yearning for the good of men; a more earnest and unselfish devotion to the Master's service; a more winsome sympathy with those who suffer; and a more self-denying readiness to help others to a better life.

The great problem of the Old Testament dispensation was to save the Church from formalism, and to train her in spirituality of life and worship. The great problem of the New Testament dispensation is to train the Church in Christian living, in Christlike ministry, and in consecrated service for the good of the world.

The fifth, and this is the last special feature of this Message of Foreign Missions to which I shall call your attention, is its ringing note of encouragement. I doubt if there is any department of Christian activity where the inspiration of encouragement is so full of glow and magnetism as is this message from the foreign fields. What blessed cheer there is in the record of missionary progress during this past century! As we survey it, we seem to be walking rather by sight than by faith. It has in it more of solid hope for the world, and more of tangible contact with the promises of God, than anything else in human history. I shall have occasion later on to refer to this aspect of our subject more in detail, but at present I must take it for granted that you are already familiar with the magnificent achievement of Foreign Missions during the past fifty years, and I will confine my remarks at the present time to some encouragements which are connected with the results of the past year or two in our mission fields.

We are fully justified in estimating that there were slightly over 100,000 conversions in the foreign mission fields of all evangelical Churches during the year 1892. This, you will notice, is an average of fully 2000 per week. Think of it, my friends! As you gathered together in the House of God from Sabbath to Sabbath during the past year, to render your thanks to your Heavenly Father for His blessings and His bounties and His benefits to you and yours, you might have added another note of thanksgiving for more than 2000 souls; a number that would pack our largest churches to their very doors, gathering together every Sabbath day of the year, literally out of every tribe and tongue and people and nation, to sit down together for the first time to partake of the communion of the Lord's Supper; and I will venture to say that you would be perfectly safe in thanking God for the same magnificent result for every Sabbath of this present year. And now let us look at some of the results reported for the year 1891 in mission fields connected with our own Presbyterian Board of Foreign Missions.

In the Tripoli field of our Syria Mission there

were 68 admitted to the Church during the year. Now in this Tripoli field there are, all told, men, women, and children, about 1000 Protestant souls. They began the year with 329 communicants, and they closed with 397. I have searched through the contemporary published records of the Presbyterian Church in the United States, and I can find only 14 churches corresponding in size to the church of the Tripoli field that have received to the communion more than 68 during the year.

In the Presbytery of Shantung, in northern China, in 1891 there were admitted to the Church 760 communicants. Now, I have taken the trouble to compare with this result the record of all the presbyteries of the United States for the corresponding year, and I find only 9 presbyteries in the country that report an addition of over 760 to the communion. They are the great Presbyteries of New York, Newark, Philadelphia and Philadelphia Central (since united into one), Lackawanna, Pittsburg, Steubenville, Cincinnati, and Chicago. Why, these are the very centers of Presbyterian influence and wealth and power in all our land; and the full force of this comparison does not appear until we note that in these

American presbyteries there is an average of 80 ministers to each presbytery—and such ministers, and such congregations!—while in the Presbytery of Shantung there are only 28 ministers, and 6 of these are Chinamen. This is an average of 27 additions to each minister.

Then there is that little Presbytery of Laos, away off in the depths of Asiatic heathenism, to the north of Siam, with its 6 churches, which in 1891 admitted to the communion 241 communicants, and in 1892 the number of churches was increased to 8, and the additions were 299. Five years ago there were 4 churches, 10 elders, and 241 members in the presbytery; now there are 8 churches, 26 elders, and 1376 members. In the first year of the past six there were 110 additions to the Church; in the second year, 129; in the third, 180; in the fourth, 190; in the fifth, 241; and in the sixth, 299. This, you will notice, is more than 40 members added to each church in 1891, and 37 in 1892, and this makes that humble foreign mission Presbytery of Laos the banner presbytery of the whole Presbyterian Church, since there is no presbytery upon record that gives an average of 40 additions to each church. In that picked nine of all our American presbyteries, the average is 14 to each minister. It is stated in the "Narrative of the State of Religion," presented to the Synod of New Jersey in the year 1892, that "in the percentage of additions upon profession of faith, the Presbytery of Corisco [connected with that synod] forges to the front. The Presbytery of Newark reports that the average accession to its churches is 22, while in the entire Synod besides it is 12, and in the Church at large only 8; but in the Presbytery of Corisco the additions average 29."

In the "Report on Foreign Missions," presented to the same Synod, occurs the following passage: "Our own Corisco last year, within its limited territory, added thirty per cent., or 290, to its membership, and contributed of its poverty $642 to church purposes."

The humble mission church at Batanga in the same foreign Presbytery of Corisco, on the West Coast of Africa, received to the communion 81 on confession in 1892. It would be the twenty-fourth on the list of our 7208 Presbyterian churches if ranked with reference to the number added on profession during the year 1891–92.

Do not think that I bring forward these comparative statistics in any invidious spirit. It is right that facts like these should be noted. They belong to the Church universal, and as such should be welcome to all who love our Lord's kingdom. They are facts in a realm where God is the chief actor, and testify to His own gracious energy. It is only when we compare results in the foreign field with corresponding results in the home field that many minds succeed in recognizing the significance of the facts and are prepared to acknowledge that results in the foreign field are worthy of attention. Notice, also, that these statistics that I have brought to your attention are not old and worn-out facts that have been made to do duty in foreign mission addresses and sermons for the past ten years; they are new and fresh; they come to us with our Columbian year; they represent what God is doing at the present time through foreign mission effort among the nations of the earth; they have the very power of the Spirit's breath still lingering about them; they are the new Columbian coins from the missionary mint, stamped freshly with the majestic insignia of the Spirit's own personality.

A few months ago I had occasion to go up into central New York, and I took the Empire State Express from the Grand Central Depot in New York City—that famous train, which is said to be the fastest in the world. At a certain point in my journey I glanced through the window, and saw, over on the parallel West Shore Road, a heavy freight train slowly making its way along an up-grade, with its engine puffing and tugging with all its might at the long line of heavy cars which made up the train. Of course the splendid Empire State Express soon left that lagging freight train far in the rear. But suppose, my friends, it had been otherwise, and that great, heavy freight train, with its immense weight of inertia upon an up-grade, had suddenly forged ahead with a mighty momentum, and leaped over the rails at such a tremendous speed that it soon left the magnificent express far in the rear. What would you have said in that case? Why, you would have said, with assurance, that somehow or somewhere there was power over there—power to overcome inertia, and to conquer difficulties, and to transcend ordinary laws by some mysterious and surpassing force. Now, this is just what is exemplified in these recent missionary statistics of our foreign fields. *There is power in them:* the power of God, the power of the divine Spirit, the power to regenerate the soul, the power which will eventually secure the long-promised triumphs of the Church, and win this lost world for Christ.

Let us believe, then, in Foreign Missions, and give them our confidence and support. They have been vindicated by history; they are the embodiment of a divine purpose; and they have been endorsed by a divine blessing. They are vindicated by history, for we are all in the last analysis children of missionary effort; our ancestors were converted to Christ through missionary agencies, and we have inherited from them the blessings of the Gospel. They are an embodiment of a divine purpose, for Christ our Lord meant foreign missions when, eighteen hundred years ago, He said, "Go ye into all the world and preach the Gospel to every creature." Notice where Christ was when He uttered that command. He was in Palestine. And what did He mean, therefore, by "all the world"? He meant the world outside of Palestine; He meant the outlying

Roman Empire; He meant Asia, Africa, and Europe; and, in His knowledge of the coming centuries, I believe He meant America too, just as much as if He had said, "Go ye into all the world, including distant America when the day of her historic appearing shall come." Therefore, from the standpoint of Christ when He uttered this text, the preaching of the Gospel here in America comes under the head of what we might call foreign mission work. It was foreign to the standpoint of Christ when He uttered this word of command.

Do not allow your minds, however, to become entangled in that distinction which we are accustomed to make between home and foreign missions. Too much is made of that distinction in the Church. It is all well enough and proper enough, if we understand just what is meant by it. It is, after all, only a geographical and administrative discrimination; it is of the earth, earthy, and has no place in the vocabulary of heaven. We have no such distinction as a home Bible and a foreign Bible, a home atonement and a foreign atonement, a home Gospel and a foreign Gospel, a home Christ and a foreign Christ.

The great word here is missions, home and foreign if you will, but missions: missions to the north and missions to the south, missions to the east and missions to the west. We read in our New Testament that "one day is as a thousand years, and a thousand years as one day," with God. Now if this is true of time, is it not also true of space? And so one mile is as a thousand leagues, and a thousand leagues as one mile, in God's sight; and there is no near and no far, but just one round world of lost and perishing souls to be rescued and saved through the world's Christ.

LECTURE II.

THE PRESENT-DAY MEANING OF THE MACEDONIAN VISION.

EXTRACT FROM A LETTER FROM CHINA.

"This is a field which I never before half appreciated. It is amazing; it almost passes belief. Numbers of cities there are yet within the oldest field—cities of from 75,000 to 300,000 population—in which there is not one Christian missionary or laborer of any name, or in which there is to be found only one native helper, lonely and feeble. In truth, the mighty cities of Nanking (with nearly a million souls) and Soochow and Hangchow (with half a million in each), and the densely peopled silk districts south and west of them, have only been touched as yet by the Church with the tips of her fingers. All the missionaries in that region combined are little more than a mockery of its needs. And I am not referring, you notice, to the far-off reaches of the Yang-tse, with its twenty millions, nor to the colossal western provinces. The section to which I allude is perfectly accessible and near at hand. From Hangchow to Shanghai, one of the longest routes, I traveled in much less than twenty-four hours in a little steam-launch, by continuous canals. I was absolutely awe-struck and dumb as I steamed, even on that short sail, past city after city, great and populous, one of which was a walled city of 300,000 souls, without one missionary of any Christian denomination whatever, and without so much as a native Christian helper or teacher of any kind. That silent moonlight night, as I passed unnoticed by those long, dark battlements, shutting in their pagan multitudes, was one of the most solemn of my life; and the hours of daylight, when other cities, still larger than many of our American capitals, were continually coming into view, and the teeming populations of the canals and rivers and villages and fields and roads were before my eyes, kept adding to the burden of the night."

REV. ARTHUR MITCHELL, D.D.

II.

*THE PRESENT-DAY MEANING OF THE MACE-
DONIAN VISION.*

PAUL was upon one of his missionary journeys, preaching and teaching the Gospel of his Lord. He came to Mysia, and essayed to go into Bithynia, but the Spirit suffered him not, and when he came to Troas God gave him a vision and a call. A man of Macedonia appeared to him, saying, "Come over into Macedonia and help us." This strange messenger from across the Ægean was to Paul a foreigner; he was a man of Europe, another continent from Paul's native Asia. It was, therefore, a call to foreign mission work, and, as such, was typical and prophetic of many a call to the Church of Christ coming from substantially the same source. A man of Macedonia, so the narrative states in fidelity to the history and geography of the times; a messenger from heaven, so the Church interprets in the light of Christ's great commission and the highest duty of His followers. Like many of the incidents of Scripture, that vision has a twofold significance: it has, on the one hand, a meaning which was local and practical and personal, pertaining to Paul and the work which he was called to do for his Master; on the other hand, it has a meaning which is typical and universal, and has a permanent application in the larger sphere of Church history and practical Christianity. It was a personal vision and a personal call to Paul. It was also suggestive and typical of a permanent call, just as real and direct, to the Church in all ages to discharge the duty of missionary service wherever similar conditions existed. That message to "come over and help us" was not for Paul alone, and it is not merely a reminiscence of his own personal experience; it was a picturesque, vivid, ever-living personification of a perpetual call of duty; it sketched forever in bold, clear outline upon the pages of revelation an immortal object-lesson in living Christianity. Its significance has received scant recognition in the history of the Church. There is still much to be learned by the average Christianity of our day, in its attitude to Foreign

Missions, from a study of Paul's reception and prompt response to that vision. It came to him, let us notice, while absorbed in earnest labors for the churches of his native land. Perhaps he did not himself at that time fully comprehend the urgency of a wider extension of his evangelistic labors. Perhaps he did not fully understand that the Gospel was to be preached to nations outside the bounds of Asia. Perhaps he fain would have lingered in Asia—dear old Asia—where the Lord was born, where He lived and taught and died, where the very ground was hallowed by His earthly presence and His deeds of love and power; Asia, which was bright with the memories of Pentecost, and was the scene of apostolic labors; where the disciples were first called Christians; where the Christian Church was already established; where truth had its home; where was centered all the spiritual culture and light which was worth cherishing in the world; and where there was "so much to be done" to keep the Church alive and prevent her from going back to heathenism. Is it possible, he might have said, that I have any duty to Europe when Asia needs me so much? Ah, do you not think that it was just because Europe was in darkness and spiritual degradation, and needed the Gospel so sorely, that God sent that man of Macedonia with his call to " come over and help us "? Now, let us candidly inquire, has the Church to-day anything in her environment, or in her spiritual consciousness, which is the counterpart to her of that vision of Paul on the shores of the Ægean? Has that Macedonian cry forever died away upon the ears of the Christian Church? Has it not rather multiplied, until it has become a many-voiced and tumultuous cry in our day? Does it not come over every sea like the " voice of many waters," in its majesty and hallowed pathos? It is not a man of Macedonia alone who speaks; it is a man of Japan, a man of China, a man of India, a man of Syria and Persia and Africa; his face is a composite photograph of every race under heaven; it is a man of many nationalities, widely scattered, and all practically in a state of moral ignorance and spiritual need, corresponding in all respects to the condition of Macedonia in the days of Paul.

To this statement some one may reply that this representation is too ideal, and it requires too severe a tax upon the imagination to accept it.

If we had an actual vision, supernatural in its character, such as Paul had, and a direct personal call of duty, with our sphere of labor clearly indicated, we should know how to respond to it. But can the Church truly claim, or can any sincere follower of Christ truthfully maintain, that there is absolutely no vision vouchsafed in this our day? Have we not something which corresponds in every essential to that vision of Paul? As we look back through the mists of the centuries, not into any dreamland of fiction and romance, but to the historic certainties of our Saviour's life, can we not see in clear outline a vision of that face which is the Light of the World, and hear Him say, "Go ye into all the world and preach the Gospel to every creature"? Is not this a vision which infinitely transcends in its dignity and impressiveness the one which was given to Paul? It is not a man of Macedonia that we see; it is the Son of Man. He speaks on behalf of humanity. He belongs to the race and cannot be claimed by any one nationality, or be identified with any single age. He stands before the eyes of all generations. He is not calling, He is commanding. He speaks at once to all ages of history. He touches alike with His personal influence and authority every century of passing time. Have we, in this our generation, in this nineteenth century, eyes of faith to see Him, and ears to hear Him, and hearts to obey Him?

It may be said that this vision is entirely ideal and can only be discovered by the aid of a most imaginative faith. It may be further said that the call to "come over and help us," which Paul recognized as coming directly from Macedonia, is in the case of our ideal Macedonian vision so vague, so confused, so scattered, and so unreal, that it can have little practical power over the conscience. We submit, however, that there is a reality in this picture which entirely eclipses and transcends its ideality. Christ is real; His command to go disciple all nations is real; the existing needs of the world are real. In truth, our ideal picture is more real, and has in it more of the permanent and substantial and incontrovertible power and pressure of existing facts than that vision of Paul itself. In the one there is simply a shadowy man of Macedonia; in the other there is the ever-living Son of God. In the one there is a voice from the realm of dreams; in the other there is a command which has in it the authority of heaven, and transcends in its reality all limitations of time and space. In the one there is reference only to one geographical locality, and the needs which are represented by it; in the other there is a mighty cry of worldwide need, which has in it all the urgency of that Macedonian appeal intensified a thousandfold. If God thought it worth while to voice that one appeal of Macedonia in the ears of Paul, is it not absolutely certain that He regards the appeal of a dying world, in its cumulative volume and its rising intensity, worth voicing in the ears of the Christian Church in this favored age of her prosperity and power, with all the magnificent resources of Christendom ready at hand, and with the Spirit of God waiting to coöperate with grace from on high?

The conclusion we reach, then, is that there is a higher than a Macedonian vision before the eyes of the Church to-day, and a louder than a Macedonian call sounding in her ears—a call which is even more emphatic, more urgent, more incontrovertible, and more directly authoritative than that addressed to Paul. If you are not convinced of this, let me ask you to sit down and deliberately undertake to prove from the standpoint of Christian faith, by the use of fair and candid arguments, that this vision and this call of to-day do not exist. If I am not mistaken, the effort will only confirm you in the conviction that there is a profound reality and a sublime authority in the missionary obligation of to-day. I am sure any loyal follower of the Master would arise from such a study with a call of unmistakable clearness and power ringing in his ears. It was Christ, after all, who spoke to Paul in the person of that Macedonian caller; so it is Christ Himself who speaks to us in the call of to-day. He not only calls but He commands; He not only commands but He calls.

I purpose now to try and give a certain verisimilitude to these thoughts, by endeavoring to voice in your hearing some of these Macedonian appeals of to-day, and I purpose to consider them as addressed to us personally, as the disciples of the living Lord, in whose name they come, and who gives them their authority. To whom are they addressed, if not to the followers and servants of Him who died for the world? They cannot be considered as addressed to the heathen themselves, or to sceptics and infidels and men of the world. They are, then, addressed to us, as assuredly as if they were in the form of a direct personal appeal to each heart. These messages I believe to be real and genuine, not fictitious or imaginative; they are weighty with high authority, and have behind them that noble and regnant personality before which we all bow. I have not manufactured these messages; I simply transmit them. Let us hear them:

Here is, as it were, a telegram from distant JAPAN. What is the purport of the message? It is supposed to come to us from Japan itself, and is signed and sealed by Japanese, whose appeal it voices. This is what they say to us:

We are a nation which has come to the front within a generation. Our traditions indicate that we are of Mongolian extraction and came from the mainland of Asia at a remote date before the Christian era. Our historical records are voluminous: one single work upon Japanese history extends to over a hundred volumes. Our government is the oldest on the face of the earth: our present emperor belongs to a reigning family which has occupied the throne for twenty-four centuries; he is the one hundred and twenty-second in a direct line of sovereigns. From the sixth century before Christ until the year 1142 after Christ Japan was ruled by one emperor at a time. A military revolution at that date resulted in a dual supremacy of a spiritual and a civil ruler, named respectively the Mikado and the Tycoon. Our Mikado was but the invisible phantom of a ruler, living in absolute seclusion, while the Tycoon was our executive and visible sovereign. In 1868 this dual sovereignty came to an end in a revolution which brought the Mikado to the throne as sole ruler of Japan, and gave him both his spiritual and his temporal supremacy. Since then a series of silent and wonderful revolutions have brought us in 1890 to representative government lodged in an Imperial Parliament, and a Cabinet under constitutional restrictions. An absolute monarchy has passed, through a miraculous evolution, into a representative system. Our people have arisen from practical serfdom to the franchise by a somewhat turbulent but bloodless revolution such as has never been known in the history of the world. Liberty has been born among us almost without a pang; our rights as citizens have been guaranteed and secured with hardly a struggle, and as a nation we are a child of this nineteenth century, freeborn to its light and privilege. To be sure, our statesmanship is unsteady and our political life full of surprises, and constitutional government is yet in the region of experiment; we are, however, in the school of experience, and we hope that we shall prove apt pupils. Our population is forty millions; our country extends from north to south for a distance equal to that between St. Paul and New Orleans, and east and west as far as Denver from New York; and in size we are about nineteen times as large as Massachusetts. We are in some respects exceptional specimens of Orientals, with peculiar virtues and marked faults. We are cleanly, courteous, kind-hearted, industrious, honorable, and intensely patriotic. Our chief defects come under the head of impurity, drunkenness, and untruthfulness, while few of us are altogether free from debt. Our land is picturesque and beautiful in its scenery, full of natural charms, brilliant with flowers, and sparkles with running water. It is, alas, in a constant tremor, which often develops into terrible earthquakes. We occupy a front rank among Oriental nations in the arts and sciences and the pursuit of literature. We prophesy that in the future one of the dreams of your own lovers of artistic beauty and intellectual research will be a sojourn in Japan.

Our religions have been Shintoism, a system of mystical nature-worship combined with religious reverence for national heroes, and Buddhism, which with us is especially atheistic, idolatrous, and low in its moral standards, so much so that we teach the Confucian system of morals to our children. The famous Jesuit, Francis Xavier, with his companions, brought Roman Catholicism to Japan in 1549, but Papal Christianity was repelled, and in less than a hundred years had disappeared from our country. With the opening of our country to intercourse with foreign nations, in 1856, by the expedition of Commodore Perry, a new era began. The changes, political, social, commercial, educational, literary, and religious, which have come since then have been unprecedented in the history of any other nation. Twenty years ago Japan had never issued a newspaper. In Tokyo to-day there are 17 dailies with an issue of over 46,000,000 copies annually, and there are 700 periodicals in the empire. Elementary education here is compulsory. There are 34,101 elementary schools and over 3,000,000 pupils. An Imperial Edict, issued some years ago, sounds the note of progress upon this line, which is to-day ringing through Japan, in the following significant sentence: "It is intended that henceforth education shall be so diffused that there may not be a village with an ignorant family, nor a family with an ignorant member."

The one change, however, which in its significance transcends them all, has been the entrance of evangelical Christianity. As we read history we see a great gulf fixed between heathen and Christian nations. We find that heathenism has never saved a nation and that Christianity has never ruined one, and we find that heathenism never gives way and loosens its grip upon a people except the Gospel of Christ finds an entrance. Japan is anxious for light and guidance in this supreme matter of religion. She is one great interrogation point as she looks toward Christendom. We find much that seems to be conflicting and uncertain in the religious and philosophical thought of western nations. Infidelity, materialism, unscriptural views of God and His relation to the universe, conflicting opinions upon some of the essential doctrines of revelation, and widely different systems of Church organization—all seem to be bidding for our allegiance. Huxley is here, and Spencer; the Unitarians are here, and the Papists, and the Greeks, and we seem to be in a place where many currents of thought surge against one another. Religious and philosophical discussions fill the air, and we often meet together in public places to consider these great themes for many hours at a time. We need a calm, strong, patient campaign on the part of the advocates of a pure evangelical Christianity in the interest of Scriptural truth. We need the visits of your best Christian teachers, men of intellectual vigor and large, clear views of truth (as Professor Ladd, of Yale University, who has recently been here), who will guide us and help us in these high themes. We need Christian journalism and the best religious literature of the age. We want your best facilities in education and your latest devices for University Extension, such as Summer Schools of philosophy and theology, and

Chautauquan organizations, and Northfield conferences. Our best young men are being trained largely under missionary auspices. We are forming our creeds, and organizing our churches, and shaping our ecclesiastical future, as you already see it coming to the front, in what we call the Church of Christ in Japan, which has recently applied for admission to the Alliance of the Reformed Churches Holding the Presbyterian System. Our young men are demonstrating their ability to take their places as the leaders and controllers of the great institutions that are growing so rapidly among us. The lamented Neesima was the president of the Doshisha University, and Kozaki is his successor. Ibuka is the president of the Meiji Gakuin. Our churches are almost entirely in the hands of native pastors. We are independent and ambitious, and often inclined to cry, "Japan for the Japanese," but we know the worth of friends, and in our sober moments we know we cannot spare you yet. We claim liberty of thought, but our strong desire is to base all our opinions and all our organized religious life upon the Word of God, and to draw our inspiration from the pure Gospel of Christ.

The record of Christian missions in Japan is the marvel of modern Church history. Your missionaries came among us in 1859. After five years of labor God gave them one convert; after twelve years there were ten. The first evangelical Church was organized in 1872, and consisted of eleven members. In 1892 we report twenty-seven evangelical societies doing mission work in our country. There are, including ladies, 604 foreign missionaries here; there are 365 churches, and a total adult membership of 35,534, of whom 3,718 were admitted in 1891, and 3,731 in 1892. We have 233 native ordained ministers and 359 theological students, besides 460 unordained preachers and helpers. Our native contributions in 1891 for the support of the Gospel amounted to $50,000. Our religious statistics change so rapidly that although they may be sent to America by the swiftest steamers that cross the seas, they grow old and out of date before they touch your shores. In 1868 Yokoi Héishiro was assassinated in Kyoto as a martyr to his Christian faith; now the Doshisha is located there, with its 522 students, and the martyr's son is preaching the Gospel in Tokyo, where there are 92 churches and chapels, 6000 communicants, 25,000 Christians, and 10,000 students in higher educational institutions, besides 30,000 pupils in schools. The Bible was given to us in Japanese by your missionaries in 1888, and its circulation, either entire or in portions, amounted to 57,894 copies in 1891.

Do not think, however, that this astonishing progress of Christianity among us has been without its struggles, surprises, and reactions. We have yet a stupendous conflict before us, and amidst the intellectual unrest, the political uncertainty, and the unparalleled spiritual opportunities of our age, we need your help at the present time in advancing the interests of evangelical religion among us. Is not our land an inviting field for the Church of Christ, if she has the heart and purpose to win a nation for her Master? If the Church of Christ will take advantage of this extraordinary opportunity, we can safely pledge Japan to be the grandest trophy of modern missions, and we can prophesy that we shall be in God's hands a chosen instrument for a wide and fruitful missionary service throughout all eastern Asia. We are sure to be the leading Christian nation of the Orient, if we read our destiny aright. Already China is sending her young men to our universities, and our Japanese churches are planning their foreign missions. Take possession of our land in the name of Christ, and you have the key to the Orient. *Come over and help Japan.*

Swiftly following this telegram from Japan comes a winged message from KOREA. This is its purport:

We are, like the Japanese, of Mongolian origin. Our compact little kingdom is in area about the size of Italy, with a population of 12,000,000. Our king is an absolute monarch, paying tribute as a nominal vassal to the Emperor of China. We are a homogeneous people, and our ethnic peculiarities correspond to our geographical situation, something between the Chinese and the Japanese. We have always been exclusive, and have hidden ourselves away from the great world, so much so that we have been called the "Hermit Nation." Our country is picturesque and mountainous; the soil is fertile, and there is immense wealth in our mineral resources. Our language is unique, being more flexible than the Japanese and less cumbersome than the Chinese. Although not the spoken language of the country, Chinese is the language of the court and of scholarship. Our present ruler, although an absolute sovereign, acknowledges the limitations of a written constitution, but in practical matters his power is supreme. The government is independent, except that China claims the right of supervision in our foreign policy, but we are surrounded by three nations, China, Russia, and Japan, any one of which would be glad to rule over us. In the fourth century of the Christian era Buddhism was introduced by missionaries from China. It was afterward supplanted by Confucianism, which is now more than any other the professed faith of the upper and middle classes, while but a remnant of Buddhism is left in the land. About a century ago Roman Catholicism was introduced, and in the absence of any earnest religious faith among us, it seemed to take root and gain headway, but was opposed by bitter persecutions in which multitudes were martyred. One of these bloody scenes took place in 1839, and another in 1868, when it is estimated that twenty-five thousand were killed. But Papal Christianity still survives, and it is estimated that it has now fifty thousand adherents in Korea. In 1882 a treaty was signed with the United States, and we threw open several of our ports to foreigners. Among them is Seoul, the royal capital, and its seaport, Chemulpo, also Fusan, in the southeast, and Gensan, to the northeast. Our entire country, however, may be said to be practically open to the entrance of foreigners.

The first approach of the Gospel to Korea was from the north, in 1873, when Rev. John Ross, a Scotch missionary in Manchuria, sought an entrance, and with the aid of a native Korean translated the New Testament into the language of northern Korea, and later baptized a few converts. He did not become, however, a resident missionary, and it was not until 1884 that a permanent missionary took up his residence in Korea, when Dr. H. N. Allen, of the American Presbyterian Mission, located at Seoul. In 1886 Rev. Dr. H. G. Underwood baptized the first convert in Seoul. In 1887 Presbyterian missionaries organized at Seoul the first evangelical church, of twenty-three members, and since then another church has been organized under the auspices of Methodist missionaries. The total membership in these churches is now one hundred and seventy-seven, and there are many promising candidates seeking admission. Six Protestant missionary societies have established missions in Korea, and at present we have sixty-two resident missionaries, including ladies. Fusan has just been occupied, and Gensan will soon be a mission station also. A missionary printing-press was introduced in 1887; a Korean Dictionary was published in 1890 by Dr. Underwood; and the translation of the Bible is now under way. A Christian college should be the next step in the march of progress. Korea is a land open to mission work. The edict against the profession of Christianity is apparently a dead letter, although, of course, there is a latent possibility of its revival, if the spirit of persecution should arise. Although our past reaches back into dim antiquity, yet we are a nation born in a day into the light of this nineteenth century. We have plodded through weary centuries, until in the present generation we have emerged from our seclusion into contact with sister nations which are the heirs of all the ages. We look to the Church of Christ, and especially to Christian America, to extend to us a helping hand and guide us into the paths of light. As we have been born in a day into the sisterhood of nations, so may it be our happy lot to be born in a day into the brotherhood of Christianity. *Come over and help KOREA.*

Following this Macedonian call from Korea we have an important and weighty plea from CHINA. Let us give ear to our brethren in that distant empire. Here is the Chinese version of the Macedonian call:

We speak on behalf not only of China proper with its population of 386,000,000, but also on behalf of the great Chinese Empire, including the dependencies of Manchuria, Mongolia, Thibet, and Turkestan, with a total population of 407,000,000.

If our message were signed by every soul in China, and we should allow four signatures a minute during twelve hours of the day, it would have been necessary that the first name should have been attached about the time that Columbus discovered America; and the line formed of the signers would have reached nearly six times around the globe, or fifty times across your continent; and during the process of attaching the signatures, a number equal to three times the population of the globe would have dropped out of the ranks in death, and their places would have been supplied by others. We were a nation before Rome was founded, and before Saul was king in Israel. We are more than one fourth of the human race; for every person in the United States there are nearly seven in China. The populations of Great Britain, Germany, France, Russia, and the United States together equal only about three fifths of the people of China. Thirty-three thousand of us die every day—sufficient to bury New York City in a month, and the entire population of the United States in five years. Our country with its dependencies is a third of Asia, and one third larger than Europe. If placed over the United States, it would extend two hundred and forty miles into the Pacific Ocean and cover a large part of the Gulf of Mexico. We have a population equal to the United States in our 1700 walled cities, several of which have more than 1,000,000 inhabitants. We have three thousand miles of coast line, and rivers longer than the Mississippi. Our rivers and canals, which are loaded with commerce, make spacious highways through the land. Our language has forty thousand characters; our literature is older than Moses; our religion than the Jewish Tabernacle; our poetry than that of Homer. Our public works are of great magnitude and antiquity. Our mineral resources are immense; we have coal-fields alone equal in size to the New England and Middle States, with Ohio, Illinois, Indiana, Michigan, and Wisconsin added. Our educational system is extensive, and our literati form a large and distinguished portion of the population. Our country was fully opened to intercourse with western nations in 1860, and we have made considerable progress in adopting the arts, sciences and inventions of the West. Our country has become accessible by the swiftest steamers, and, were we allowed to do so, we would soon turn the Pacific Ocean into a Chinese ferry. Our foreign relations with the United States, especially the Chinese Exclusion Bills, have filled our minds with astonishment and perplexity, and now the climax has come in the Geary Act of 1892, which seems to us both unfair and unjust.

So far as present treaties are concerned, the Christian religion has its Magna Charta in the twenty-ninth article of the United States Treaty with China, in which it is guaranteed that "those who quietly profess and teach the doctrines of Christianity shall not be harassed or persecuted on account of their faith." This applies to the foreign missionary and also his Chinese converts, since in either case neither the native nor the foreign Christian is to be interfered with or molested in peaceably teaching and practicing the principles of Christianity. We cannot deny that a strong feeling against foreigners exists throughout large portions of the empire, having its storm-center in the fanatical province of Hunan, from whence the vile literature urging a crusade against foreigners usually comes. Our country is wide and vast, and it is extremely difficult for a central government to control a spirit so subtle and intangible as the anti-foreign sentiment, but we have reason to believe that strenuous and serious efforts will be made on the part of the authorities to check all excesses. We have not as yet followed the example of America and passed our Exclusion Bill against innocent and inoffensive foreigners living among us; nor have we opened as yet our international rogues' gallery where we impale our foreign guests on the point of the camera.

We have three great religions among us: two of them Chinese in origin, and the third an exotic from India. Our Chinese religions are Confucianism and Taoism; both of which originated about the sixth century B. C. Confucius was a historic person, a moral sage, a prophet of reason. He made no claims to divinity, but was a human teacher of what is due between man and man. Confucianism is a religion without a revelation, a worship practically without a God, a code of morals without an ultimate personal authority. The system finds its springs in earthly and temporal relations, rather than in reverent worship of the living God. It exalts the parental relation into a system of worship extending even to remote ancestors. Its realm of moral duty includes human government, social manners, practical precepts, and religious formalism. Its moralities have reference almost exclusively to what is due from inferiors to superiors, and in this connection it teaches, as one of its precepts, "What you would not have others do to you, do not to them." But it fails to reach the Gospel standard that we should return good for evil. Its code of precepts has to do with the moral etiquette of the state and the family, and reaches out into the realm of the dead, requiring an elaborate worship of ancestors, with its enormous expense and its burdensome exactions. Confucianism seems to be the patriarchal relation developed into a religion of veneration for superiors, living or dead. It is a deification of man, and its natural result is to lift the soul no higher than its own plane, while it gives to human nature an irresponsible power which opens an easy path to tyranny. There is in Confucianism no supreme God, no soul-destroying sin, no mediating sacrifice, no Saviour, no real prayer, no inspiration to righteous living. Its highest goal is, good order in the state, good manners in the home, religious veneration of the departed, while it leaves the immortal soul to struggle with its sin, without a Saviour. Taoism is simply the deification of material mysteries, and its natural outcome is material idolatry. Buddhism came to us from India. We find in it no moral guidance in righteousness, no spiritual life for the soul, and no uplifting worship. Our native religions cannot save us, and we are the victims of superstition in a thousand fantastic and tyrannical forms. Sin reigns in China, and we need Him who came to seek and to save that which was lost. The Papal and Greek forms of Christianity have entered here, and both, especially the former, are aggressive and gaining ground.

Evangelical missions came to us early in the century, when, in 1807, Morrison took up his residence at Canton. The struggle to make headway was a long and desperate one. After sixty years there were about one hundred ordained missionaries in China, and three thousand communicants. This was one ordained minister to every four million people, which would be at the present time equivalent to about fifteen Christian ministers to the entire United States. Although missions began early in the century, it was only in 1842 that the treaty ports were opened, and it was in 1860 that existing treaties were made, and not until 1865 did missions begin to penetrate into the interior. Our progress in the last twenty-five years has been rapid. We have now 600 ordained missionaries, and, including ladies, 1500 foreign laborers in China, representing 42 different societies. We have 250 ordained and 3000 unordained native laborers, and 522 organized churches. The work of medical missions among us is extensive, as we have 61 hospitals and 44 dispensaries, in which 350,000 patients are treated annually. We have 50,000 communicants, including an addition during the past year of nearly 3000. There is a remarkable readiness in China for the reception of Christianity. The faith of the people in their superstitions and in their dumb idols is wonderfully shaken. The Tai-ping rebellion showed us the folly of trusting in the help of idols, since those who trusted in them were everywhere defeated, and only foreign interference saved our empire from destruction. Christianity has ministered to us in times of famine and flood. We have been helped by those whom we distrusted, and many of us have learned to respect and love them. In one of those famine-stricken districts a Buddhist temple was afterward given by the people to the American missionaries to be used as a Christian church. Our native ministers and evangelists are many of them eminently successful, and we hope for great results through the labors of natives themselves who are called of God to His service. Our great needs at present are a standard translation of the Word of God to take the place of the confusing multiplicity of versions that have been prepared in various parts of the empire, and also an earnest missionary campaign throughout China without delay. The recent conference at Shanghai, under the guidance of the divine Spirit, took the preliminary steps toward the preparation of three great standard versions of the Bible: one in the High Classical, or Wenli language, which is the universally written but unspoken language of the empire; another in Low Classical, or Easy Wenli, for those who are unfamiliar with the higher classical tongue; and still another in the Mandarin, or the great colloquial language of northern, western, and central China; and from these standard versions other versions in various local dialects can be made wherever the necessity exists. This grand step forward in giving the Word of God to China is one of the most important events in the history of missions. And what shall we say of the call for personal missionary work throughout our vast empire? The China Inland Mission, with its one hundred and three stations and over five hundred resident missionaries in fourteen provinces of the empire, shows the possibilities of missionary work in the interior; and the call of the Shanghai Conference in 1890 for one thousand missionaries only fairly represents the immediate demands of the work. Our converts have increased of late years in something like a geometrical ratio, so much so that in the past thirty-five years they have multiplied at least two thousand-fold; and at the same rate of increase for another thirty-five years there will be in China twenty-six million communicants and one hundred million adherents. China is destined to be a land of Pentecosts. She needs only the religion of Christ to become one of the dominant powers of the earth. As yet we have only the first sheaf of the harvest. It is truly an "age on ages telling" in China, and the Church of Christ has an opportunity here such as has never been opened to her in the history of our Redeemer's kingdom. *Come over and help* CHINA.

Far to the east of China, dotting the vast waters of the ocean, are the ISLANDS OF THE PACIFIC. They, too, send us a Macedonian message. Let us listen to this appeal from the waiting isles:

Recent geographers have given to our island world of the Pacific the general name of Oceania, and this is subdivided into Malaysia in the northwest, and Australasia to the southward, and Polynesia to the eastward, with a still further subdivision of the central groups north and south of the equator into Micronesia on the north and Melanesia on the south. Where we came from we do not know, but it must have been from the continent of Asia, probably from both Malayan and Caucasian origins. We are the lost sheep of the human race. Isolated in our island homes, we have been the prey of barbarism and cannibalism and cruel strife for centuries. Our islands vary in size from a vast continent to a tiny speck on the bosom of the pathless seas. New Guinea is larger than France, and Borneo is only a trifle smaller. Sumatra is a thousand miles long, and as large as Great Britain. Our climate for the most part is balmy, and bright with perpetual summer. Nature has enriched us with some of her choicest treasures, but our human hearts are in poverty and our human lives have fallen into the lowest depths of superstition and ignorance and misery. Only within the century have we been taught of God, and from island to island the tidings have spread. If the "feet of those who bring good tidings" are "beautiful upon the mountains," they are no less beautiful upon the seas. The tidings of salvation have come to us as upon the wings of the wind, and the white sails of the "Morning Stars," the "Daysprings," the "Southern Crosses," and the "Ellengowans," have been hailed with delight, and to some of us the missionary visit has been the crowning event of the year. Ours is a wonderland of missions, a land of transformations, of romance, of heroism, of "perils by land and by sea," of patient faith, of arduous toil, of noble sacrifices, of heroic martyrdoms, of unparalleled successes, and gracious victories that must have rung through heaven. Under the cocoa-trees, in the perpetual summer of lonely islands, are graves which the Christian Church might delight to honor as monuments of the sweetest heroism and the truest loyalty and the most unselfish service to which the Church can point in modern history. The dim obscurity and deep loneliness of our isolation have hidden away from the knowledge of the world the Christian life which has sprung up among us in this nineteenth century, until these isles of the Pacific, like the catacombs of Rome, have sheltered a Church in exile, whose only channel of communication with fellow-Christians has been the secret pathway of the waters, through which the herald ships have passed with their messages of cheer and hope, while in our ocean solitudes we have often held our love-feasts far out of sight of the busy world. From north to south through the midst of our islands runs the 180th parallel of longitude, where the world's day nominally begins; but to us has dawned a brighter day of Gospel light and sunny hope.

The first messenger of modern missions came to us just before the century, when the London Missionary Society landed its first missionaries in Tahiti in 1797, and since then the work has developed in two great divisions, that north of the equator, largely in the hands of American missionaries, and that south of the equator, in the hands of English and Europeans, making a total of fifteen missionary societies which have entered the Pacific. In the north the main centers are the Sandwich, the Gilbert, the Marshall, and the Caroline groups; in the south the main centers are the Marquesas, the Society, the Hervey, the Samoan, the Fiji, the Loyalty, and the New Hebrides groups, with the large single islands of New Guinea and Borneo and those of the Indian Archipelago. Some of the most conspicuous and transforming victories which the Gospel has ever achieved have been won among our people. The Sandwich Islands on the north and the Fiji Islands on the south are examples of what God's grace has accomplished among us.

Our entire island world includes about thirty-eight clusters or groups, varying in number from four separate islands, as in the Loyalty group, to four hundred, as in the Philippine, and included within the whole circumference of our watery realm there are not less than two thousand inhabited islands, with a total population estimated at ten millions. Of these distinct groups twenty-seven are already under the protection or control of civilized governments, besides seven separate islands. Evangelical missionary societies have occupied fifteen of these groups, having in all 2260 stations where mission work is conducted. In connection with these various missions many of our languages have been reduced to writing and made a medium of communication through printing, and the Word of God has been translated entire into nine of these, and in part into thirty-three. We have 1369 churches, served by 1200 native pastors, and in addition to these there are 9074 unordained native helpers engaged in the service. The total of communicants in these churches is 58,000, and the total of professed adherents of Christianity in the Pacific Islands is 225,000.

There are fourteen groups of islands which may be said to be practically Christianized, as the Sandwich, Marquesas, Fiji, Gilbert, Ellice, Caroline, Samoan, Friendly, Hervey, Loyalty, Tokelau, Austral, New Hebrides, and Society, besides numerous separate islands, making a total of three hundred and five distinct islands where Christianity may be said to be the religion of almost every household. In addition, there are other groups that are partially Christianized, as the Banks, the Solomon, and the Santa Cruz Islands. Hundreds of native missionaries have been educated and trained in institutions like the model Samoan Missionary

Seminary at Malua, and St. Barnabas College on Norfolk Island, and the Training Institution at Fiji, with its one hundred and nine candidates for the ministry. At the latter school, when an appeal was recently made for fifteen helpers to enter upon missionary service in New Guinea, fifteen hundred miles away, and a service of great peril and hardship, there were forty volunteers offered themselves at once. It has been a bright feature of Christian life among us that it has been missionary in its spirit, and our native missionaries have been largely instrumental in carrying the Gospel to other islands. The work in New Guinea and in the Samoan group and in Micronesia has been largely through native instrumentalities. We have 2398 mission schools, attended by 68,000 pupils, and our churches contribute annually over $72,000 to help on the progress of the kingdom. The Samoan Islands sent in 1890 an offering of $9000 to the London Missionary Society, and have given an average of $6000 annually to the same society for the past twenty years.

Christian missions among us have been at

tended with enormous difficulties and ever-threatening perils. Already Williams, Harris, George Gordon and his wife, James Gordon, McNair, Patteson, and Atkins, eight devoted missionaries, besides hundreds of faithful native laborers, have yielded up their lives in martyrdom. They have received an earthly as well as a heavenly crown in the erection of Christian churches upon the very soil which was stained with their blood, and in Gospel triumphs like that recorded upon the memorial tablet of Geddie, at Aneityum, with the glorious legend: "When he landed here in 1848, there were no Christians; and when he left here in 1872, there were no heathens." There have been single missionaries, like Titus Coan, who have baptized with their own hands about 15,000 converts, and in one single day 1705. We have given this record in detail that the Church of Christ may be stimulated and encouraged to continue this work, which has been so fruitful and so manifestly blessed of God in the past. Of the total of 2000 islands, only some 350 have been as yet touched, even in part, by the power of the Gospel, and there remain 1650 still waiting for the tidings of a Saviour, with a population of not less than 9,000,000 still unevangelized. While Christendom has its ninety-and-nine safe within the fold of light and knowledge, think of the lost sheep of this distant realm of darkness and danger. *Come over and help the* ISLES OF THE PACIFIC.

Let us turn now from the isles of the Pacific and listen to an urgent summons from SIAM and BURMA—lands that are comparatively little known, but which have already been the scene of notable progress in mission work. These countries, which are geographically contiguous, forming the bulk of a great Indo-Chinese peninsula which extends toward the south between China on the northeast and India on the northwest, are little visited by travelers, but together they represent a population of 15,000,000, among whom the Gospel has won some conspicuous victories. They voice their appeal to us as follows:

We are a collection of nationalities and races with innumerable tribal subdivisions. Our languages, however, are not many, and seem to have much in common. Our religion is chiefly Buddhism and Demon Worship. The caste system, however, is not found among us, and we consider ourselves higher in the scale of civilization, especially in our treatment of woman, than many of our Oriental neighbors. The interior tribes inhabiting the mountainous regions are wild and warlike races, yet display a singular readiness to welcome Christian instruction. The Laos tribes in the north of Siam, and the Karens in Burma, have received the Gospel seed as into good ground, and have yielded a generous harvest.

Christian missionaries entered Burma early in the century. Judson, who arrived in 1813, baptized the first convert after six years. In 1834 he completed the translation of the Bible into Burmese, and flourishing missions of the American Baptist Union have been long established, with at present 23 stations, 139 missionaries, 610 native preachers, 550 churches, and 30,253 communicants, of whom 1936 were received in 1891. Mission schools number 500, with 11,000 pupils. Six other societies have also entered Burma. In Assam also there are 7 stations, with 33 missionaries, and a church-membership of 2400. An encouraging feature of our work is that native evangelists, especially among the Karens, are our most successful workers. The Karen Bible was completed in 1853, and still another translation in a different dialect in 1883, so that the entire Word of God is in circulation among all the Karens of Burma. In 1878 a jubilee celebration was observed, fifty years after the baptism of the first Karen convert, Ko-Tha-byu. It was found at that time that the membership of the Karen churches was over 20,000.

In Siam the Gospel is making rapid progress among the Laos tribes, and our appeal for help is most earnest and importunate. The American Presbyterians have here a most encouraging mission, and an open door into southwestern China. Christian missions in Siam are regarded with favor and treated with unusual courtesy and generosity by the king and his government. In 1878 a proclamation of religious liberty for the Laos was made by the King of Siam. The Bible is already in the Siamese language, and the material facilities are now sufficiently advanced to give the hope of its early translation and distribution in the Laos tongue, in which the Gospel of Matthew is already issued. Our past history is a promise of great and fruitful results, if Christian missions will come to the help of this distant land, hidden away in the depths of comparatively unknown Asia.

Come over and help SIAM *and* BURMA.

We lay aside the message from Farther India and Siam and open another from the teeming realm of INDIA. What myriads of voices mingle in this appeal of India, which is said to contain more distinct and separate nations than Europe. It is a country whose greatest length from north to south and its greatest width from east to west are equal, and in either case measure about 1900 miles. Its area is as large as all Europe, including Russia. Its total population, including that of the British provinces and native states, is 287,000,000, and has increased 33,000,000 in ten years, according to the census of 1891.

It has, therefore, twice the population of the two Americas, North and South, with 40,000,000 to spare. The single province of Bengal has more people than the United States. Two of its languages, the Hindustani and the Bengali, are spoken by more people than inhabit the two American continents. One of its religions, the Hindu, is professed by more than three times the population of the United States, and another, the Mohammedan, by a number nearly equal to the population of our country. The recent census was taken in 17 different languages, and there were 950,000 enumerators. The average population per square mile for all India, including Burma, is 184, and in some sections, as in Bengal, it reaches 460, while the average population of the United States is 17.9 to the square mile. The danger of famine is constant, and the ravages of disease are frightful. There are 500,000 lepers, while 417,000 die annually of cholera, and 3,500,000 of fever. In the official returns for 1891, it was reported that 24,841 people in British India were killed by wild animals during that year, of whom 22,134 died from the bite of snakes. Three fifths of India are under direct British rule, while the remaining two fifths, consisting of 460 native feudatory states, are in vassalage to the British government. The Portuguese and French have small settlements scattered about upon the seacoast.

The original inhabitants of India were Turanian, and at a distant period, at least ten, and perhaps fifteen, hundred years before the Christian era, there was a great Aryan invasion which dominated the history of India until about 1000 A.D., when the Mohammedan invaders after repeated efforts gained the ascendency. The Mogul power was established in 1526 and held sway until, in 1757, by the victory of Plassey, under Lord Clive, the British rule was begun and the mighty Indian Empire of Great Britain was founded. One hundred years later, in 1857, at the time of the mutiny, the Indian Empire was firmly established, and came fully under the power of the British Crown and Parliament. The providence of God is wonderfully revealed in all this, and it is a blessing beyond compare to a country like India, so liable to be torn by civil strife and overrun by tyranny, to have the strong, firm, and just rule of the British government exercising its benign sway over these vast, restless, and turbulent races. The outlook for the future is that all things are now ready for India to become a Christian empire, and it is a reasonable hope that not many generations will pass before we shall see marvelous and startling changes in this land. Already the native Protestant Christians of India, Burma, and Ceylon number 671,285, a number which may safely be regarded as fully equal to the total number of Christians in the Roman Empire at the end of the first century of the Christian era. Let us listen now to the resistless plea of India, which comes to us as follows:

We are the children of Providence, and God has reached out His hand to help us in wondrous ways during the past century. He has put an end to cruel customs, and has alleviated many of the awful miseries that afflicted us. We have a government which assures peace and administers justice, and which, although it is not free from painful failures in the past and strange insensibility to some pressing evils, is yet an immense boon to our country, and life and property are now as safe in India as in any Christian land. Our material progress is full of the spirit of Western civilization. Our postal facilities are admirable, by which 320,000,000 letters and newspapers are transmitted in a year; and our telegraphic system is equally good, with 37,000 miles of wire, by which are transmitted 3,500,000 messages a year; and there are already 18,000 miles of railway in operation, by which 120,000,000 passengers are carried annually. Society is being revolutionized, and already a new moral and social tone is pervading it. Our giant system of caste is receiving constantly innumerable blows from every direction, especially from the silent and vigorous influence which general education exerts in breaking down its barriers. The government has conferred an imperial benefit upon us in the system of national education, established in 1854. We have 130,000 educational institutions of all grades under government auspices, attended by 3,700,000 pupils, and there are at present in India more than 14,000,000 readers, and the educated classes who have been through our higher institutions are almost without exception familiar with English.

Our religious life is many-sided, and enters into all the phases of our social system. We have pantheism and mystical philosophy for Brahmans, and we have idolatry and gross ceremonialism for those of lower religious instincts. Hinduism has a wonderful flexibility and capacity to adjust itself to all classes of society, and as a religion it does not trouble itself with the sins of men, but rather with their external observance of superstitious rites and ceremonies. It absorbs and assimilates the mighty system of caste, and at the same time uses it as a facile instrument for its own ends. Modern Hinduism is a lapse into grosser forms of idolatry and into deeper depths of superstition than those which characterized the earlier and purer forms of Brahmanism. The Hindu of to-day is a worshiper of false gods, a slave to gross superstitions, a Pharisee of the Pharisees in ceremonialism, and is seeking to work out his own salvation by methods which are both degrading and puerile. While the Hindu faith is held by nearly three fourths of the people of India, yet there is still an immense following to Islam, numbering in all over 57,000,000. There are besides 7,000,000 Buddhists and over 11,000,000 divided up among smaller sects, and among them is a remnant of the Parsees, numbering about 90,000. Among all this variety there are 2,284,380 recognized as Christians, but of this number only 559,661 are enrolled as Protestants. If we include also Burma and Ceylon the number will be 671,285.

Protestant missions in India were permanently established when Carey, as a representative of the Baptist Missionary Society, arrived in 1793, although as early as 1705 Ziegenbalg and Plutschau were here as the representatives of a Danish mission. Carey and his friends with difficulty secured a footing, owing to the opposition of the English authorities. The London Missionary Society began its work at Madras in 1805, and the Church Missionary Society sent Henry Martyn in 1807. Judson and Newell arrived in 1812, although a year later Judson went to Burma. The Wesleyan Missionary Society of England entered in 1813. In 1830 the Scottish Presbyterian Church sent Alexander Duff to be the leader in the great educational movement in India. In 1833 the Presbyterian Church of the United States of America sent her missionaries Lowrie and Reed. The American Methodists entered in 1856. There are at present 36 large missionary societies and 29 smaller organizations doing work in India, making a total of 65 agencies.

The progress of Protestant missions during the century has been such as to kindle the largest hopes of wonderful changes in the near future. If we compare the statistics of 1851 with those of 1890 we can note astonishing growth covering the period named. Foreign ordained missionaries have increased from 339 to 857; native ordained preachers from 21 to 797; native lay-preachers from 493 to 3491; lady foreign missionaries from none in 1851 to 711, and native female evangelists from none in 1851 to 3278. These last significant figures indicate the rapid growth of zenana missions, that new and powerful agency which has so recently taken a front rank among the missionary forces of India. In 1881 there were 7522 zenanas visited, and 40,513 in 1890. In 1881 the zenana pupils were 9132, and in 1890 the number had increased to 32,659. Protestant missions have given special attention to educational agencies in India. There are at present 81 theological and training schools, with 1584 pupils. Mission schools of all societies number 6737, and their pupils 238,171. The work of medical missions was not begun until 1867, and at present there are 97 foreign medical missionaries and 168 native, with 166 hospitals and dispensaries. The native Protestant communicants in 1851 were 14,661, and 182,722 in 1890. The Protestant adherents in 1851 were 91,092, and 559,661 in 1890.

How inadequately these figures represent the changes of the century! Christianity has entered India as a living religion, and its leaven is working among her vast population, until, in 1892, there are indications of deep upheavals and great mass movements toward its acceptance. The higher castes are intellectually and spiritually restless, and are seeking by such compromises as the Brahmo Somaj and the Arya Somaj to establish a *modus vivendi* between Brahmanic philosophy and Christian revelation. The Gospel has found a larger and more effective entrance among the lower castes, and is silently reaching down to those strata of society which are below the caste line. Unless all signs fail, India is being prepared for Pentecostal scenes. The American Methodist missions report 25,000 conversions during 1892, and thousands more are pressing on into the kingdom. The average reported by the Methodists of 1200 conversions per month for the last two years seems a wonder of divine grace, and yet if it should become 12,000 a month, it would require even at that rate two thousand years for the conversion of India. Even a million converts a year would mean nearly three hundred years before India was won for Christ. Surely the King's business requireth haste. The rapid development of the native agencies of India is a conspicuous sign of the coming of the kingdom. The great empire will soon be in the hands of native Christian converts, whom God will use for the evangelization of India, and for missions into neighboring lands. Native Indian missionaries will soon represent a native Indian Church in a foreign missionary campaign. Our appeal is backed by a marvelous century which has now just closed, and it is emphasized by the magnificent promise of the coming century which has now just opened. In the name of these vast and needy millions we call to the Church of Christ: *Come over and help INDIA.*

Leaving India and going toward the west, the vast continent of AFRICA is before us. It seems to fill the vision, and overwhelm the mind, and awaken a feeling of awe, mingled with yearning zeal, in a heart inspired by the spirit of missions. We try to picture its colossal proportions of 11,500,000 square miles, noting that it is more than three times as large as Europe, and that all of North America and Europe together would not occupy the same space. Then its teeming population, equal to nearly one seventh of the human race, roughly estimated from 160,000,000 to 200,000,000, adds a picturesque and at the same time an affecting interest to the scene. Africa has waited long for its day of visitation. It has been like a submerged continent for centuries, and only of late has it loomed up before the eyes of the world and fixed at once the united gaze of statesmen, explorers, scientists, historians, merchants, and Christian philanthropists. It is a new world for the nineteenth century to conquer. More has been learned of Africa in the past fifty years than has been known before since the Creation. The world has been both entranced and appalled as its enormous interior populations have come to light, and its natural mysteries have been disclosed, its gigantic problems revealed, its colossal woes uncovered, its piteous story of suffering and wrong recited, and the irresistible appeal of a sorrow-stricken, world-forgotten continent has been unfolded in current literature. A startling emphasis is also given to this story of African wrong when we find that even the contemporary relations of civilization to Africa are not free from new perils; that while philanthropy has been slowly awakening to the urgency of its duty and the grandeur of its opportunity, human greed has been shipping its rum and its weapons of destruction to the untold injury of Africa, while the inhuman cruelties of the slave-trade have not as yet been suppressed.

The story of African exploration in its early and primitive period reaches back to the fifteenth century, when the Portuguese made some efforts upon the West and East Coasts and ventured somewhat into the interior. The Dutch in the seventeenth century obtained their footing in South Africa. In the years 1768–73 James Bruce, the first modern explorer of the interior of Africa, made his venturesome journey, and has been known since as the discoverer of the Blue Nile. It was in 1795, however, just about the time that Carey was establishing his mission in India, when the past century of modern missions began, that systematic exploration was undertaken. In this same year Mungo Park made his first journey, lasting two and a half years, and in 1803 he undertook a second journey, which resulted in his death. As late as 1851 the president of the Royal Geographical Society said, "All beyond the coast of Central and Southern Africa is still a blank in our maps." Among the earliest of modern explorers were Krapf and Rebmann, two missionaries of the Church Missionary Society, who made their entrance upon the East Coast in 1844. In 1849 David Livingstone began his explorations, extending over a period of twenty-four years. He died in 1873 at Ilala, on the south shore of Lake Bangweolo. His heart was buried under a tree near by, but his body was removed to England and interred in Westminster Abbey. The Royal Geographical Society of England has recently placed a memorial tablet of bronze on the tree near which he died, with the inscription: "Livingstone died here, Ilala, May 1st, 1873." Other distinguished explorers since Livingstone were Burton, Speke, and Grant (1857-62), Baker (1863-65), Schweinfurth (1868-71), Stanley (1871-90), Cameron (1873-75), and Thomson (1884). Recent years have only added to the efforts at exploration, so that at the present time there are at least fifteen exploring parties conducting operations in Africa, and every European government which has its protectorate or sphere of influence is desirous of discovering as soon as possible every unexplored mystery and unknown possibility of its new possessions. There are still vast regions in Central Africa, north of the Congo Free State, about which little is known.

A language map of Africa has recently been constructed, chiefly through Dr. R. N. Cust, who has made careful and learned researches into the modern languages of Africa. It divides the people into six linguistic groups—the Hamitic, in North Africa; the Semitic, including those in North Africa and along the valley of the Nile, using in the main the Arabic language and identified with Mohammedanism; the Nuba Fulah, in the Eastern Soudan; the Negro, in West and North Central Africa, with 195 distinct languages and 49 dialects; the Bantu, south of the equator, with 168 languages and 55 dialects, as far as at present known; and the Hottentots, in the southern extremity of the continent, the lowest in the scale of civilization. The total of languages represented in these linguistic divisions is 438, with 153 separate dialects. The Bible has been translated wholly into 13 of these African languages and dialects, and the New Testament entire into 10 additional languages, while portions of the Bible are in 43 others, making a total of 66 languages and dialects which have been made a medium of Scripture truth.

The religions of Africa are not in the main attended with idolatry such as prevails in India, but may rather be classed under the general name of fetichism. A fetich is some material thing which is supposed to contain a spirit, and this spirit, either for good or evil, possesses supernatural powers. Almost anything may be a fetich, and in that case must be regarded with the reverence and superstitious fear with which the ignorant regard demons and evil spirits. The result is that the great mass of the people of Africa are the victims of innumerable superstitions, and the only religious life they know is one of bondage to the cruel and relentless exactions of barbarous custom, or to the malicious caprice of the evil spirits which are supposed to inhabit the material things with which men are surrounded, which they therefore regard with superstitious fear, and to which they continually offer their religious sacrifices. Fetichism is not always unaccompanied by idolatry, but as a rule idols are not used. Mohammedanism has a large following in the north of Africa, and in the Soudan, East and West. It is also found on the East and West Coasts. It is difficult to form an accurate estimate of the number of Mohammedans. It has prevailed in the sections of Africa mentioned since the Mohammedan invasion of the seventh century, and it is possible that at the present time one fourth of the population of the continent may be ranked as Moslems. As regards some aspects of external civilization, the African Mohammedan may be considered as the superior of the fetich worshiper, and when the faith in one God is intelligently held as a matter of conviction, a manifest advance has been made into the realm of higher religious truth; but, after all, measured by the moral and spiritual standards of the Bible, there is little, if any, difference between the practical religious life of an African Mohammedan and an African pagan. Both are far out of touch with a holy God and the Gospel standards of righteousness which He has given us. The Christians in Africa number about three and a half millions, one half of whom are Copts and Abyssinians. The remainder may be divided between Roman Catholics and Protestants. There are nearly a million Jews, mostly on the shores of the Mediterranean, and about 250,000 Hindus, chiefly on the East Coast.

The recent partition of Africa among the European nations has been one of the foremost events of the century, and has committed the statesmanship, civilization, and philanthropy of the leading nations of the world to the oversight and development of the material and moral well-being of Africa to an extent beyond the bounds of imagination a few years ago. Let us hope that the higher interests of these vast and ignorant populations will become a special charge upon the humanitarian sympathies and the Christian consciences of these mighty nations which have accepted so impulsively the vast responsibilities involved in these self-assumed protectorates. In actual extent of territory France leads the list, having 2,902,624 square miles under her supervision, to which Dahomey has been recently added, completing her supremacy over almost the entire western section of the northern half of Africa. As regards population, however, Great Britain, with a protectorate of 2,570,926 square miles, is immensely in advance of all other nations. Germany follows, with 866,000 square miles, Portugal, with 735,304, and Italy, with 602,000. Spain has her possessions mostly in islands off the West Coast, with an area of 243,877 square miles. Then there are countries tributary, as Egypt and Tripoli to Turkey, and independent, as Morocco in the north, some of the Soudan States in the interior, the South African Republic, the Orange River Free State, Swaziland in the south, and Liberia in the west. Not the least remarkable among the recent political changes in Africa is the creation by an International Conference at Berlin, in 1885, of the Congo Free State, which was placed under the personal sovereignty of the King of the Belgians. In 1889 the king by will bequeathed to Belgium all his sovereign rights in the State, and at a convention held July 3, 1890, between representatives of Belgium and the Congo Free State, the right of annexing the latter was reserved to Belgium after a period of ten years.

Missionary work in Africa has developed rapidly within a generation. The Moravians, who entered Africa on the West Coast as early as 1736, were the pioneers, but were obliged to give up the struggle on account of the deadly climate of that region. They entered South Africa in 1737, but were bitterly opposed and practically expelled by the Dutch. Subsequently, in 1792, they renewed the effort, and have established permanent and useful missions. The great missionary siege of the African continent has been entered upon by all the leading missionary societies of the world. The London Missionary Society established itself in Africa as early as 1798, and was followed by the Church Missionary Society in 1804, the Wesleyan in 1811, the American Baptist Missionary Union in 1821, the Basle Missionary Society in 1827, the Rhenish and the French Evangelical Missions in 1829, the American Presbyterians, Methodists, and Episcopalians and the American Board of Commissioners in 1833, the Berlin in 1834, and since then the English Baptists, the Free Church of Scotland, the Universities' Mission to Central Africa, the Scotch and American United Presbyterian Churches, the Established Church of Scotland, and many others have added their forces to the advancing hosts. Among the recent developments in this noble campaign is the occupation of Uganda by the Church Missionary Society, the opening up of mission work in the Congo Valley, the new push of the Church Missionary Society into the Soudan by way of the Upper Niger, and the North African Mission among the Berbers. The total result at present is represented by 42 missionary societies, 1000 stations, 1168 missionaries, and about 1,000,000 Protestant adherents, of whom 101,212 are communicants. The Christian world has received no Macedonian call more startling and pathetic than that which comes from Africa. We listen with wonder and awe to the voice of a continent which speaks to us as follows:

Our cry is out of the depths; we belong to the submerged millions of the race; our existence has been shrouded in darkness for centuries. A whole continent of forgotten humanity has suddenly awakened to consciousness, and appeals to the human brotherhood of favored nations for help and hope, and a share in the blessings of heaven. We have long dwelt in ignorance and misery, the slaves of unhappy destiny, banished from the world's light, and strangers to the world's civilization. Within a generation we have found the white man pressing in among our vast populations for political and commercial ends, but not always to our own highest welfare. To the long and dreadful chapter of wrong and cruelty which the slave-trader has written in blood upon the quivering heart of Africa must now be added the sad story of the introduction of intoxicants, which to our amazement and sorrow have come to us from lands of Christian light, although brought by the hands of unchristian greed. We have wondered if this new era would not bring us also our share of those "good tidings of great joy which shall be to all people." Here and there around the vast circle of our seacoasts there are already centers of light, which have moved inward at some points as if to illumine the central darkness. But, after all, these centers of light are few in comparison with our need, and the movements of Christianity in our behalf seem to be slow and inadequate. We are thankful for the lives and labors of some of the world's noblest missionaries. We see in them, and in others who have come to carry on their work, what Christianity can do for man, and our own hearts yearn toward this far-off ideal.

The brief history of Christian missions in Africa has in it less of discouragement than would naturally be expected. We point to the trophies of the Gospel in South Africa, where the venerated Moffat labored, to our martyrs in Uganda, to such fruitful institutions as Lovedale, and the Gordon Memorial, and the Huguenot Seminary at Wellington, and to the results of evangelistic and educational work in Egypt, Uganda, Livingstonia, Transvaal, Madagascar, South Africa, the Congo, Gaboon, and the valley of the Niger. The London Missionary Society has 51,250 African names on its church rolls; the Wesleyan Missionary Society, 18,000; the Berlin Missionary Society, 11,456; the Church Missionary Society, 8700; the Paris Evangelical Society, 9662; the United Presbyterians, 3571; the American Presbyterians at Gaboon, 1563; and the American Board, 1300. A little handful of 101,000 have been redeemed in Africa, while Christian missions have touched in all a million of our people. Yet there is a tract in the interior north of the Congo, as large as all Europe, without a single missionary. The religion of Islam has brought no blessing to Africa, and it can never regenerate our people. Wherever it has made for itself a pathway among us it is found to be associated with polygamy and slavery. The former is an old curse of Africa, and the latter has never been so cruel, so blighting, and so bloody as by the hand of the Arab Mohammedan.

We hear that the discovery of America four hundred years ago had in it the making of a nation where civilization, freedom, and moral culture have ripened and bloomed as never before in the history of the world. We believe that this has all happened under the inspiration of Christianity, and now at the opening hour of our own era of progress we pray for a mighty infusion at the outset of Christian instruction and guidance, that our own Columbian future may have in it the power of that heaven-sent religion whose mission it is to regenerate the world. As Columbus sailed across the seas to America, so Livingstone and Stanley and the noble missionaries of recent years have trod the silent paths of the African forests, and have brought to us the very Bible that is enshrined in the modern history of Christendom. We plead for the religion of Christ. Who like us can plead from such depths of need? Who can reveal such a pitiful past to give urgency to the prayer? Who can show such present wrongs in the slave-trade and the traffic in rum, and such new perils from the very presence of civilization, as we who implore, not the worst, but the best that you can give us?

Come over and help AFRICA.

From the great continent of Africa we turn to the TURKISH EMPIRE, the heart of the Mohammedan world. Since the Mohammedan conquest in the seventh century Moslem power has been predominant in western Asia, and since the establishment of Turkish supremacy in the thirteenth century these fair lands of the Levant have been dominated by the Turkish government. The rule of the Turks has brought no hope or inspiration to the subject Christian races, and the haughty and fanatical Islamic spirit has been a constant menace to the rights of Christian populations, who have lived in abject deference to the ruling Moslem power. The wide and absolute supremacy of the Turk has been much curtailed within the past half-century, and yet he is still the civil and military ruler of the Christian races of his empire, and claims, moreover, absolute lordship over the consciences of his Moslem constituency. The progress of religious liberty in Turkey has had a notable advance during the past fifty years, and yet the results are rather theoretical than practical, as the strong hand of religious bigotry and military power still rests upon every Moslem, and he accepts Christianity only at his imminent personal peril. The Christian races of the empire have been expected simply to exist upon sufferance, and while their religion has been tolerated freely among themselves, it was with the understanding that they should not assert themselves or assume toward the government any other attitude than that of abject humility and constructive non-existence.

Missionary enterprise entered Turkey in a quiet and almost unnoticed way some seventy years ago, when missionaries from the American Board first landed at Smyrna in 1820 and in Palestine in 1821. Since then slow but steady progress has been made, very largely under American auspices, until of late years magnificent and inspiring results have developed, and the Turkish Empire has been the scene of the partial regeneration and revival of the old Christian races, who have caught the inspiration of the age from the missionaries, and under the stimulus of education and the uplifting power of biblical Christianity have become the leading races of the empire. The Mohammedan populations have kept up the old Islamic spirit, cherishing their haughty self-complacency, living in an atmosphere of religious pride, and boasting of their political ascendency. The Oriental Christian Churches, meanwhile, have been the scene of one of the noblest and most substantial missionary triumphs of the past century. The Christian races of the Orient have responded quickly and vigorously to the touch of a living Christianity. Colleges and schools for both sexes have been established. The Bible has been translated, and a religious literature created. Churches have been established, and generations of the young have been trained in Bible knowledge. The result is that the Christian races are now leading in the intellectual progress and modern development of the empire, to the dismay and chagrin of the Moslem element.

The Turkish government has taken offense at the impulse which the Christian subjects of the Porte have received from missions, and is thoroughly alarmed by this silent revolution which has come without excitement, and almost without observation, and is irresistibly reversing the relations of the Moslem and the Christian. The policy of the Turkish government has been increasingly inimical and aggressive in its attacks upon mission work. It has endeavored to close schools; to suppress literature; to deal a staggering blow to the rising ascendency of the awakening Christian element of the empire. The American colleges are all under suspicion; mission churches are regarded with disfavor; village schools are especially disliked. The energy, intelligence, and hopefulness of these despised subject races have become too pronounced to be longer endured. Turkish dominion must assert itself anew, and must bring again into moral, intellectual, and civil subjection these rising nationalities that have always sat in silence at the feet of the haughty Moslem. The Christian world has here an interesting and fascinating drama of contemporaneous history to study. The story of the Moslem and the Christian has its pathetic past, and it has also its stirring present. An acute and startling phase of this conflict is hastening on. The Christian has the Providence of God, the power of education, the inspiration of a religious reformation, the impulse and stir of modern thought, the public sentiment of the age, and the sympathies of Christendom on his side. He has a haughty and long-dominant foe to deal with, and the immemorial ascendency of the Moslem will never yield without a desperate struggle.

Deeper than this question of Christian revival is that of liberty of conscience to Moslems themselves. This is stoutly and defiantly denied to them by the Sultan, and by the whole religious and military power of Islam. With the inspiration and glow of a living Christianity must inevitably come the problem of a Moslem's possible attitude toward Christianity. There can be but one goal; there will be but one final solution of this great question. It must end sooner or later in entire and untrammeled religious freedom for every soul in western Asia. The world moves on toward light and freedom. No human will and no human sword can stay its advance. Christian missions in the Orient have had in the past, and have still in the present, a great duty in reëstablishing a pure and biblical Christianity in the

East. The further and perhaps mightier task of securing the supremacy of Christianity over all hearts must also be taken up. Where the sword of the Moslem waved in victory in the seventh century, "the sword of the Spirit, which is the Word of God," must win its triumphs in the twentieth. A half-century of preparation has already wrought wonderful changes, and all things are now in readiness for a rapid and vigorous and successful advance toward the goal of all true missionary effort. Let us listen to the appeal which is presented to us on behalf of evangelical Christianity in the East. The yearnings of awakened multitudes are voiced to us as follows:

We are living in Bible lands, but we are sadly destitute of Bible Christianity. We desire deliverance from the religious tyranny of the Christian hierarchy of bishops and priests, and from the formality and superstition of Oriental Christianity. We look especially to America, since God in His providence has committed our spiritual welfare to the hands of the American churches. We rejoice in the success which has attended the labors of American missionaries throughout the Turkish Empire. Within fifty years they have given us the Bible in eight different languages. A Protestant community of 80,000, of whom 18,000 are communicants, now exists in Turkey, and the native churches number 200. There are six American colleges located at different points in the empire. The total of students is 1200. Seventy students are in training for the ministry. Education has been steadily pushed, through village schools, of which there are now 700, with 50,000 children. Our native languages before the coming of missionaries were barren and empty so far as saving truth and modern knowledge were concerned. The mission presses now print about 40,000,000 pages annually, and over one half of these are pages of God's Word. Medical missionaries have rendered a blessed service, and thousands are helped continually by their healing touch. We plead for Christian literature on behalf of the fifty millions who speak the Arabic language, and who look to the American Mission Press in Beirut for the Word of Life. We plead for evangelical religion on behalf of those who have been taught of man rather than of God, and whose Christianity has hitherto been so sadly corrupted by external ceremonialism and vain superstition. We plead on behalf of our children, that they may have the advantages of Christian education. We point to the harvest which has been already gathered, the first-fruits of that great religious reformation which is coming. "It is daybreak everywhere" throughout the Turkish Empire, and with the coming of the day we hope for providential changes which will give full scope to the intellectual and spiritual aspirations that have been kindled through the return of a biblical Christianity to the land of its birth. When our day of deliverance comes we shall hope to stand alone, and to become ourselves centers of missionary activity in the East. At present we are too weak and too helpless under the shadow of irresponsible power to carry our burdens and fight our battles alone. We still need the American missionary, with his moral stamina, his civil standing, his courage, his faith, his energy, his varied resources, and his financial backing. His work among us has attained a magnificent and permanent impulse, and we beg for your constant and unwearied efforts at this critical period in the history of the revival of Christianity in Bible lands. God has chosen American Christians to be the saviors of Christianity in the East, and a saved and regenerated Christianity in Eastern lands will become a mighty and aggressive power in commending Christ and His Gospel to those who have long rejected it with defiance and scorn. The time is soon coming when we shall surely need all the moral support and the national sympathy that we are sure American Christianity will give in our time of trial. We shall hope to be found faithful, and one of the sources of our strength and hope will be the prayers and sympathies of Christian America, by whose ministry we have learned again of Christ and His Gospel. *Come over and help the* TURKISH EMPIRE.

To the eastward of the Turkish Empire is PERSIA, a land which was an integral part of the ancient Medo-Persian Empire, and whose present condition resembles in many respects the sister-empire of Turkey. Its area is estimated at 628,800 square miles, about three times the size of France. Its population is about 9,000,000, of which nearly 2,000,000 are nomadic. Its prominent races are the Turks, Persians, Arabs, and Kurds. The Mohammedans of Persia number

8,000,000, but they are mostly of the Shiah sect; the Armenian population is about 43,000, and the Nestorian 23,000. Until the third century of the Christian era the Armenian, Nestorian, and Persian Churches were in existence, but in the fourth century a terrible persecution swept over these Christian Churches, annihilating the Persian branch, and leaving only the remnants of the Armenian and Nestorian. These ancient, historic Churches have survived in a corrupt and feeble state until the present day, when Protestant missions have occupied Persia, and, with the Armenian and Nestorian Churches as a basis, have entered upon a missionary campaign.

Henry Martyn, a chaplain in India, came to Shiraz in Persia in 1811, where he spent nearly a year working upon the translation of the New Testament into Persian. It was finished in 1812, and Martyn ended his work with the following prayer: "Now may the Spirit who gave the Word, and called me, I trust, to be an interpreter of it, graciously and powerfully apply it to the hearts of sinners, even to gathering an elect people from the long-estranged Persians." Martyn left the country on September 12, 1812, for England, without any knowledge of a single Christian convert in Persia, and stopping at Tocat, Asia Minor, *en route*, died after a week's illness, and was buried there.

Rev. C. G. Pfander, of the Basle Missionary Society, followed in 1829, but when in 1834 Georgia was annexed by Russia, the missionaries were expelled. In 1833 Rev. Frederick Haas began mission work at Tabriz, but left in 1837. The mission of the American Board was commenced in 1834, and has been conducted with energy and devotion under the care of that society until 1871, and since by the Presbyterian Board of Foreign Missions of the United States, to whom at that time it was transferred. The Church Missionary Society in 1875 formally adopted a mission which had been started by Rev. Dr. Bruce in 1869. They have stations at present at Julfa and Bagdad. In 1869 what has been known as the "Archbishop's Mission to the Assyrian Christians" was founded. Its object is rather the restoration of the old Nestorian Church than an incisive and thorough conversion of the people to spiritual and biblical forms of Christianity. The historical pedigree of the Nestorian

Church is regarded by the patrons of the Archbishop's Mission as so satisfactory and unexceptionable that its spiritual degeneracy does not seem to call for a radical and thorough evangelical reformation, but only for a reëstablishment of the old organization and a quickening of its ancient forms.

The progress of mission work in Persia has been attended with many difficulties. Moslem fanaticism, backed by the government, is alert and virulent. The Christian hierarchy is also jealous and unscrupulous in opposition. Much has been accomplished, however, in establishing a pure Christian Church in these ancient seats of early Christian history. Persecutions on the part of the Moslem authorities, and especially the fanatical populace, have been frequent and severe, and only the past year has revealed in the story of Mirza Ibrahim a record of heroism and fearless devotion to religious conviction which has ended in his martyrdom in a Persian prison.

The revised Syriac Bible has recently been issued under the superintendence of Rev. Dr. Benjamin Labaree, at the expense of the American Bible Society. The past year has been one of severe strain, on account of the prevalence of cholera, by which it is estimated that 50,000 people died. The heroism of an American lady physician, Miss Mary Bradford, of Tabriz, was the means of saving many lives, and was an inspiring illustration of that courage and devotion which Christian womanhood has revealed upon the foreign mission field. During recent years throughout a rapidly widening sphere, a new and powerful impulse has been given to the cause of world-wide missions by the magnetic influence and the sweet ministry of woman. She has lovingly assumed an ever increasing share of toil and responsibility. A message from Persia voices to us the Macedonian call of that distant land as follows:

We are far removed from the touch of Western civilization, and yet recent years have brought us, to an unexpected extent, some of the advantages of the modern world. Our cry, however, is not for mere civilization—we want the Gospel of Christ. American missionaries have sought us out, and have brought to us the teachings of the Bible and the benefits of education and the ministry of healing. We have churches and schools and hospitals. Men and women of noble and lovely characters have spent their lives among us as the messengers of your American churches. They have trained our native preachers and teachers, so that we have 361 native Christians engaged in mission work. We have 37 organized churches, and many more places where the Gospel is preached. The communicants gathered into our mission churches number 2443, while 3341 of our children are under mission instruction. These statistics but faintly represent the influence of evangelical Christianity. A new era has dawned, and the hope of a wider and more quickening Christian revival throughout Persia is kindling our hearts. We are a little group of Christ's followers in the midst of an overshadowing and overwhelming hostile element, but our influence over our Mohammedan fellow-countrymen has not been without its results, and we plead for help to go forward with firmness and energy, and with God's blessing we shall yet have a noble part in the victories of the Gospel over its giant Moslem foe. *Come over and help* PERSIA.

From western Asia we now cross the seas to the Western world, and before us is the continent of SOUTH AMERICA. A Macedonian cry of continental proportions again sounds upon our ears. South America has been called in its missionary aspects "The Neglected Continent." It is a vast region of the earth, over which the deepest shadows of Romanism have rested for centuries. The need of Gospel light and instruction is pitiful. The reign of ignorance and superstition is despotic and unchallenged. The total area of the continent is nearly 7,000,000 square miles, and its population is estimated at 34,000,000. It consists largely of Spanish and Portuguese mixed races, numbering about 23,000,000, while there are about 3,000,000 Negro freemen and 4,000,000 pagan Indians. It is a continent largely of republics, numbering ten in all, the only exceptions being the provinces of Dutch, French, and British Guiana on the northeast coast. The natural features are on a scale of magnificence unexcelled by any other section of the world. Chief among these physical wonders is the river system, comprising the Orinoco, the La Plata, and the Amazon, the latter being the largest river of the world, with 25,000 miles of navigable water-way, penetrating the continent in every direction to the base of the Andes. The mountain system is equally grand.

The continent was discovered A.D. 1500 by a Portuguese navigator, so that its Columbian anniversary is only eight years later than that of our own continent; but the destiny of the northern and southern divisions of the Western world has been marvelously different. North America has developed under Puritan influences; South America has been under the sway of Papal power. One has been largely Protestant; the other has been wholly Romish. The development in the north has been along the lines of freedom, intelligence, and morality, under the enlightened training of a spiritual and biblical form of Christianity. The result in the south has been marred and shadowed by priestly tyranny, gross ignorance, and defective morality, combined with superstitious bigotry and the lowest forms of external and hollow ceremonialism. The spirit of the Inquisition still hides in the Papal system of South America. The blind intolerance of medieval Romanism still fights for supremacy, and the battle of the age for liberty of conscience is yet to be fought and won in a large portion of the southern continent.

The pioneer missionaries to South America

were the Moravians, who entered Dutch Guiana in 1735, and after a long and weary struggle with the deadly climate finally established a work which has resulted in missionary efforts that have made the three Guianas the brightest lands on the South American continent. In 1854 a final entrance was secured to Tierra del Fuego, after the heroic struggles of Allen Gardiner and his companions had closed with the tragic story of their death. Thus the continent in its northern and southern extremities was consecrated to missionary effort by heroic exhibitions of the martyr spirit. Since then various mission agencies have entered, until at the present time it is occupied by seventeen societies, as follows: the southern branches of the American Baptist, Presbyterian, and Methodist Episcopal, and the northern branches of the American Presbyterian and Methodist Episcopal Churches, the London Missionary Society, the British and Foreign Bible Society, the American Bible Society, the American Episcopal, the Moravian, and the South American Missionary Society, besides Bishop Taylor's Mission, the Help for Brazil Society, the West Indian Conference, the Society for the Propagation of the Gospel, the Plymouth Brethren, and the Salvation Army. An effort to estabtablish still another centre of work is about to be made by a band of young men recently graduated from the missionary training-college of Dr. Guinness, in East London. Their objective point is Peru, one of the most neglected places upon the continent, where, as in the case of Venezuela, Ecuador, and Bolivia, there is practically no missionary work in operation. Let us listen now to the message of "The Neglected Continent," which comes to us as follows:

We regard our appeal as a Macedonian cry in a sense as significant and historic as any which reaches the ear of the Christian Church from any other section of the earth. We consider our appeal, at least to the American Churches, as containing this special element of urgency, that we are in a sense neighbors, and therefore plead the interests of those who for this reason should not be forgotten in the missionary plans of your home churches. We have modeled our systems of government after the example of the American republic, and we have ten great States having constitutions framed after the pattern of our mighty sister-republic of the north, although we must confess that republican institutions are not as yet regarded by us with that sense of personal responsibility and that reverence for truth and righteousness which are the only safeguards of popular government. We have learned that a republican form of government will not in itself create and mold a great nation. We need the Bible and the religion of the Bible, and the enlightening and uplifting power of biblical morality, to give to the republics of South America the stability, the moral earnestness, and the Christian patriotism of the favored nation of the north.

A careful study of our religious state will convince the conscientious student of missions that our need is disproportionately great, and that we have not received that attention from the friends of Christian missions which our destitute condition deserves. Some of our large countries are still practically untouched by any serious effort on the part of the Protestant Churches. Ecuador, with a population of over a million, has no missionary; Bolivia, with a population of 2,300,000, is also without a missionary; Venezuela, with a population of over 2,000,000, has only one Protestant missionary; Peru, with a population of 3,000,000, has only one missionary with a few native helpers; Colombia, with a population of 4,000,000, has only eleven missionaries; Brazil, with a population of 14,000,000, has eighty-one missionaries; and a comparative presentation of our need with that of other lands where foreign missions have entered would reveal the fact that of all the countries where work has been established hardly any is so poorly supplied with men and resources as the continent of South America. It is not an exaggeration to state that we have 30,000,000 people practically untouched by missionary effort.

The total number of missionaries at work in South America, including men and women, is not more than 325, and the communicants do not exceed 15,000; yet in some sections where the work has been pushed with aggressive energy, as in Brazil, there has been a manifest response, and a spirit of individual responsibility and local interest has led to the formation of a national organization of Protestant Churches, from which good results are hoped for in the future. In Chili also the work of the American Presbyterian missionaries has assumed a hopeful aspect, and even in the midst of civil strife and turbulence progress has been made. We desire a better and nobler religious life, and we have no hope of obtaining it except through a stronger infusion of biblical truth, and a purer exemplification of righteous living on the part of our religious leaders and of our entire Christian population than we have ever yet had under Papal auspices.

South America is sadly destitute of evangelical religion, lying in the deepest depths of medieval apostasy, and only the Spirit of the Living God and the inspiring contact of the Living Word can arouse and refresh us with the sweet uplifting power of spiritual Christianity. Our cry for help, while it is not that of heathenism, is just as earnest and intense as the mightiest appeal of lands that are utterly shrouded in darkness. We are as destitute of spiritual, saving Christianity as those who have never heard the Gospel message of salvation. *Come over quickly and help SOUTH AMERICA.*

From South America we turn northward and traverse the Central American States to MEXICO. On every side there is the same woful need of missionary effort. Through all Central America, consisting of the five little republics of Honduras, Guatemala, Nicaragua, Costa Rica, and San Salvador, there are signs of the unbounded influence and unchallenged dominion of the Papal Church. A spirit of toleration, however, is in the air, and religion is becoming less and less a matter of State regulation. Freedom of conscience is winning recognition more and more. The Wesleyan Church of England, the Moravians, and the Presbyterian Church (North) have already established missions in Central America, and some other minor societies have inaugurated work there, but in San Salvador, with a population of 777,895, there is still not a single voice from all neighboring Christendom proclaiming the glad tidings.

As we enter Mexico we come in contact with a story of civil progress and missionary success which is an occasion for gratitude, and gives large hope for the future. Within a generation a downtrodden and priest-ridden nation has won civil liberty and come out into the light of modern republican civilization. Protestant missions fully established twenty-one years ago have just come of age in our neighboring republic. Twelve missionary societies are already at work there, with a record full of promise. The missionary statistics of Mexico yield such encouraging results as the following:

There are 385 organized churches, 177 foreign missionaries, 512 native workers, 16,250 communicants, 50,000 adherents, over 7000 of the young under instruction in mission schools, and over 10,000 in Sabbath-schools. Literary agencies have not been neglected. During the last year the agent of the American Bible Society sold 4361 Bibles, 7475 Testaments, and 9240 Gospels.

The government is professedly friendly, and guarantees full protection to its citizens, and is ready to forcibly interdict all religious persecution. The advance of Mexico in material, commercial, educational, economic, and international respects has been phenomenal, and there is an open door for aggressive missionary effort. The appeal of Mexico is brief but urgent, as follows:

Our interests are largely identified with those of the great republic. We look to the Christian Churches of America to give us sympathy and help in our struggles to throw off the dominion of our Papal masters, who have ruled us to our detriment and misery for centuries. We have caught now the spirit of free institutions, and we believe in a religion of light. We desire an open Bible, a free Gospel, a living Christianity, and a biblical standard of morality. Give us freely of the spiritual help, and lead us quickly into those paths of peace and hope and happiness which have been the lot of Christian America. We think that we can absorb all that you can give us, and we beg that without delay we may have a generous share of the spiritual riches of the pure Gospel. *Come over and help MEXICO.*

Were there space to incorporate them, we might record Macedonian calls of similar import and urgency from other, though less conspicuous, portions of the earth, many of them in a still more needy and destitute condition. We could listen to the appeal of some of the larger islands of the East Indies, of the Malay Peninsula, Siberia, Russia, Thibet, Afghanistan, Baluchistan, Arabia, Greece, Greenland, and the West Indies. Are not the examples which have been given, however, sufficient to show the urgent and thrilling significance of this Macedonian appeal to the Church of Christ in our present generation? Let me ask further, was there anything in the state of the Roman Empire in the age of the apostles, and subsequently, which made it more important that the Gospel should be given to the world then than that it should be given to the world now? In truth, every great argument for an aggressive and world-wide Gospel which was effective then applies with equal pertinency now. There is the same divine command in existence, with its authority unimpaired and its urgency undiminished. There is the same need, which has grown even more manifest. There is the same awful, solemn, pitiful, and urgent fact of heathenism. There are the same serious and perplexing obstacles to be overcome. There are the same claims of brotherhood, the same possibility of rescue, the same power and value to the Gospel, the same evidential worth to a triumphant Christianity, the same training and spiritual culture needed in the Church and in the personal character of Christians. In fact, we cannot discover one single claim which the heathenism of the Roman Empire could bring forward which does not exist to-day, nor one single reason which applied to the Christianity of apostolic times in the interests of aggressive missions in that day which does not apply with equal force at the present time.

Let us advance a step further, and consider the additional reasons which give even greater urgency to the claims of missions in our own age. Compare our present knowledge of the heathen world and its needs with that of earlier ages. How much more is known by us than was known even a hundred years ago, when Carey studied these great problems! Consider the present facilities of travel and access to all parts of the known world, and the resources of present organization, either on the field or at home. There are missionary societies at the present time which in home administration and foreign resources and facilities will compare favorably in organized efficiency with the foreign offices and state departments of civilized governments. Consider also the present international restraint which rests upon hostile governments in their treatment of foreign residents, and the possibility of missionary residence in almost every foreign field, in easy and constant communication with society and churches and friends in the home land. Note also the enormous wealth of the Christian Church, which can guarantee the support of the missionary and his work, and also the rising interest in mission work, which is a sustaining and cheering incitement to those who labor in distant and obscure localities. No religious newspaper of the day could afford, even if it were so inclined, to dispense with its missionary intelligence, and in one of our most prominent religious weeklies, which is conducted with exceptional alertness and discrimination, a special missionary department has been lately established, with a monthly budget of letters fresh from the prominent centers of foreign missionary service. Does it not seem as if our Master, with the same supreme purpose in view, and the same promises and rewards for faithful service, while making it even more imperative upon the Church of this age to go into all the world with the Gospel for every creature, was at the same time making it a simpler, more inspiring, and more attractive thing to do? And thereby, while the cross is made easier, the failure to take it up and carry it is made the more conspicuous and inexcusable and disloyal.

If the condition of our fallen world was such as to call for the sacrifice of Christ, then the condition of heathenism in our day would require the sacrifice of Christ at the present hour, had it never been made before. If this is true, then this grand fact comes to the front, that after eighteen hundred years of delay, the Church of Christ, with a finished atonement, a printed Bible, the coöperation of the Holy Spirit, and an unparalleled array of magnificent material resources, has the privilege of accomplishing triumphantly a service which is worth the sacrifice of the Son of God. If Christ had never given Himself, He would be ready to do it now for the heathen world of our own present day, and what He would be willing to lay down His life for the sake of accomplishing, He calls upon His Church to do in His name, with the surpassing promise of His own presence and leadership, and the assurance of success. "The brother for whom Christ died," says Paul; "the brother for whom Christ *would die*," says the Spirit and Providence of God to a Church holding in her hands the sacred trust of the Gospel, and possessing the material facilities, the spiritual resources, and the readily accessible power to bring this world into subjection to Christ before another century of modern missionary history shall close.

LECTURE III.

THE PRESENT-DAY CONFLICTS OF THE FOREIGN FIELD.

"*To the missionary laborer in far lands, mastering with difficulty unknown tongues, surrounded by unfamiliar arts and dusky faces, toiling for years to make a few souls know something of Him who taught in Palestine, the future is as certain as if he touched it; and that future, to his exulting expectation, is to be as radiant with glory as the sky over Calvary was heavy with gloom —as resplendent with lovely celestial lights as to his imagination, if you hold that the faculty chiefly concerned, was the mount of the Lord's supreme ascension. He expects long toil, and many disasters, incarnadined seas, dreary wildernesses, battles with giants, and spasms of fear in the heart of the Church. But he looks, as surely as he looks for the sunrise, after nights of tempest and of lingering dawn, for the ultimate illumination of the world by the Faith. And however full of din and dissonance the history of mankind has seemed hitherto, seems even to-day, he anticipates already the harmonies to be in it, as under the guidance of Him of Galilee it draws toward its predestined close, 'not sentimental or idyllic, but epic and heroic.'*"

REV. RICHARD S. STORRS, D.D., LL.D.

III.

THE PRESENT-DAY CONFLICTS OF THE FOREIGN FIELD.

CONFLICT is a condition of progress in all great reforms. Reformation implies a struggle with existing evils. Great wrongs cannot be righted, nor crying evils remedied, nor giant abuses corrected, without sharp and vigorous contention. The history of human progress yields abundant testimony in support of this statement. Nations have fought for freedom and self-government, the people have found deliverance from oppressive taxation, unjust discrimination, and the overshadowing claims of selfishness, only by agitation and strenuous opposition. Restraints have been put upon cruel customs and inhuman abuses only through strife. Society has to fight against the giant evils which threaten its security and happiness; it must wage a perpetual warfare with crime, intemperance, impurity, anarchy, political corruption, and socialistic license. The Church is in perpetual conflict with sacerdotalism, formalism, superstition, bigotry, unreasoning traditionalism, and rationalistic liberalism. Conflict is therefore a sign of aggressive efforts in every sphere of reform.

The foreign missionary enterprise is simply an organized effort to accomplish a spiritual reformation. It is a marshaling of religious and moral forces for a universal campaign against sin and error. Its purpose is to dislodge Satan, to dethrone superstition, to overthrow human usurpations, to deliver man from spiritual slavery, to institute moral reforms, and to introduce the life-giving and soul-inspiring spiritual energies of the Gospel into the individual and social and national life of peoples who have been long under the sway of false teaching, and who are wedded to their sins and errors. It is a reform which aims at sweeping and radical changes, which cannot be properly understood and appreciated at the outset by the unconverted multitudes. It strikes at universal sin and wrong; it disturbs evil in all its forms, searches it out in all its lairs, unmasks its sophistries, exposes its cunning devices, and brands it in whatever disguises it may pose, or whatever alluring forms it may wear. Foreign missions may be considered simply as God at work in the world, with His own chosen instruments and methods, for the amelioration of the woes of the race and the lifting of mankind into contact with the one supernatural agency that can start the soul toward heaven and give it strength to pursue the upward pathway.

Any intelligent survey of foreign missions at the present stage of their progress will therefore inevitably reveal a broad and varied realm of conflict, and we shall now ask your attention to some of the more prominent phases of this strenuous struggle, which has been precipitated by the very success which marks the progress of the cause. We note as worthy of attention:

I. The conflict with a self-centered Christianity in the Church at home. The expression seems like a contradiction in terms, for one of the first and most characteristic triumphs of Christianity in the heart is to dethrone self and clothe it in the livery of service, and bid it center its thoughts upon others; yet so tenacious and despotic is the sway of self, and so subtle and disguised is the approach of the tempter, that these high behests are often ignored until Christianity itself may become self-centered. We would guard this statement carefully, so that it shall not be understood to apply to that inner circle of unselfish followers of the Master who count it their joy and privilege to seek the good of others, in the name of Christ. There are many such, and they are the salt of the Church, and Christianity is kept from corruption and collapse by their sweet loyalty to the Master's spirit. They reach out after the needy, the distressed, and the wandering; they shed a glow of sympathy, of comfort, and of inspiration into chilled and darkened hearts; they love the kingdom, and rejoice in its advancement, and pray for its progress wherever there are souls to seek and save. They are faithful to the claims of home Christianity, and they are loyal, too, to the claims of a world-wide stewardship. The cause of foreign missions is borne up as upon wings by their prayers, their gifts, and their indefatigable labors for its advancement. I have called this an inner circle, and rightly so, for it is the very heart of the Church, and it is inner in relation to the larger outer circle of Christians to whom the cause of foreign missions is little more than a name, and many of whom regard it with aversion or distrust or entire indifference.

There are many, too, who, while they heartily respect Christianity, and honor its mission of service, are inclined to argue that the whole duty of the Church is done when it is faithful to the work near at hand. They draw the line at foreign missions, and will not allow their Christian sympathy and their sense of duty to reach out beyond the circle in which their own lives move. Among all such there is a lamentable ignorance with reference to the history, the progress, the surpassing claims, and the stirring triumphs of this great cause. There is hardly any realm of current knowledge in which they are so utterly lost. There is no sphere of the Church's activities which they so studiously ignore as that of missions. The world knows more of its actors, its statesmen, its soldiers, its explorers, its scientists, and its latest and lowest records in every sphere of contest than the majority of Christians know about the missionary enterprises of this century. The literature of missions, which is now so able, so voluminous, and so packed with stimulating facts, is hardly allowed even a place in their current reading. The result of this ignorance is that many false statements that are carelessly or cruelly made with reference to missions find a ready credence where they should only receive a prompt denial.

There is also a deep-seated indifference in the hearts of many as to the whole missionary movement of the Church. It is a matter which is treated with invariable apathy, and sometimes with positive contempt. It is simply kept outside the circle of serious thought or conscious interest. A sermon on foreign missions is never welcome, and all contact with the whole subject is avoided as wearisome and distasteful. The natural result is consistent illiberality in all gifts to the cause. It is an astonishing fact that there are by actual count 2224 Presbyterian churches in our own communion in America which gave last year absolutely nothing to foreign missions, while there were only four presbyteries in which every church gave something. Could the statistics be accurately tabulated, it would no doubt be found that in the churches which gave, the gifts were largely from the inner circle of those who know something of missions, and give out of love to Christ, and with a profound appreciation of the cause as God's latest and clearest sign to His people, and the freshest touch of the Lord in the exercise of His mediatorial sovereignty as the Head of His Church. The great mass of Christians, if they were honest with themselves, would confess that they give little, and that little they give with less interest than to any other department of church benevolence.

With this self-centered spirit in the Church the cause of foreign missions has to contend as if for its life. Its work increases, and it cannot reach the great constituency of the Church to secure the support it needs. If Christians but realized it, there is nothing more inimical to the true power and the high spiritual welfare of the Church than this same self-centered spirit. The law of Christianity is self-communication; its strength grows by extension. Self-communication is a law of the divine existence, and God has made Christianity after His own likeness in this respect. The Church lives only by an effort to give life to others. A Christianity which is not aggressive becomes regressive. A state of inaction sinks at once into a state of degeneration. A reclining Church soon becomes a declining Church. It is a philosophical and practical truth that the only way to save religion from extinction is to extend it. It has been objected to foreign missions that this country has no religion to spare; but the only way that a country or a Church can have any religion to spare is through an unsparing effort to impart that religion freely to others. Self-sacrifice is the condition of self-preservation, and giving impoverisheth not, but rather enriches. Oh that this unnatural, this unhallowed conflict with a self-centered Christianity might come to an end, and the Church of Christ be more Christ-like in this one sublime and unique characteristic of the Master—His mission "to seek and to save that which was lost." A Christianity that seeks is a Christianity that saves. A Christianity which simply nourishes itself soon loses its power. The true and sufficient antidote to spiritual coldness and feebleness in the Church, to worldliness and religious indifference in the hearts of Christians, and to the encroachments of rationalism in doctrine, is the glow and sacrifice of a true missionary zeal. A Church which is absorbed and inspired by missionary activities has little to fear from heresy or worldliness or spiritual degeneracy. Christ Himself walks in the midst of the golden candlesticks that are lighted with the flame of His own consuming zeal for the souls of men.

II. We turn our attention now to conflicts with rival and intrusive missions. We speak here of conflicts rather than of rivalries, for Protestant missions are usually bitterly opposed, often through violent and unscrupulous measures, by competing missions, who conduct their work not in a spirit of generous rivalry, but of desperate and dogged conflict. It is unhappily true that Romish, and especially Jesuit, missions are not content simply to push their own work side by side with evangelical agencies, but they wage war upon Protestant missions, and seek with unscrupulous zeal and bitter determination to destroy them. The missions of the Romish Church are active, vigorous, and extended. Upon almost every field of Protestant missionary activity we have these cunning and implacable foes plotting against us, and seeking through every channel of influence to stay our progress. In many countries, especially in Mexico, in the South American republics, in Madagascar, in several groups of the Pacific Islands, to a certain extent in the Turkish Empire, and in some parts of Africa, they are able to count upon the sympathy and even the practical aid of the government, either native or foreign. In other lands, as in China, Japan, and India, they are diligent and active in using every available resource to accomplish their purpose. Their attention seems to be about equally divided between pushing their own missionary efforts and thwarting those under Protestant auspices.

Roman Catholic governments in Europe, however much they may distrust the Jesuits at home, are ready to use them as political agents in their colonies, and thus it often happens that State and Church are banded against Protestantism through this alliance between Romish missionaries and local government officials. At the present time Romanism is making progress in Japan, and a hierarchy has been recently established there, with an archbishop at Tokyo, and under him bishops at various points throughout the empire. Although Romish missionaries were once expelled from Japan, yet they are slowly winning again a formidable position there, which we may be sure they will use to the detriment of evangelical missions. In China it is estimated that there are 500,000 converts to Romanism, and the missionary staff of the Church, with its 600 Europeans and 550 native priests, are opponents not to be despised; while in Tonquin and Cochin China Romanism has an open field, and this is true of a large part of Malaysia. In the Caroline Islands, since the occupation by Spain, there are islands, such as Ponape, for example, where the people are strictly prohibited from holding religious service except under Catholic auspices. The aggressions of the Church of Rome in the Punjab have recently been made a subject of special attention by the Protestant missionary societies of that region. In Syria Jesuit intrigue and opposition are a most serious hindrance to Protestant success. In Mexico the intolerant hatred of Romanism, although much restrained by the present government, often breaks out into violent and bloody attacks upon evangelical missionary agents, and the administration hitherto has been so largely under the power of the Papal party that there has been hardly any check to intrigue, while the authority of officials too often lends itself to the service of the Romish Church. The latest and most conspicuous phase of this conflict is in the distracted state of Uganda, where Romanism has been busy plotting and scheming, by fair means or foul, to banish Protestant missionaries and destroy their work.

While the Romish Church is our most formidable foe, yet we must not forget the animosity of the Greek and Armenian and Coptic Churches; nor should we ignore the efforts of the extreme High-Church party, wherever they come in contact with evangelical missionaries, to conduct their work in a spirit of exclusive and often somewhat haughty rivalry, where we should at least expect a broad charity and a generous fellowship. What is called "The Archbishop's Mission to the Assyrian Christians," in Persia, is a leading illustration at the present time of an uncalled-for and distracting intrusion into a mission field already successfully occupied by a vigorous Protestant mission. The efforts of the Plymouth Brethren have often given great annoyance to missionaries, but the harm which they have done has usually been temporary, and those who have for a time been led to accept their singular perversions of Christian truth have in the end returned to their first love.

III. Still another of these conflicts which is worthy of notice, although its results are probably of little serious injury to the cause of missions, is with the misrepresentations of those who willfully, or through ignorance or prejudice, are disposed to bear false witness against missionaries and their work. There are many would-be critics of missions who often make public statements with reference to the characters and lives of missionaries, their methods of conducting the work, and its results, which are either utterly false, or pervaded by such a spirit of disparagement, and sometimes of contempt, that many fair-minded people are unduly influenced, and those who are already prejudiced are confirmed and encouraged in their unfavorable convictions. The authors of these adverse criticisms are sometimes travelers or foreign residents, who may be supposed to have had good opportunities to form a judgment from personal observation, and yet some of the most unjustifiable and misleading animadversions have come from this source. We cannot account for it, except as the result either of failure to ascertain the facts, or an indisposition to treat missions with fairness, or an irresistible inclination to deal them a blow. These statements have been abundantly answered and refuted by the testimony of other witnesses of the highest integrity, and often those who occupy positions of great dignity and honor in the service of the State. We have time only to mention such names as: Lord Lawrence, Sir Donald McLeod, Sir Bartle Frere, Lord Napier, Sir Richard Temple, Sir William Muir, Sir Charles Elliott, Hon. W. E. Gladstone, Sir M. Monier-Williams, Lord Dufferin, Sir Charles Aitchison, Mr. H. M. Stanley, Mr. Charles Darwin, Lieutenant-General Baker, Mrs. Isabella Bird Bishop, Miss C. F. Gordon-Cumming, and United States Ministers Angell, Denby, Lew Wallace, and Whitelaw Reid, and lately Mr. Charles S. Smith, president of the New York Chamber of Commerce, who in various parts of the world have spoken in terms of unstinted admiration and profound respect of the practical good accomplished by missionaries, the sterling value of their personal characters, and the substantial results of their work.

It may be said, also, that while no doubt there are many beautiful and noble exceptions to the statement, yet as a rule the spirit and tone of European society in foreign lands is entirely out of sympathy with the purpose and work of missions. The too prevalent spirit of pride and worldliness, the questionable, and sometimes scandalous, lives of many foreign residents make contact with the missionary upon any terms of cordial sympathy and coöperation impossible, and the result is often an ill-concealed impatience at his presence, and a desire to be rid of him, and free from the rebuke of the Christianity which he teaches. Again, the whole purpose of missions is often regarded with extreme distaste and disparagement by many in foreign lands, who consider the missionary as a fanatic, or a fool, and the effort to teach Christianity as an unwarrantable intrusion into ground already preoccupied by religions which, if not so good as Christianity, are at least good enough for Hindus and Chinamen.

Misrepresentations from other sources have come to the front of late, as in the unspeakably scurrilous placards of the Chinese; and even the contents of the Chinese "Blue Books," published under government auspices, are not free from scandalous statements.

No doubt the great mass of criticisms and misrepresentations referred to can best be met with a dignified silence, and yet much harm is done to the cause of missions among many credulous and uninformed people by such misstatements from apparently authentic sources. We must trust to the dissemination of reliable missionary information, and to the progress of a winning cause, to triumph in the end.

IV. Another dread battle which our foreign missions have to fight is the conflict with dangerous climates and an unhealthful environment. This is not the case in every instance, as many of our missions are in healthful and bracing climates; but throughout the entire tropical belt of the world missionary life is often a serious struggle with depressing and dangerous climatic conditions, and with unsanitary surroundings. Many faithful and valuable missionaries have been the victims of poisonous malaria, deadly fevers, or prostrating sun-strokes, or have yielded to the nervous strain of work where every breath had in it the taint of pestilence. Every large Eastern city is full of lurking danger, which even the utmost prudence and care cannot fully overcome. The water is often foul with contamination. Pestilential diseases are unceasing in their ravages at many points in the East. Leprosy, cholera, malignant fevers, small-pox, diphtheria, and blinding affections of the eyes are so frequently met with in Eastern life as to be rather a matter of every-day than of epidemic experience. Some of the statistics furnished by the British government in India will give an idea of the magnitude and virulence of these dangers to health. It is estimated that there are 500,000 lepers in India, and that there are 417,000 fatal cases of cholera in a single year, and that 3,500,000 annually die of fever and 125,550 of small-pox, even though vaccination is compulsory and nearly 6,000,000 children were vaccinated last year.

These hidden dangers are now rendered less fatal by caution and prudence as a rule of missionary life, a lesson which costly experience has taught. More salubrious localities are selected for mission stations, and a proper regard to the laws of health, in the light of experience, is recognized as a duty which the missionary owes to himself and to his cause. It is now also a part of the policy of missionary societies to provide in some convenient locality missionary *sanatoria*, where in inexpensive but healthful surroundings worn and prostrated workers may have the healing touch of mountain air, and the needed relief of rest and change, and where at certain seasons of the year during the heated term mission conferences may be held, and questions discussed, and plans made, so that the time spent there often sends not only the life-blood bounding through the veins, but throws a new vigor into all the channels of missionary service.

V. Another serious hindrance to foreign missionary effort is occasioned by its conflict with the political and commercial projects of European governments, and with the malign influence of vice and greed as exhibited in the lives of unworthy representatives of Western civilization in foreign lands. Mission work is frequently carried on in countries which are under the political or commercial control of some foreign government, and in such instances it is frequently, although not invariably, true that there is a serious conflict of interest between the government on the one hand and the aim of missions on the other. We must not forget to note, however, that while these conflicts are sometimes a serious hindrance, yet, on the other hand, it is frequently the case that the political or commercial projects of foreign control secure the introduction of modern facilities in the advantages of which mission enterprise has its full share.

At the present moment the illustrations of this painful conflict which stand out most conspicuously before the world are the opium traffic in China and India, the labor traffic in Malaysia and the Pacific Islands, and the Kanaka traffic among the islands of Polynesia for the supply of laborers upon the sugar plantations of Queensland. These latter, as conducted at present, are little else than an organized system of slavery on a very large scale, as we find it illustrated in the case of Chinese coolies at Singapore, which is made a distributing center for the Malaysian Islands. We also mention the trade in intoxicants and firearms in the New Hebrides, the oppressive policy of the Dutch in Java, the rum traffic and slave-trade in Africa, and what is called the liquor traffic in India. To be sure, we cannot hold European governments strictly responsible for all these evils, and yet the relation of the British government to the history of opium in China is too well known to be ignored, and the traffic in rum should be everywhere prohibited where Christian governments have the power to do so; and now that so much of Africa is coming under European control, one of the first and most sacred duties of civilized governments is to deal a death-blow to the slave-trade. The restrictions upon the traffic in intoxicants in the Congo Free State seem to be merely a sham, whereas there should be no difficulty in dealing efficiently with this monstrous evil. While the missionary is offering the cup of salvation to the African, reckless greed and heartless cruelty are pressing the cup of ruin to native lips.

An effort is being made at the present time to secure restrictive legislation as regards intoxicating liquors, firearms, and ammunition throughout the South Sea Islands, especially in the New Hebrides, and it is to be hoped that our own government will heartily join with European powers in some international regulations with a view to the suppression of this evil. Laws of this kind are already in operation in the British colony of Fiji, where the sale of intoxicants to the natives is made an offense punishable by a considerable fine and imprisonment. It is to be hoped that righteous and just consideration for the dictates of humanity, to say nothing of religion, will in the end induce civilized governments to exercise their authority in forbidding these evils, and in the name of civilization and humanity to cast them out.

Few of us realize the terrible ravages of opium among the Chinese. It is now fifty years since the British government forced the entrance of opium into China at the point of her bayonets, and who can picture in imagination the dreadful results that have followed? Between five and six thousand tons are sent from India to China annually as an article of English trade, from which the Indian government derives at the present time an annual revenue of about $32,000,000, while the Viceroy of India is the largest manufacturer of opium in the world. It is estimated that there are in China at the present time not less than eighty million victims to this scourge, and Dr. J. Hudson Taylor stated in the London Missionary Conference in 1888, that, if we take into consideration the families of the victims of opium, there are not less than one hundred and fifty millions of souls suffering, directly or indirectly, from this evil in China. The protests of Christian England against this iniquity have been loud and long, and an anti-opium movement has been fully organized. Numerous and influential public meetings are constantly held for the purpose of staying the evil, and even in the British Parliament in 1891 a majority voted in condemnation of the traffic as "a morally indefensible source of Indian revenue." This vote, however, was taken when there was only a partial attendance in the House, and seems to have been practically inoperative. The declaration has met with much opposition in influential quarters, and even the London *Times*, in commenting upon the fact, remarked that the "House of Commons was simply having one of its too-familiar spasms of cheap

Puritanism." China herself has begged and struggled to be delivered from this curse. Korea is also in the field as a new victim to this vicious habit, which seems to be gaining a hold upon the people of that land, and, judging by the experience of the past, it will not be long before it will be firmly and widely established in that kingdom.

The ravages of opium in India, although not so generally known and discussed, are attracting the attention of philanthropists at the present time. The attitude of the British government in the case of India seems to be utterly indefensible and inexplicable. A recent official inquiry, under the auspices of the Indian government, as to opium consumption set forth that it was "merely a luxury, indulgence in which the government could do nothing to hinder, except by preventing the use of illicit opium, and keeping the licit article at a high price." It is an easy thing to suppress illicit opium, but to suppress the prime article which brings in the revenue is another matter. In the face of the rapid increase of the habit among the Hindus, which in the Bombay Presidency alone, according to official reports, has been at the rate of 549 per cent. since 1876, the government freely offers for sale at public auction a license to sell the drug, which is disposed of to the highest bidder. The singular and sinister restriction which is put upon this license is not with reference to limiting the amount sold, but, on the contrary, fixes the minimum quantity which *must* be sold during the term of the license, and in the case of failure to dispose of the stipulated amount, the owner of the license must pay to the government a "penalty at the rate of five rupees per pound on the quantity of opium required to make up the said minimum."

Could the British-Indian government make a more deliberate and cold-blooded conspiracy with Satan to ruin souls for hire than in this fearful compact with the Indian opium-seller? It is estimated that during the last three years the number of opium joints in India has increased by about fifteen hundred, and now that the British have annexed Upper Burma, where before the annexation the introduction of opium was prohibited by the law of the land, there seems to be imminent danger of British rule opening the door for the introduction of the dread poison among the people of that country. Already

Burma may be said to be literally on its knees praying the British government not to introduce the scourge. There has been as yet no formal and official action on the part of the English government sanctioning the iniquity in Burma, but there is virtual connivance at the illicit traffic, and official licenses are sold to Chinamen, ostensibly to sell the drug to their fellow-countrymen, in places where there is hardly a Chinaman, and where the license becomes merely a pretense for evading the law and selling the poison to the natives of the land.

Another alarming indication of the rushing tide of wretchedness and ruin which is gathering such fearful headway in the Eastern world in connection with the use of opium is the fact that the Chinese themselves have now commenced to cultivate the poppy in their own fields, and in place of the familiar placard in China, which indicates that rice from the province of Szchuen is for sale, there has of late been substituted a sign which advertises that "Szchuen earth" may be had, by which suggestive term the Chinese designate Szchuen opium.

The great arguments of those who oppose government action on the part of Great Britain in the matter of opium are that it is impracticable and impossible; it is urged, moreover, that if the British government should lift its hands from the monopoly, others would take it up, and a less pure quality and cheaper species of the drug would still be produced, so that little would be gained. It is a specious and utterly indefensible line of argument. It means that England can afford to do wrong, and cannot afford to do right, and the whole financial argument collapses in view of the fact that government plans might be made to supplement for a time the revenues of the Indian dependency until the financial difficulties were obviated. The injury to missions by opium is something incalculable, and the issue between righteousness and humanity on the one hand, and iniquity and callous greed on the other, is both sharp and irrepressible. This traffic in opium has been called "England's greatest contribution to the world's wretchedness."

We have little space left in which to speak in any detail of the dire and dismal story of rum in Africa. It is even a more infamous and unspeakable wrong than that of opium. Before the recent prohibition it was estimated that 10,000,000 gallons of intoxicants were introduced by foreigners into the Congo Free State and the basin of the Niger. The official statistics of the Boston custom-house for the year ending June 30, 1891, show that America is responsible for nearly 1,000,000 gallons of liquor exported to Africa. Germany, however, sends far more than any one country. The British government a few years ago prohibited the liquor traffic in Basutoland, at the earnest request of the native chiefs, with most satisfactory and wonderful results.

In Central and Western Africa, however, a constant river of ruin is still pouring into the bodies of African victims. It is one of the most unmitigated sins that has ever been committed with the connivance of civilization, by the hand of unscrupulous greed. Those in authority who have the power to check it seem to have spasms of conscience and flashes of shame over the dreadful business, but nothing is done with a strong and persistent purpose to remedy the evil, and, in the meantime, every ship that carries a missionary to Africa is likely to have enough rum on board to ruin a thousand souls.

We have time only to refer to the other phase of this conflict which was mentioned, and that is the malign influence of Western vices and commercial dishonesty as exhibited in the lives of unworthy representatives of Western civilization in foreign lands. The missionary teaches a religion of righteousness, purity, truth, honesty, Sabbath observance, and Christian kindliness; but alas, the lives of many who are inevitably associated with Christianity in the minds of the surrounding heathen exhibit an unblushing disregard of the most fundamental principles of truth and righteousness. The conflict is a painful and delicate one, and the damage to missions is serious and far-reaching; but we can only hint at these facts, and must pass on to other subjects which claim our attention.

VI. Another great conflict of mission fields is with the opposition of civil governments and ecclesiastical hierarchies. The Gospel in many instances brings the civil and the religious rulers to bay. The State is often in such close union with the Church that it feels called upon to place its interdict upon the Gospel, lest the official prestige of its State religion should be injured; and for other reasons, sometimes on account of political suspicions or fears, and sometimes through dread of the enlightening, quickening, and progressive influence of Christianity, the State interposes its authority, either openly or secretly, to stay the progress of missions.

In the case of ecclesiastical rulers, the Gospel is, of course, an enemy to be feared by them. Its doctrine, its worship, its fundamental principles of church polity, its ethics, and its exaltation of the mediatorial office of Christ, as well as its condemnation of the pride of the heart and sins of the flesh, are all in hopeless hostility to the whole ecclesiastical system and practice of false religions. The priesthood of all Oriental religions is, with, of course, some individual exceptions, unfathomably base and defiled. They teach formality and superstition in their speech, hypocrisy and deception in their ecclesiastical service, immorality and covetousness in their lives, and pride and self-complacency in their official lordship. They hold the souls of men in darkness, terror, and abject dependence, and they hate the Gospel of light, liberty, humility, purity, and free salvation, because it strikes at once a deadly blow at their ecclesiastical usurpations, their official duplicity, and their scandalous lives.

The question of the civil status of missions and the treaty rights of missionaries is one that has come to the front of late in China, Turkey, Persia, Africa, and in the Caroline Islands of the Pacific.

In China the lives and property of missionaries have been during the past year, and may be at any moment again, in serious peril, although it cannot be fairly said that the Chinese government exhibits any official or open enmity to our missionaries.

In Turkey, however, the case is different, and the anti-missionary spirit in the government is strong and determined. The Turkish authorities are studiously endeavoring to carry on their crusade against evangelical missions in such a way as to avoid open and flagrant transgression of treaty rights. American missions entered Turkey seventy years ago, and have conducted a quiet but aggressive work along all the lines of Christian influence and progress, until the government has become thoroughly alarmed lest Christianity should carry the day, and the prestige of Islam, both civil and religious, should wane. It must be said that our missionary operations have been treated in the past with remarkable tolerance by the Turkish government, although no doubt the timely exactions and restraints of Christian governments have had a large influence in checking the instinctive bigotry of Islam. But of late years, and increasingly so within the past year, the Turkish government has given very deliberate and serious attention to imperial legislation, for the express purpose of laying its heavy hand of authority upon American missionaries and their work. They have legislated, however, so sweepingly and so pointedly that our own government, which has been admirably served at Constantinople by Ministers Wallace and Straus and Hirsch, has been able, with the coöperation of the Protestant powers of Europe, to interpose an effective protest against the Turkish plans. It remains to be seen whether the apparent cessation of active hostilities on the part of the Turkish government is permanent, or merely temporary. It is probable that our missions are to meet with vigorous and determined efforts on the part of the Moslem authorities to hinder their further progress and deprive them of their facilities.

The problem is not without its difficulties to the Turkish government, since treaty rights have been very explicitly defined in the case of almost every Christian government, and, moreover, there exist large Christian communities and nationalities throughout Turkey, each one of which may be said to be under the patronage and protection of some European government, which feels it to be for its advantage to have an ally in the Orient, so that the Turk is placed in an attitude which is at once delicate and dangerous in case he undertakes to legislate in any general way against the interests of these Christian communities. If, on the other hand, he attempts to single out the Protestant community as a point of attack, he is entangled in embarrassments which even his astute and double-faced diplomacy can hardly overcome. If he levels his guns at evangelical Christianity, after having officially recognized the existence and rights of the Protestant sect by an imperial firman, he is in danger of sending his deadly missiles in a too promiscuous fusilade throughout the whole Christian camp of the empire. We may feel assured that the God of missions is master of the situation in these old Oriental empires, and that He who has watched over the interests of His kingdom in all ages of history will vindicate in our day His marvelous power to make "even the wrath of men to praise Him."

There has been bitter and cruel persecution of late in Persia; in the Caroline Islands there have been flagrant outrages by the Spanish authorities; in Russia the Stundists have had to face horrible ordeals for righteousness' sake; and in Japan there are still lurking signs of hostility on the part of the government to the free and open propagation of the Gospel. In Korea a hostile animus against not only missionaries, but all foreigners, is from time to time manifested. Along the northern shores of Africa, where the Moslem influence is still predominant, and in the storm-center of Uganda, there are serious difficulties of the kind we have mentioned. The God of missions is also the God of nations, and in His name the Gospel must fight its battles.

The opposition of ecclesiastical authorities, and, in many cases, of the fanatical lay element also, becomes more and more noticeable as the power of the Gospel begins to be manifest among the adherents of false religions. In many Eastern lands ecclesiastical leaders have also civil powers, which they can use to carry out their ends. In Turkey the patriarchs and bishops have power to arrest and imprison those who are inclined to Protestantism, to confiscate their property, and indirectly to secure, or at least encourage, the cruel and violent personal treatment of members of their own religious constituency who are not entirely submissive to their authority. Little or no restraint on the part of the Moslem authorities may be looked for, as they have tacitly handed over the civil rights of the various Christian communities into the hands of their ecclesiastical superiors, with the understanding that the religious rulers are responsible for the good behavior of their spiritual followers. We may be sure that unscrupulous men who find their ecclesiastical authority in danger and their constituency diminishing by evangelical conversions will not hesitate to use their power, with terrifying effect, to check the influence of Protestant teachings and keep their religious following intact.

VII. Another conflict which must be noted in this connection is developed by the aroused and quickened antagonism of devout and loyal adherents of opposing religions. This opposition has been stimulated by the very fact that the progress of the Gospel has put them on the defensive, and in many instances the intellectual stimulus which has come with the Gospel, and the very intelligence, knowledge, and extension of resources which missions have brought, are turned against Christianity. Mission success has aroused the bigotry, kindled the fears, quickened the zeal, and put weapons into the hands of those who recognize the necessity of self-defense and brace themselves for the contest.

We have illustrations of this in India, in such movements as the Brahmo Somaj, and the more recent Arya Somaj, a society which was not in existence twelve years ago, yet it numbers now many thousands in its membership, has already established a college at Lahore, and has its preachers in the bazaars. The Brahmo Somaj is an older movement, and may be described as simply a struggle or spasm of Hinduism to free itself from idolatry and polytheism, and absorb the ethics of Christianity without its supernaturalism. It is a cold and bald attempt at an ethical salvation, its conscience casting off the baser and grosser cult of Indian heathenism, and reaching out after more satisfying ethical standards, yet with no recognition of the unique character of Christ, and no humble dependence upon His mediatorial work. We may expect religious evolutions like this amidst the turmoil of thought, and the unsettling of traditional convictions, and the unbalancing of the religious poise, which the entrance of the Gospel must surely bring, as it asserts its exclusive and sublime claims in the presence of these great ethnic religions that have hitherto reigned without a rival in Eastern lands. It is hardly to be expected that the Mohammedan, the Buddhist, the Brahman, the Confucianist, and others like them, will yield to the supremacy of the Gospel without many curious and even pathetic attempts to build their "half-way houses to Christianity," or to invent some compromise between the old and the new. It is only a soul that is born from above by the power of the divine Spirit that "rings out the old and rings in the new" in humble, total, and final surrender to Christ. It is true still, especially among the heathen nations, that "whosoever believeth that Jesus is the Christ is born of God," and he it is only that, in the power of that faith, overcometh the world.

VIII. We are thus led to consider another of the conflicts of missions. It is a battle at close quarters in the realm of the inner life, and it is always fought at a serious disadvantage. We refer to the struggle of evangelical truth with the prejudices, superstitions, jealousies, traditions, and conscientious convictions of the native mind. The Gospel of Christian missions seeks to enter a preoccupied realm. Its function is still to cast out devils, and to scourge money-changers from the temple; to rebuke the Scribes and Pharisees and idolaters; to call into question the cherished convictions of the heart, and challenge the daily practice of the life.

It is impossible for us fully to realize what a mental and spiritual revolution is implied, what a breaking of intellectual and religious caste, and what a thorough and far-reaching reorganization is necessitated by the entrance of the Gospel into heathen communities. All things literally must become new, and man himself must be made a new creature if the Gospel is to become his guide, his hope, and his song. Right in the path of the Truth, at the very entrance of its influence into the spiritual nature, stand, with keen alertness in the aroused consciousness of danger, the superstitions of a lifetime, the prejudices that have sunk their roots into the very depths of consciousness, the customs that have become a second nature, the hopes that have been fondly cherished, the traditions that have gathered weight through generations; and the Gospel does not simply regenerate the heart, but in so doing it stirs up fearful questions about the fate of ancestors, and trembling apprehensions about the prospects of children. It must cross the trend of national expectations, and seem to reverse the whole meaning of history. It must shiver the old intellectual and religious formulæ, break the old molds of thought, ruin the old haunts of the imagination, and make the deepest and strongest religious experiences of the soul as if they had not been. Things that are must become as if they were not. Things that seem to be foolish must put to shame those that have hitherto seemed wise, and things that have been considered weak and base, and things that are despised, must bring to naught the mighty things that are. Old friendships must be broken, family glory must be dimmed, long-cherished pride humbled, natural timidity must be conquered, social inertia must be overcome, irresolution must be cast aside, hereditary indisposition to change must be banished, personal interest must be sacrificed, worldly loss must be faced, the alliance with civil and ecclesiastical power must be forfeited, and a leap into the unknown and untried experiences of an absolutely new religion must be taken, and all upon the basis of what seems to be comparatively slender historical evidence, and what appears to be a somewhat questionable voucher of superiority, without the familiar *éclat* of public approval and the support of government sanction. The native convert is, in fact, about to accept deliberately and finally a religion without an emperor, without a ruler among men, without a visible representative from the official ranks of the nation, without an army at its back, without a verified promise of material good or an assurance of physical protection, with absolutely nothing to cling to except perhaps the loving heart-throb of some missionary teacher, the soul-subduing tenderness of a new-found

Saviour, and those wondrous promises of an invisible Lord.

Do you wonder that there is a conflict here which has taxed all the resources of Christian missions, and which has made every victory of the Gospel a spiritual marvel in which "one has chased a thousand, and two have put ten thousand to flight"? I believe we cannot and do not realize the spiritual glory and sublimity of our missionary triumphs. I believe there are miracles of grace in our day which are not surpassed in power by any in human history. How it would startle the world if a modern railway train should go shooting across the continent of Africa, clearing its own way, laying its own road-bed, building as if by magic its own bridges, and leaving behind its spinning wheels a permanent achievement which would represent millions of money, and an incalculable expenditure of toil and triumph of skill! Yet there is to-day more of God, more of His Spirit, more of His power, more of His manifest intervention in that magnificent "highway for our God" which the missionary toils of the century have opened up into the wilderness depths of the world's heathenism than in any mere miracle of physical achievement. "A little one *has* become a thousand, and a small one a strong nation," and the Lord *is* hastening it in His time. Let us recognize His hand, and give Him the glory.

IX. I have only time for a brief word in conclusion, with reference to the conflict of Christian missions with the Prince of Darkness and his immemorial ally, the fallen nature of man. It is the old story of the Gospel at war with sin and ignorance. It is the old mysterious conflict with "principalities and powers, and the rulers of this darkness, and the spiritual hosts of wickedness in the heavenly places." The sinful heart is Satan's stronghold. All other difficulties would vanish if ignorance, apathy, and love of sin would give place to humble teachableness, sincere penitence, and a cry for mercy. The heathen the world over are sinners, salvable, but, so far as we have any reasonable basis of hope, in the immense majority of instances as yet unsaved. They are possible (perhaps in many cases more possible than we realize) but yet not actual subjects of mercy. Judged by any standard, they cannot be admitted to heaven without the atoning mediation of Christ and the spiritual transformation of the Gospel. There is, then, just as much need of sending them the Gospel, and just as much propriety in giving it to them as to any other class of human beings. The vital question for us to discuss and decide is not whether the heathen will be saved without the Gospel, but can they be saved by it? The former question is too mysterious, too speculative, and too difficult to be decided by the light either of reason or revelation. The question, Can they be saved by it? is clear, practical, stimulating, and hopeful. It is enough for us to have settled the salvability of the heathen as over against the immensely preponderating danger of their perishing in their sins without it. In the presence of the lurid glare and the terrific roar of the flames in a burning building, we never stop to discuss with reference to those in peril the question of the probability of their escape without our help. We decide rather the possibility of rescue with our help, and, that question once decided, we give the help without delay, and our reward is the joy of rescue, and this is the crowning joy of missions.

Out of all the difficulties and conflicts of missions comes, however, a measure of success which gladdens earth and heaven, and brings refreshment and cheer and solace to humble and prayerful souls. There is already enough of substantial results in missions to justify a modern edition of the Acts of the Apostles, to add another chapter to Christian apologetics, to make luminous with new light the prophecies of God's Word, and to add a clearer, deeper, and sweeter strain to the as yet faint and far-away melodies of the golden age. Let the Church awake to the realities of Christian missions. The kingdom is too shadowy to the children of the King. The history of this wondrous century is too much of a dream, passing time is too much of a plaything, and this mortal is as if it were not destined for immortality. The great Reformation brought us life in doctrine; the missionary reformation of this century is more and more to bring us life in service. The former delivered the Church from the dark ages of formalism and spiritual slavery; the latter will deliver the Church from the dark ages of indifference and spiritual inaction. The true life of the Church is coming in the triumphs of the missionary idea.

LECTURE IV.

THE PRESENT-DAY PROBLEMS OF THEORY AND METHOD IN MISSIONS.

"More and more am I convinced that the hope of this great land [India] lies in the educated Christian natives. The missionary cannot Christianize the land. No foreigner can evangelize another country than his own; the springs of religious life must be found in the soil itself. For many a year, perhaps for many a century, the work of the missionary will not be finished in India, but after all, however long continued, it is essentially pioneer and foundation work. Wisely have the American Board missionaries, like the Pilgrim Fathers, everywhere planted the schoolhouse side by side with the church. In these twin buildings lies the hope of India."—REV. FRANCIS E. CLARK, D.D.

"Looking, then, at our churches in their relation to the missionary work, what we wish for those at home is a paramount loyalty to Christ, and a sense of direct, personal responsibility to Him for the spread of His Gospel. We wish, also, the simplest, most economical, and efficient possible organization for reaching the unevangelized world. For the churches abroad, gathered by missionary labor, we wish the earliest possible period of self-guidance and self-support. This is the result of our labors that we wish to see—self-guiding and self-supporting churches. For self-guidance we prepare them by instruction and by giving them the Scriptures. Self-support in its principle we insist on. This we do for the sake of the mission churches themselves as well as our own."—PRESIDENT MARK HOPKINS, D.D., LL.D.

IV.

THE PRESENT-DAY PROBLEMS OF THEORY AND METHOD IN MISSIONS.

WE have considered the present-day conflicts of mission fields, and have found that, under existing conditions, these conflicts are the inevitable outcome of aggressive missionary activity. There arises, however, in connection with the successful advance of missionary effort, a succession of perplexing and serious difficulties, which may more properly be considered as problems to be solved than as conflicts to be fought out. Conflicts arise in connection with hindrances to be overcome, obstacles to be removed, and active opposition to be subdued and conquered. Problems arise in connection with difficulties to be solved, methods to be adopted, principles to be enforced, and adaptations to be made in adjusting the Gospel to new and untried conditions in the world.

Problems, like conflicts, are inevitable, and we

need not be discouraged if they press hard and long, and seem to be for the time being insoluble. God has trained His Church in the school of problems, and we have no reason to doubt His presence and favor in connection with missionary enterprise because of perplexities and difficulties which call for wisdom, patience, and prayerful dependence upon divine help for their solution. "The blood of the martyrs is the seed of the Church," and in the same sense the problems of practical Christianity have a noble mission in quickening thought, arousing energy, developing power, teaching dependence, and giving wisdom, patience, and facility of adaptation to the Church in pushing on her work in the world.

The problems of mission fields are often especially complex and disheartening, and beyond the scope of human wisdom to master. They arise out of such a variety of conditions, touch such a multiplicity of interests, involve such intangible forces, deal with such multiform phases of human nature, and seem to be so barren of possible solutions, that the only way to deal with them is slowly and patiently to feel our way along in the dark, until some glimmer of light gives the clue to an exit to the region of hopeful solution. Each mission field has many problems in common with all others, and at the same time is likely to develop some which are special to itself. We have now to invite your attention to some of these problems which are pressing at the present hour.

I. I shall venture first of all to say a few words with reference to the problem of theory. This is perhaps a matter which has more to do with the home side of foreign missions than with the distant fields of labor, and yet a moment's reflection will convince us that this is a far-reaching problem, and that it concerns the interests of the foreign field in a very direct and important sense, inasmuch as the proper support and efficient conduct of missions depend so largely upon a correct theory of the whole enterprise in the minds of Christians at home. This subject has always been important, but it has come to the front of late in current discussions upon missions in a way which has made it at the present time a question of keen and vital interest in its relations to the whole work of foreign missions.

There is no doubt in many minds a feeling of painful perplexity, disturbed poise, vague questioning, and unhappy uncertainty with reference to the whole subject of foreign missions. Many plausible, bold, and even passionate statements have been made, either by the opponents, or in some cases by the supposed friends of missions, which seem to give such a very uncertain sound, and to introduce such an intangible element of doubt into the realm of missionary activity, that many conscientious and loyal Christian people hardly feel sure that missions are necessary, and scarcely know why they are undertaken. One of the desiderata in current religious thought throughout the Church seems to be a true, clear, practical, genial, rounded, and wholesome theory of missions, which, while loyal to the Bible, should yet be free from narrow, extreme, and disproportionate emphasis upon any one aspect of a subject which is necessarily somewhat complex and composite.

A true theory of missions involves correct ideas concerning the motive, the object, the necessity, and the result of missions. We must strike a true note with reference to each of these aspects of the subject, in order to sound a full and harmonious chord of theory. We have only time to offer a suggestion or two along these different lines of approach to a full and true and comprehensive philosophy of missions.

As regards the *motive*, it is plainly love to Christ, and obedience to His command. This may include more or less of love for lost souls—the more the better—and of pity for those in ignorance and misery; but above all other motives which have a sustaining, inspiring, and impelling influence over the Christian heart is love for the Saviour, and a consciousness of obligation to Him, and a desire to do His will with reference to the proclamation of His Gospel.

As regards the *object* of missions, it is to give the Gospel to those who need it. If the heathen do not need the Gospel, then our human race could have done without it. If it is not a blessing to them, then how can we consider it a blessing to us? If it is a work of supererogation to take it to them, why was it not a prodigious mistake to bring it to us? What blessing or solace or hope for time and eternity has it brought to us which it cannot also carry to them? The object, then, of missions is simply the extension among all men of the manifold benefits of the Gospel. If Christ is the best gift of Heaven to earth, if the Gospel is the sweetest message of God to man, if the benefits of contact with Christianity are unique and obtainable, so far as we have been informed, only through the dissemination of the religion of Jesus Christ, if we who have it are responsible for the introduction of that religion where it is not known and where it cannot be found, except as we make it our business to give it, then there is no object which is worthy of fixing the purpose of the disciples of Christ which transcends in its dignity the simple gift of the Gospel to those who need it.

As regards the *necessity* of the Gospel to heathen nations, there is much in current literature, and in the lurking doubts which have taken possession of many Christian minds, which would either give an entirely uncertain response to this question, or, in varying degrees of boldness and vigor, deny altogether that missions are necessary. The difficulty in most minds seems to be a speculative one. It is to reconcile the justice and love of God with the condemnation of a heathen soul. If the question were with reference to the actual moral condition of a representative heathen, there would probably be practical unanimity. If we could inspect his character and observe his life and know him thoroughly within and without, we should in the vast majority of cases form a decided judgment as to his moral standing. His heart would be pronounced sinful, his nature morally depraved, his mind filled with superstition, and his whole spiritual and external life would be recognized as moving in an atmosphere of stolid selfishness and hardened depravity. If the heathen commit crimes against international law or against human rights, if they murder, or pillage, or practice their cruelty or duplicity upon those outside of their immediate circle of nationality or tribal kinship who are entitled to the legal protection of civilized governments, then there is no question whatever with reference to their condemnation and the necessity of punishing them; but when their relations to divine law are in question there is much vague and obscure speculation.

Now, we may lay down some clear general principles, which have a governing influence in these matters, and in the light of them we may hope to reach some clarified convictions. We must maintain that God is just and loving; we must maintain also that the heathen are morally depraved and worthy of condemnation, not because they sin against *all* the light which God has given to *men*, but because they sin against that *special measure of light* which He has given to *them;* and that just as the Word of God where it is fully known shall be the judge of those who sin against its light and instruction, so the light which God has given, either through nature or the conscience, to those who sin against that light will be their judge, and that judgment will be rendered in strict and even transcendent accord with all the principles of justice, and will be not one whit less under the modifying power of love and pity than the condemnation which shall be visited upon those who sin against greater light. Proportionate guilt and proportionate condemnation, in harmony with strict justice, and under the full cognizance of love and mercy, is the lot of an impenitent heathen, just as it is the portion of those who sin in presence of greater light. The full recognition of this element of *proportion* in

God's judgment of the heathen at once relieves the mind of all vague and painful apprehension of the possibility of wrong or injustice. It is impossible that there should be any cause of complaint with reference to the divine dealings with impenitent heathen which does not also apply to the impenitent who die in their sins where the Gospel is fully known. There never can be, or never will be, any *injustice* arising out of undue or disproportionate severity in the divine judgment.

If, then, the principle of justice be fully conceded, a large part of the difficulty is removed. Much of the current arraignment of Christian teaching with reference to the guilt and danger of the heathen is based upon the imaginary idea that it necessarily involves injustice to ignorant, helpless, and doomed humanity. Let us then, in the light of a clear, emphatic, and unqualified recognition of the fact that the justice and love and mercy of God will condition His judgment of the heathen just as much as His judgment of Christendom, look once more at the question of the necessity of missions, and, if the Gospel is the power of God to save, why is it not the power of

God to save the heathen from *his own measure* of guilt and condemnation, just as much as it is the power of God to save the dweller in Christendom from *his* sin and its penalty? If it is a necessity here, why is it not a necessity there? The only possible escape from the force of this reasoning is either to consider the heathen guiltless and meritorious, or it is to postulate the divine mercy and love as accomplishing for the heathen what it cannot be supposed to accomplish for other sinners, except in utter disregard of fundamental biblical teachings.

Of the two possible solutions suggested above, the supposition that the heathen is a guiltless and meritorious being is one which cannot be maintained without the annihilation of moral distinctions, and, as regards the second supposition, that in some way and at some time by virtue of some extra-biblical provision there is assured hope for the heathen, we must exercise extreme care that we should not advance in connection with this idea any theories which are contrary to Scripture, or destructive of established principles. It is just here that the currents of thought are apt to develop some whirlpool of untenable theory. Probation after death is unscriptural, and cannot be maintained except by an uncandid, forced, and perilous wresting of the Scriptures. Supposed contact with and conscious rejection of the historic Christ at some stage of the soul's history as a necessary pre-essential of condemnation is a speculative theory, adopted as a relief to a painful dilemma, since there is plenty of sin in the world which deserves judgment, where Christ is not known nor His Gospel rejected. Mercy without penitence is an untenable thought, as it admits pride and immorality into the presence of God.

There is, however, a measure of relief in addition to that secured by the certainty of scrupulous fairness and absolute justice in God's attitude toward all men, which has been already referred to, in that God is absolutely sovereign in the dispensation of the benefits of Christ's redemption. He has been pleased to make explicit requirements which condition the securing of these benefits wherever Christ and His atoning mediation are revealed to human consciousness, but He has nowhere declared that in cases where Christ's mediation is absolutely unrevealed there *is no hope* whatever of obtaining its benefits. He has nowhere said that humility and penitence and trust and prayer, with the conscious recognition of demerit and dependence, shall be inevitably in vain where Christ is unknown. This would be making divine mercy and pity and compassion and love merely the servants and attendants upon divine revelation in its full and completed form. It would mean that where the Bible does not go, there divine mercy cannot enter, and Christ's work is unavailable, and divine pity is necessarily inoperative. The result would be to close absolutely the door of hope, as by a divine fiat, to the great mass of the human race.

Now, if this is going to be done, God is the only one who should do it, and we know that it never will be done unless both His love and justice assent to it. There seems to be nothing, however, in the divine character, or in the divine dealings with humanity, or in the revealed Word, which forbids the hope that God in His sovereignty *is able*, if He wishes, to exercise His mercy, where it does not conflict with other attributes, in cases where the object of mercy is in such an attitude of humble, childlike self-renunciation and dependence upon divine help that there is no obstacle to his receiving the benefits of Christ's death as the gift of divine grace; just as these benefits are granted to one who, in the full knowledge of the Christian scheme, seeks reconciliation with God, through humble acceptance of an offered Saviour. Who of us would dare to close this door of hope, and to decide *ex cathedra* that God is helpless, even though Christ has died, and the Spirit lives, to save a soul to whom He has not been pleased to transmit in its fullness the revelation of His redemptive methods? It has been His plan, moreover, to leave the distribution of the knowledge of Christ to a Church full of human imperfections, which He knew, even though the matter were committed unreservedly to its hands, would be careless and selfish about this sacred trust to an extent which would involve the possible loss of unknown millions of souls. It may be noted also that it is not fullness of knowledge, or clarified intellectual comprehension of divine methods, that God requires, even in Christian lands, so much as humble recognition of unworthiness, and sincere penitence, and trustful reliance upon His divine compassion and power to save.

We would not advance this message of hope as an essential doctrine of Christian theology, or even a clear and specific teaching of the divine Word, since God has been pleased to keep His own counsel with reference to the possibilities of divine mercy; but as we hope and believe in the application of the benefits of Christ's redeeming work to all infants dying before they reach the age of responsibility, so we may hope and believe that there is a possibility also of the extension of this principle of grace to those of adult years among the heathen who consciously, whether under the guidance of the natural conscience or in response to the influences of the divine Spirit, take before God an attitude of humble dependence, and seek salvation, not upon the basis of merit, but on the basis of mercy, and look to Him in penitence and prayer. God would not be God were He to turn a deaf ear to the cry of the humble, penitent, and trustful soul, even though that cry came out of the darkness of the heathen heart. Would not God be strangely untrue to Himself were He utterly unresponsive to a prayer which must have been prompted either by the conscience which He has implanted, or the Spirit which He has sent? The poet Southey, in some lines which he has written in imitation of the Persian, has voiced such a prayer in the following touching petition:

> "Lord! who art merciful as well as just,
> Incline Thine ear to me, a child of dust!
> Not what I would, O Lord, I offer Thee,
>   Alas! but what I can.
> Father Almighty, who hast made me man,
> And bade me look to heaven, for Thou art there,
> Accept my sacrifice and humble prayer;
> Four things which are not in Thy treasury
> I lay before Thee, Lord, with this petition,
>   My nothingness and wants,
>   My sins and my contrition."

It is entirely another matter, and simply a question of fact, whether many or few take this attitude of humility and trust before God. In no case could such an attitude be regarded as acceptable to God were it not accompanied by an earnest struggle after righteous living and true obedience. Alas! we have reason to fear that few in the heathen world are seeking God and asking His mercy in the spirit we have indicated.

It may be said, moreover, in this connection, even were it true that many honest and sincere heathen souls were seeking God in a spirit of humble teachableness, penitence, and trust, and were making a strenuous endeavor to walk in obedience to the light which God has given them, that this would not make it one whit less important and obligatory that the full light and guidance of the Gospel should be carried not only to them, but to those around them who are living in violation of conscience, and in the indulgence of every known sin. Whatever measure of relief may be brought to this appalling problem of the fate of the heathen by the hope of the *possible* salvation of *some*, it still remains overwhelmingly true that the Gospel is necessary both to those concerning whom it might be possible to cherish hope, and to those whose relations to God are, so far as we have any light to judge, utterly hopeless. It is necessary in order to give full light and guidance to those who may be feeling and searching after God, and also to the great mass of humanity who are doubtless living in utter indifference and callousness, willing slaves to sin, and shallow devotees to empty formalism.

The necessity for the Gospel may still be urged, not upon the sole plea that there is absolutely no possibility of salvation, even theoretically, without it, but rather that it is the divinely ordered, the divinely effective, the divinely blessed agency for enlightening, persuading, convincing, and winning the soul from nature's darkness, weakness, and peril to the light and life of assured reconciliation and peace. It is the accredited instrumentality for transforming character. For all these purposes the Gospel has been commissioned, and we have been commanded to disseminate it, and wherever it has been tried it has proved an unfailing resource. It is the power of God put into our hands, and we are bidden to use it as the one transcendently wise and permanently effective agency for saving all men. Nothing else has been given us by God, and has been so chosen and honored by Him as the one supremely blessed instrumentality for illumining the mind, arousing the conscience, leading to repentance, subduing, melting, and humbling the heart, and giving a gracious energy to the will, as this Gospel of our Lord and Saviour Jesus Christ. To cast a doubt upon its value, its efficiency, its necessity, is to substitute human opinion for the wisdom of God. Whatever hopes we may cherish with reference to the possibilities of divine mercy, we must ever recognize the atoning work of Christ as the basis and condition of the exercise of mercy, in the sense that divine mercy is operative only in connection with Christ's atonement, whether that atoning sacrifice is intelligently accepted by the sinner, or its benefits unconsciously received in response to prayer for pardon. God has given us the Gospel as His own chosen means for bringing all men into the kingdom, and it is absolutely the only means which He has commissioned us to use. We believe, then, in the Gospel first and last, as the prime necessity in the case of all men, and that we are bound to preach and teach it throughout the world.

It remains to say a word with reference to the fourth essential of a rounded theory of missions, and that is the *result* to be aimed at. It is not simply preaching the Gospel for a witness, or, in other words, the mere evangelization of the earth in distinction from its conversion. This is a very insufficient and imperfect statement of the scope, magnitude, and significance of this great duty of the Church to the world. It is a most inadequate conception of the result proposed, that it is simply to proclaim the Gospel in all human ears, and bear witness to its existence before all men. The result which we should seek is broader, more comprehensive, more permanently fruitful than this. It is to plant Christianity among the nations; it is to bring individual souls, entire communities and whole nations into living contact with its power; it is to propagate and establish the spiritual kingdom of our Lord and Saviour Jesus Christ throughout the earth, and at the same time to develop, as far as possible, self-supporting, self-perpetuating, organized agencies, which shall be Christian in their animus and influence and power.

The result aimed at in Christian missions involves as essential to their permanent success:

First. The material plant, which is educational, literary, philanthropic, and evangelistic, and in its scope includes Christian education, Christian literature, Christian philanthropy, and Christian evangelization. It implies organized churches, native agencies, and Christian institutions planted in heathen soil upon a self-supporting and self-propagating basis.

Second. In addition to the material plant, it implies the Scriptural leaven which represents the power of the truth working to produce conviction, to guide, persuade, and instruct the mind, undermining prejudices, overthrowing superstitions, dislodging formalities, producing humility, and leavening the mind and heart with the transforming influence of God's truth.

Third. To the material plant and the Scriptural leaven we add the spiritual energy which is the result of the working of the divine Spirit, and includes regeneration, conversion, and righteous living, kindling the zeal, deepening the consecration, quickening the sympathy, and developing the piety of the heart. The aim of Christian missions is to Christianize this earth, to transform humanity by the power of truth and by the agency of the Spirit, through the message of the Gospel, and it is to do this in the case of individual lives among the old and the young, grouping these lives into organized churches, and lifting the Gospel, with all its ministries and with its divine authority and divine efficiency, to the supreme place in the individual heart, in the social life, and in the national organization. Christianity, like ivy, grows upon some solid support. From the days of the apostles it has sought to identify itself with substantial, permanent bases and institutions.

If it is objected that there is not enough of the witnessing element in all this, we affirm that it is the very best kind of witnessing; it is material, intellectual, social, systematic, declarative, evangelistic; it is a rounded, permanent, pervasive, incisive, self-perpetuating, cumulative, loyal, persuasive, loving, personal witnessing for Christ, and to Him. It tells the whole story of His Gospel and its mission. It lives, it breathes, it throbs, it sways, it impels, it solidifies results, and fixes the Gospel with a permanent grip and an abiding power in the hearts and homes, the schools and churches, the social and religious experience of heathen peoples and nationalities, whose future is just beginning to take shape, and who are on the threshold of the twentieth century of human history. It will make it the joy of heathendom to live in the twentieth century, as it is now the joy of Christendom to live in the nineteenth century.

And now in the light of these considerations

we gather up our thoughts, and state what we believe to be the true theory of missions. It is the preaching and teaching of the Gospel out of love to the Master who commands it, to those who need it, and to whom, so far as our knowledge or information goes, it is a universal necessity, with the purpose of propagating Christianity throughout the earth, and bringing all men into both the visible and invisible kingdom of our Lord and Saviour Jesus Christ.

II. We turn now from the problem of theory to that of finance. This, although primarily rather a problem belonging to the home administration, is also one of great practical importance in the conduct of missions abroad. Our foreign mission work has been conducted by the voluntary contributions of Christians at home, with the exception of small amounts which have been raised on the field. The administrative agency of these funds has been either a society, such, for example, as the London Missionary Society, and the American Board, or an authorized board or committee appointed and delegated by the Church to serve in that capacity. There have been also a few agencies of a more private character, and some independent missionaries supported by personal contributions. It is almost an axiom of policy in this great and complex work that some responsible administrative agency is essential to secure wisdom, efficiency, economy, and orderly control in a work so extensive, and so liable, without constant oversight and firm guidance, to lapse into confused, irregular, and sporadic methods. The policy of establishing direct and independent relations between foreign missionaries and their work on the one hand, and individuals or individual churches on the other, while it might produce a temporary development of interest and a new sense of responsibility, would soon result in confusion, misunderstanding, and disjointed administration, involving a loss of efficiency and a general slovenliness of method which would work serious injury to the cause. The plan of the organized society, or the delegated board, or the official committee, is the one which has commended itself to the Christian Church by long experience, and increasingly so in these days of administrative responsibilities and perplexing problems. The large financial interests involved call for the most careful, wise, and conscientious distribution of sacred money.

In connection with this problem of finance, two points are of special importance:

First. While conserving the voluntary element in the contributions of the churches, to secure at the same time a firmer hold upon the conscience of the giver, and bring the contribution to foreign missions into closer touch with a sense of responsibility, and a conviction of duty, and an abiding spirit of loyalty to the Master. Some method must be devised by which these voluntary contributions to foreign missions shall appeal not simply to impulse or to choice or to inclination, but to an abiding conviction, a profound sense of duty, a consciousness of sacred obligation, and a deep spirit of personal loyalty to our Lord. Giving to foreign missions must become in our churches a matter of Christian honor and unfaltering consecration. Just as a man of high business integrity honors his note, so Christians should honor this debt to Christ and humanity. It is felt by prominent societies, and especially by our own Presbyterian Board, that some wise method must be devised for securing a more assured stability to the income, and a more conscientious attitude on the part of the giver. Responsibilities of administration to the extent of over a million a year are now regularly assumed, with the possibility of a shortage in funds which may become paralyzing in a single year. It is plain, moreover, that the resources of the Church in this matter of foreign missions are very imperfectly and disproportionately drawn upon by the present methods.

Second. Another point which calls for consideration in this connection has to do rather with administration in the foreign field. It is to make such an economical adjustment of expenditures in our mission fields that we shall not be unnecessarily duplicating work and wasting resources. We must not allow any spirit of rivalry or denominational pride to lead to the multiplication of educational facilities, or of other missionary agencies, where by mutual arrangement the work could be done by one institution, and so avoid the expense of several. This is an aspect of foreign missionary finance which is being carefully considered by missionary societies occupying the same field. There is reason to expect that the spirit of coöperation will secure a wise economy of expenditure, and to this end there is at the present time a concerted movement toward consultation, and mutual adaptation of resources on the part of missionary organizations at home. A conviction is growing that there is danger of waste in the multiplication of agencies in many fields, and that practical coöperation is the true method for reducing expenses, especially where churches of the same polity are working side by side, whose differences in creed are rather matters of shading in doctrine than of divergence in essentials. This policy of coöperation must extend also to a reasonable uniformity in salaries and disbursements, both in the case of foreign missionaries themselves, and of native agents. The Church must have the surest guarantees that its contributions are spent wisely and to the best advantage, and to this high purpose all minor differences and rivalries, or merely personal preferences and ambitions, must be made strictly subservient.

III. The next problem which we shall consider briefly is that of coöperation, which suggests also the larger problem of unity in the foreign field. The duty and rule of missionary comity is now generally recognized, and almost universally observed. Our large societies are governed by a spirit of scrupulous courtesy in this matter, and missionaries upon the fields are in full sympathy with the obligations which this rule imposes. In the recent Conference at Shanghai, which was attended by four hundred representatives of the forty-six missionary agencies in China, a Permanent Committee upon Comity was appointed, to whom should be referred all questions of the division of fields. This rule of comity, however, is only a step in the right direction, and leads us to the more important subject of coöperation among Protestant denominations in the same fields. We distinguish here for the present between coöperation and organic union; the former is possible, and even obligatory, where the latter may be as yet impracticable, or even undesirable.

By coöperation we mean consolidation of agencies in the practical conduct of the work where different branches of the same denomination are conducting work side by side. This coöperation may be accomplished in the foreign field without in any way interfering with separate administration in the home churches. We have conspicuous illustrations of it in Japan, where the "Church of Christ in Japan" is a united organization which has developed out of the missionary activities of six different branches of the Reformed Church holding the Presbyterian polity; and at the last meeting of the Presbyterian Alliance at Toronto, an application was made by our Japanese friends to be admitted to the Alliance, as entitled to a representation in that body. Steps looking to a similar result have been taken for the formation of a united Presbyterian Church of India, under the auspices of the Indian Presbyterian Alliance. A basis for union has already been agreed upon, which deals with the questions of polity, doctrine, and local organization, looking to one General Assembly and a number of synods and presbyteries. The polity is to be essentially Presbyterian, and the doctrine essentially evangelical, embracing the Apostles' Creed, the Nicene Creed, and some modern statement of doctrine to be agreed upon, which, while conserving the essentials of Christian orthodoxy, shall be conceived in a broad and genial spirit, and be free from all needless dogmatic entanglements. The Alliance recommends in this connection that the proposed Presbyterian Church of India, while acknowledging first of all its allegiance to its own constitution, shall also hold in veneration the Westminster Confession, the Westminster Shorter Catechism, and the Heidelberg Catechism. A movement similar in purpose and plan has also been inaugurated among the Presbyterian missions in Korea and China.

This spirit of coöperation is at work in other denominations, especially the Methodist Episcopal and Congregational. It has not as yet, however, reached a degree of spiritual enthusiasm and practical power sufficient to bring together such kindred denominations as the Congregational and the Presbyterian. An effort to this end has been made in Japan, but in view of the many delicate questions and threatened embarrassments which soon came to the front, it has been deferred indefinitely, and it seems more than likely that the time has not yet come for a larger organic union of the historic Christian denominations, even on the foreign field. Perhaps at the present stage of missions more effective work and more vigorous administration can be attained through denominational agencies; but certainly a strict minimum of denominational distinctions should be observed in all our foreign missionary operations.

If we cannot have union between Presbyterians, Congregationalists, Methodists, Baptists, and Episcopalians, let us at least wipe out all minor distinctions and subdivisions, so that there shall be but one front and one organization to each of these great denominational divisions. The signs of the times indicate coöperation and union within denominational lines, as the watchword on the mission fields. This is wise and timely, both as a practical object-lesson to the churches at home, and in the interests of unity and efficiency in the evangelical churches of the foreign field. In the meantime, much may be done without disturbing in the least the cordial relations or the denominational susceptibilities of the churches at home, by securing unity of counsel and method in home administration. Our boards and societies of kindred polity and creed should have, in connection with questions of policy, method, and administration, one council-chamber, where, in a spirit of fraternal consultation and conference, lines of policy may be marked out, and lessons of experience may be gathered, and unity of purpose may be stimulated. A conference for these purposes, held under the auspices of the Alliance of the Reformed Churches, embracing the representatives of the Churches of the Alliance, was held recently at the Presbyterian Foreign Mission Rooms in New York. This conference became the basis of a still larger fellowship and union of the representatives of all the Protestant missionary societies, who met in convention at the same place upon the day following the previous gathering. Representatives of seventeen missionary organizations passed the day in conference, and in the discussion of important subjects upon which unity of aim and method was desirable. Many questions of importance took definite shape under the impulse of that conference, and the fruitfulness and value of such a gathering was manifest, and the cordial and delightful fellowship and harmony of the occasion was unmarred by a single discordant note.

It seems probable that problems that have been practically insoluble in the atmosphere of church life at home may be fully solved in the practical working plans of the foreign field, and one of the blessings which foreign missions may bring to Christendom will be an inspiring impulse in the direction of Christian union, and a deeper spirit of harmony throughout the Church.

IV. We turn our attention now to the problem of method, which has given occasion for prolonged and earnest discussion, and has developed some considerable diversity of opinion among the friends of missions. The prominent methods of conducting mission work may be included under five divisions—the evangelistic, the educational, the literary, the medical, and the industrial. It should be noted carefully here that this classification of methods is with reference to the instrumentality rather than the aim proposed. The evangelistic method must not be regarded as monopolizing the evangelistic aim, which should itself pervade all the other methods. In fact, it is the aim which should be the guiding and controlling element in all missionary operations, and the absence of a Christian purpose and an evangelistic spirit in any of these methods would be fatal to their usefulness as a true missionary agency. On the other hand, so long as the goal is Christian instruction, heart conversion, and spiritual edification, we will find in each of these methods a way of approach to this goal, and each method will be useful in its own way and place. Evangelistic preaching is addressed chiefly to adult minds assembled for religious worship. Educational teaching is addressed to the young, and may be made a most hopeful and blessed instrument for bringing them early into the kingdom. Literary work is addressed to a more general constituency, and through the Bible and religious books and tracts a far-reaching and powerful influence may be exerted. Medical ministry reaches those in suffering and weakness, and through it the Gospel of spiritual healing may be brought into close and vital touch with the soul. Industrial agencies are useful where it is desirable to give practical education in the arts of labor, united with religious influences and instruction.

It will be noted that the method is nothing if it is not dominated by the spiritual aim. Evangelistic services may be formal and perfunctory; educational agencies may be merely secular; literary efforts may be subservient to mere intellectual culture; medical work may be merely philanthropic; industrial schools may have no higher mission than mere manual training. Under any of these conditions the distinctively missionary character of these methods has been forfeited.

The discussion of this subject has been marked by considerable misunderstanding and misconception. The exalted and exclusive place which some have been inclined to give to the preaching of the Gospel, or the oral proclamation and exposition of divine truth before an audience, has been based largely upon a mistaken conception of the availability and usefulness of other methods to accomplish precisely the same end as that which the preacher of the Gospel has in view, namely, the spiritual guidance and edification of the soul. Under the impression that evangelism was neglected in the sphere of educational, literary, and medical service, many zealous friends of missions have advocated the exclusive claim of simple evangelistic agencies to be ranked as the legitimate missionary method. A wiser and more discriminating opinion is now almost universally accepted, and all these methods are recognized as having a useful function and a legitimate place in missions, with this important and vital provision, namely, that the purpose should be always and predominantly a spiritual one, and in the interest of practical Christianity.

The supreme purpose of missions is to disseminate the Gospel and teach men the way of life and obedience, and in the carrying out of this purpose the preaching of the Gospel is a method which has been divinely ordered and divinely blessed, and it must never be underestimated or ignored; but preaching is manifestly not the only method of reaching the conscience, instructing the mind, and moving the heart. It is not recognized as such here in our own land, where Christian instruction in Sabbath-schools and day-schools and in private classes is recognized and used, and where Christian literature has such a wide, salutary, and beneficent influence, and where medical ministry is a recognized department of Christian work. Why, then, should not these methods be sanctioned and approved in the foreign mission fields? Education is important there, that the school may be recognized and adopted as a religious rather than a secular institution; that the Bible and the whole system of biblical truth may be brought into contact with young minds; that the seed may be sown in the best soil; that the influence of a heathen atmosphere and the temptations of heathen surroundings may be anticipated by preliminary training; that the spiritual nature may be fortified against the assaults of Satan; and that enlightened and educated natives may be trained for mission service. It is a mistake even to limit the educational efforts of missions to the children of native converts, as has sometimes been advocated, since our schools are often most efficient and valuable agencies for rescuing heathen children from heathenism. It seems hardly necessary to say that this plea for education as a missionary method involves no exclusive or paramount claim of usefulness, and that it is a plea for Christian education in distinction from secular, and implies the employment of Christian rather than heathen teachers. It is, in fact, simply an extension of the whole idea of the Sabbath-school in our home church to the needs of our foreign mission field. The fact that the school is conducted every day of the week, and that branches of secular education are taught in it, does not necessarily destroy its religious influence and power, or interfere with its evangelistic purpose.

The same line of argument, did time permit, might be pursued in connection with literary work. In this age of the world, when Christian missions enter a foreign field to carry the Gospel, it is almost an inexcusable oversight to ignore the power of the press and the influence of literature. One of the first steps of a true missionary campaign is the translation and distribution of the printed Bible, and this must be followed by the creation of a Christian literature in all its departments. Under the circumstances in which our missions are working, to neglect education and literature is almost equivalent to acknowledging that Christianity has no message to the human mind. Good service also has been done of late in several mission fields by the use of the magic-lantern as a popular method of education. Sacred scenes upon the canvas can be made the text for much Gospel instruction.

The place of medical work, if done with Christian sympathy and tact, and followed up with Christian instruction, is vindicated both by the example of Christ and by all experience. In the hands of lady physicians it is at present practically the only method of reaching the women in many heathen communities.

As regards industrial schools, they are, of course, limited to a narrow range of missionary effort, but in some portions of Africa, among simple and ignorant people, they have been found eminently helpful in giving a direction to life, and opening up a sphere of usefulness at the same time that they afford an opportunity for religious instruction. They seem to rescue young lives from inanity and idleness, and give them a start in a career of self-respecting usefulness, with the Gospel planted in their hearts.

If we were called upon to place the emphasis upon any one of these methods, or to select one to the exclusion of others, we could not hesitate to regard the preaching of the Gospel as entitled to the supremacy; but where all these methods are available and useful, there is no necessity of confining our missionary operations to any one. We should rather make the best use of them all by preaching, teaching, printing, and living the one Gospel of truth and light and knowledge and service. We may use all these methods as different ways of drawing, attracting, winning, persuading, helping, and compelling souls to come into the kingdom of our Lord. Possibly different fields may call for different degrees of emphasis and prominence in the case of some one of these methods of influence. It has been found, for example, that medical work has been especially useful in China, and educational work is just now at a premium among the low-caste children of India, and in the Turkish Empire. Could Christian missions have the opportunity to educate a generation of Moslem children, it would be a telling blow against the giant system of Islam. Possibly the same field at a certain stage of missionary effort may indicate one method as more promising than another. Possibly the circumstances may be such in certain fields that some one of these methods may be allowed to lapse so far as the foreign missionary is concerned, because the natives themselves are prepared to assume the responsibility in a satisfactory way. However this may be, it has been, and is still, the almost universal practice of Christian missions to avail themselves of these various methods, and to make all subservient to the one great aim; and we cannot but believe that it would have been a misguided policy, involving a disastrous mistake, to have conducted our Protestant missions with special reference only to the needs of those adults who could be gathered together to listen to the preaching of the Gospel, and so ignore the wants of the children, disregard the claims of the suffering, and fail to consider the intellectual needs of the people. And while it is true that in some sense all these methods may fail unless they are inspired with the right aim and receive the divine blessing, it is, on the other hand, true that in a very vital and precious sense they may all succeed if they are faithful to the supreme purpose, and conducted in a way to secure the divine recognition.

V. There are still questions of great complexity and difficulty which remain to be considered, and they may be included under the general title of the problem of native development. Successful missionary work results in a Christian constituency in the midst of surrounding heathenism, and whether we regard the convert as an individual or consider him in his collective capacity as a community, it will at once be recognized that his situation is unique and almost startling, and must be beset with many difficulties and perplexing embarrassments. Even his contact with Christian truth is in some respects novel, and his individual relations to kindred and friends, to his government, to his local community, to the manners, customs, and traditions of his country, to his former co-religionists, to the religion which he has given up in embracing Christianity, and to the Christian Church and his place and service therein, are all new and untried to him, and frequently involved in entanglements which are full of casuistry and practical embarrassment.

If we look still further into this special phase of missions, we will find questions of great practical importance in connection with the coöperation of native teachers and pastors in the conduct of mission work, and further still in connection with the organization and development of the native church, and the relation of the native assistant or associate to the foreign missionary, and of the native church to the home society. We will find that a careful study of this class of problems will reveal many serious questions of policy and many delicate and embarrassing difficulties, which call for consummate tact, wisdom, patience, charity, firmness, dignity, and the pervading, controlling spirit of Christian love, to deal with them successfully.

Time will permit only a brief reference to these problems. I can do little more than indicate them, and as some of them are still in process of solution, it would be presumptuous to attempt to speak in any spirit of assurance concerning them. We may class them under the two general heads of, first, the individual native, and, second, the organized church.

In connection with the individual native, we have the question of coöperation: How far, and in what capacity? What is the place and function of native agency in mission work? To what extent is it necessary, and what importance must we attach to it? What should be the character and limits of training which native agents should receive? What practical regulations should be made with reference to wages? What should be the proper proportion between foreign funds and native contributions? What is the relation of the native agent to the missionary, and to the board or society at home? In fact, the whole economy of the native arm of missionary service is bristling with questions which may at any time become acute in their complications; yet the speedy development of an efficient and self-reliant native agency is without doubt at the present hour one of the most pressing and vital problems of the foreign field.

In connection with the organized church we have the question of creed, which at first may be quietly settled by the acceptance without scrutiny of the creed of the missionary, but which subsequently may come up for discussion by the native church itself as it reaches the stage of independent thought. Then there is the question of organization, including the measure of self-government which may properly be demanded on the one hand, and wisely conceded on the other. And in some cases the matter of polity becomes an open question, and then the subject of a native pastorate soon comes to the front, and the relation of the native pastor to the mission, and to his own people, and the proper provision for his support, all require attention. The matter of self-support—that is, the assumption by the church itself of its own financial obligations—is a subject which has been attended with much embarrassment and many perplexities; and now that our mission work is becoming more successful, the larger question of the organization of national churches is in some fields already pressing itself upon the consideration of both missionaries and native communities, and involves, of course, the relation of such a church to the home church which has been instrumental in giving it the Gospel.

There is still another set of questions involved in the proper attitude of the native church to certain national customs and manners, and others with reference to the proper requirements for church-membership and suitable rules of church discipline. Finally, there is the whole subject of the missionary responsibility and duty of the native church in its own local field of opportunity.

We have not time even to discuss in the most general way these problems. In fact, they may be more properly left to the missionaries themselves upon the fields, in their conferences and ecclesiastical gatherings. Their importance may be discovered at once if we consult the records of the great Missionary Conferences recently held at London and Shanghai, where elaborate and able papers were presented upon almost all of these phases of missionary policy. It is considered here at home one of the essentials to successful preaching of the Gospel to make such an application of divine truth to modern life and the daily practice of men that the Word of God shall be brought into living contact with the conscience, and shall touch every phase of practical morality and of social and religious duty. If this is a difficult thing to do here, and taxes the intellectual ability, the spiritual insight, the practical talent, and the philosophical acumen of a trained, educated, and sympathetic preacher of the Gospel, how much more difficult must it be in the atmosphere of these foreign lands, and in that new and strange and alien environment, to apply wisely, tenderly, and effectively the great fundamental truths of the Gospel, and the vital principles of Christian morality, and the essentials of ecclesiastical polity, and the governing regulations of church life, and the obligations of missionary service, to the Christianity of missionary lands, in such a spirit and method as to secure native coöperation, purity of church life, high moral standards, and a true conception of the supreme and exclusive place of Christianity among the religions of the earth.

Let us ask divine wisdom that these great problems of His kingdom, as it advances among the nations, may all be finally solved in a spirit of wisdom and love, to the glory of His name, and to the honor and exaltation of His Church.

LECTURE V.

THE PRESENT-DAY CONTROVERSIES OF CHRISTIANITY WITH OPPOSING RELIGIONS.

"*Go forth, then, ye missionaries, in your Master's name; go forth into all the world, and, after studying all its false religions and philosophies, go forth and fearlessly proclaim to suffering humanity the plain, the unchangeable, the eternal facts of the Gospel—nay, I might almost say the stubborn, the unyielding, the inexorable facts of the Gospel. Dare to be downright with all the uncompromising courage of your own Bible, while with it your watchwords are love, joy, peace, reconciliation. Be fair, be charitable, be Christlike, but let there be no mistake. Let it be made absolutely clear that Christianity cannot, must not, be watered down to suit the palate of either Hindu, Parsee, Confucianist, Buddhist, or Mohammedan, and that whosoever wishes to pass from the false religion to the true can never hope to do so by the rickety planks of compromise, or by the help of faltering hands held out by half-hearted Christians. He must leap the gulf in faith, and the living Christ will spread His everlasting arms beneath, and land him safely on the Eternal Rock.*"

"*I have said enough to put you on your guard when you hear people speak too highly of the sacred books of the East, other than our own Bible. Let us not shut our eyes to what is excellent and true and of good report in these books; but let us teach Hindus, Zoroastrians, Confucianists, Buddhists, and Mohammedans that there is only one sacred Book that can be their mainstay, their support, in that awful hour when they pass alone into the unseen world. There is only one Book to be clasped to the heart—only one Gospel that can give peace to the fainting soul then. It is the sacred Volume which contains that faithful saying worthy to be accepted of all men, women, and children, in the east and in the west, in the north and in the south, 'that Christ Jesus came into the world to save sinners.'*"

SIR M. MONIER-WILLIAMS, LL.D.

V.

THE PRESENT-DAY CONTROVERSIES OF CHRISTIANITY WITH OPPOSING RELIGIONS.

RELIGION is a theme of wondrous fascination and supreme importance, and the controversies of religion have absorbed the highest energies and taxed the deepest capacities of the human mind in all ages. Christianity as a final and authoritative expression of truth may be regarded for this very reason as the mother of controversy. Her mission is to reveal truth and controvert error. Her Founder and Supreme Teacher came to bring not peace, but a sword. Christian missions are destined, I might almost say designed, to develop controversy. They come with a clear, clean-cut, exclusive, and authoritative system of truth based upon and identified with historic facts, which is the direct and irreconcilable antithesis of false religions. This system of truth is bound to challenge, to controvert, and to supplant existing religious opinions, and substitute its own teachings and its own historic verities in the place of long-cherished convictions. It has no other course open to it. Christ came to save; He came also to enlighten, guide, and deliver the human mind from the spell and bondage of error. Christian truth, therefore, with its supreme and exclusive claims, cannot enter where errors and superstitions hold sway without at once challenging them, and in its turn receiving a challenge, and being called upon to give an account of itself.

In earlier stages of the modern missionary enterprise, when Christianity was still in the shadow and its presence hardly recognized, little controversy was excited, or at least it was confined within a narrow circle. Now, however, that missions have advanced so rapidly to a position of influence and dignity, the era of controversy is upon us, and we can already discern the signs of an impending struggle, which will probably surpass in its intellectual intensity, its spiritual pathos, and its imperial triumphs any of the great controversies of history. It looks at present as if Christianity, with noble earnestness and high courage, would at one and the same time engage in a life-and-death grapple with universal error, under the leadership of Christ her King. With the Spirit and Providence of God as its allies, it seems to be preparing for a single-handed and simultaneous struggle with every giant system of religious sophistry which for long centuries has held the human mind in darkness and bondage. It is face to face to-day with every great dominant religion of the earth, and it will soon be a question of the survival of the fittest and the triumph of the best.

Religion is a term which is used to indicate that spiritual relation between a Supreme Being or Power and His intelligent creatures which results from a mutual search for and recognition of each other, and which, when successful, secures communion of spirit, and leads, on the part of the creature, to reverential worship and cheerful obedience. When unsuccessful, however, the relation is not marked by proper and happy contact with the true God on the part of the creature, but develops into vain and superstitious beliefs and practices. The proper sphere of religion is therefore that realm of thought and practice where God, or what stands for God, and man meet and commune, and assume, each in his place, the proper relations to each other. Religion, then, may be true or it may be false. It may imply and include relations which are right in theory and measurably perfect in practice, or it may utterly fail in both these respects. In its spiritual aspects, as related to the inner experience of the heart, it is subjective; in its external aspects, as related to organization and formal rites, it is objective. Religion has been a factor in the life of mankind since the creation, and the evidence is constantly accumulating that it has been in some form a part of the experience of all men in all ages and countries. Even atheists are simply those who have forced themselves into a rejection of religion. The science of comparative religion has come into prominence of late, and has as its field of research the origin, history, and related as well as differentiated teachings of the world's religions.

The genesis and development of religions has been a subject of much research among modern students, and has given occasion for many rationalistic speculations and various elaborate theories based upon naturalistic premises, but the light which Scripture casts upon this somber and fascinating theme all points to one sufficient explanation of these false systems. God gave man a religious nature, and also gave him a religion in Paradise, both before and after his fall, which He expanded, emphasized, and confirmed by subsequent revelation. This fair, sweet gift of God has been neglected, misused, defiled, and dragged down into the depths of ignorance and superstition, whither fallen man has sunk, until it has become so transformed into the likeness of man's spiritual and intellectual degradation that it has become a delusion rather than a blessing to the vast majority of the race. The light which was in man has become darkness, and "how great is that darkness!" The result has been idolatry in all its forms, which is simply the substitution in the realm of religion of the creature for the Creator. Out of the vanity, ignorance, and despair of the human mind in its proud and helpless struggle after some satisfying solution of the problems of life and destiny, have come those great ethnic religions which, by virtue of the distorted and mutilated fragments of truth which they contain, as well as their concessions to weakness and sin, have held sway for long centuries over so many millions of our human race. It is plain that however clear God may make the original revelation of Himself and His will to man, that revelation may be willfully misunderstood, or misinterpreted, or overlaid, or distorted, or mutilated by the fallen being to whom it is addressed, until it loses finally all essential correspondence with its original form, and is supplanted by the speculations, superstitions, and philosophical theories of the darkened reason of man, until religion becomes in fact a reflection of human ignorance, rather than an exponent of divine wisdom.

This, in the briefest possible words, seems to be the real historic relation of false religions to divinely revealed truth. They are the corruptions and perversions of a primitive, monotheistic faith which was directly taught by God to the early progenitors of the race. They are not even after the pattern of things in the heavens, much less the heavenly things themselves. They are rather gross caricatures and fragmentary semblances of the true religion, which have departed so far from the original model as to be in many essential things positive contradictions and reversals of the truth. God by the severe discipline of the Old Testament economy, and by His special dealings with a chosen people, kept alive and propagated the truth in the hearts of men, and preserved it from total and final extinction. This truth grew brighter and brighter, and was revealed more and more clearly in symbolism, prophecy, and experience, until the glories of that long-concealed mystery of the Incarnation burst at length upon the world. Since the Incarnate Word came among men Christianity has assumed its function as the supreme light of the world, the only divinely authenticated revelation, the true philosophy of religion, the sacred spiritual force which is to enlighten, guide, regenerate, and transfigure human life and human history. And now, in these latter days, in which we are born to a mission of exalted privilege and blessed service, Christianity is reaching out after its place of power among the nations of the earth. With Christendom as its material base, Christian men and women as its chosen instruments, the Spirit of God as its effective agent, and the reigning Redeemer as its King and Leader, it has commenced in earnest its search for these wandering nations, to bring them back to God. Like John the Baptist of old, Christianity is crying to-day in the wilderness of prevalent worldliness, "Prepare ye the way of the Lord!" Ah, that the Church would give heed more diligently to this message which the providential "fullness" of our present time has brought to our ears.

We have designated the false religions of the world as lapses from the true. They are poor counterfeits which rationalism would palm off upon men in the name of revelation. They are the result of an apostasy more or less complete. They are aberrations of the religious faculty in man. Insanity is unhappily a recognized fact among mental phenomena, yet, as the name implies, insanity is simply the unbalancing of a sound mind; so these false religions are a species of spiritual insanity. They result from the unbalancing of sound religion. They are the overturnings and convulsions of the soul of man in the darkness and despair of its wanderings from God. So it is that we find in many of these ethnic religions that certain phases of primitive truth have lingered, and we can trace therein the faint and haggard and pain-worn features of the original likeness. We usually find in them, in some form or other, the doctrine of God, the claim of revelation, the idea of propitiation by sacrifice, the formal ceremonies of worship, the débris of original ethical standards, the function of the priesthood, the demand for some measure of righteous living, the hope of immortality, and an expectation of judgment; and yet their relation to the divine religion may be described by the single word usurpation. They have supplanted the true with infinite effrontery and glaring caricature. It is very much as if some vain and weak man should attempt to assume the astronomical control of the universe, or to become the supreme regulator and disposer of material forces, or the originator of social and economic laws by which, according to his claim, the whole moral system of the world would be revolutionized and righted. We have in the realm of sociology something which is analogous to these false religions in the spiritual realm, in the doctrines of nihilism, socialism, and anarchy, the prevalence of which would destroy society, just as the prevalence of spiritual error has limited and almost destroyed religion as a saving force in the world.

No one can study these human religions without being impressed, on the one hand, with the fact that they are the shadows of a great unknown which must have been stamped with a divine likeness, and, on the other hand, that they have been conceived in deference to human pride, vanity, weakness, and fleshly desire. Could we imagine the unaided reason, the undisciplined affections, and the carnal appetites of fallen humanity to have held a council to deliberate upon the subject of a religion and formulate its principles and practices, we may find what we would naturally anticipate to be the result of such a movement in most of the existing religions of the earth, Christianity excepted.

It follows from these considerations that Christianity as a missionary religion enters a preoccupied realm. It addresses itself, as Paul did among the Athenians, to a "very religious" as well as a very sinful people. It does this, moreover, without the aid of material force, without visible éclat, and without the use of spectacular and sensational methods. It is sometimes long years, perhaps an entire generation, before a single convert is won. The extension of its influence, like the action of leaven, is often silent and obscure. It contends with the deepest and strongest currents of human thought; it clashes with immemorial customs; it seems to the disciples of other religions to be a presumptuous intruder without sufficient credentials, with little visible or self-manifested power to attract and subdue a mind thoroughly under the spell of superstition, with a seared conscience and a darkened understanding, and no spiritual aptitude to receive its teachings or appreciate its high mysteries. It is a mistake to represent non-Christian nations, except as God's Spirit touches individual hearts, as longing for the Gospel and ready to receive it. They are, as a rule, misguided and thoroughly deceived by their false religions. The whole realm of religious thought is darkened and hushed like some chamber of death, while thronging superstitions, like ghostly watchers, guard every approach lest the glad tidings of the Gospel should enter. The spiritual condition of the heathen world has been painted in dark colors, but we doubt if the picture has ever been overdrawn, or its awful shadows made deeper than the reality.

This subject of the religious state of the heathen world has sometimes been presented by students of comparative religion in what has been called an unprejudiced or judicial spirit, which, however, has led to conclusions which are scholastically shallow, morally sentimental, and practically false. The representations which have been given of ethnic religions have been highly idealized, and have been drawn, often in a spirit of literary dilettanteism, exclusively from the sacred literature which represents the original aspirations and ideals of the founders and leaders of the various systems, who were in many cases men of genius and intellectual power and high ethical ambitions. However well these early founders may have wrought under the guidance of the reason, and however much they may have succeeded in borrowing the light that God has given to the world, they have nevertheless built with wood, hay, and stubble. Their ideals have crumbled, and their followers have lived and moved only amidst the ruins of ideal systems. These ruins were soon infested with living creatures of the degraded imagination, with vile forms of creeping lusts, with every species of superstition, and with the loathsome monsters of revolting idolatry, which have turned the very shrines of religion into a refuge for that nameless brood of creatures which have defiled sooner or later every temple which the hand of man untaught of God has vainly reared in the name of religion.

The heathen world as it really is is a very different thing from the heathen world as it aspired to be. The struggle of the human mind to formulate and carry into practice a helpful religion has been sadly and completely in vain. Even if we take these false religions at their best, if we follow them back to their purest sources, if we sit at the feet of their founders and study their philosophic and ethical ideals, we still find them to be the products of reason, or of the religious faculty in man moving in partial light and feeling blindly after God. There is usually also a spirit of compromise with sin. They fail, and fail hopelessly, in the essentials of a true religious system. What they teach of God is obscure, distorted, and in many respects fictitious and blasphemous. If it is theistic in any sense it is either dualistic or polytheistic or pantheistic, and even where it is monotheistic it gives no adequate conception of the divine character. The blessed Deity is gone beyond recognition in almost all these systems, and in His place is gross idolatry as in Hinduism, substantial atheism as in Buddhism, a mutilated conception of the Godhead as in Mohammedanism, or sacerdotal usurpation and ceremonialism as in lapsed Christianity. What they teach of the essence and function of religion is simply the heights and depths of formalism divorced from practical morality. Their teachings of the nature and power of sin are grossly defective. Sin, as we understand it in the light of Scripture, may reign in their mortal bodies while they still play the rôle of religious devotees among their fellow-men. They have no remedy to propose for sin except a vain and childish, or a severely ascetic, cult of self-righteousness combined with shadowy forms of sacrifice; and in that inner realm of the affections, as well as in the outer arena of life and duty, there is a notable failure to realize those graces of the character and those virtues of the life which it should be the mission of religion to secure.

In view of this deep and painful and fatal lack in the greatest and best of human religions, what a thrilling pathos there is in the cry of unconscious need which comes to the Church of Christ to-day from the vast majority of our human race; what a desperate urgency there is in this call for guidance and help, amidst the ignorance of the mind, the deadness of the conscience, the pitiful inadequacy of the resources, and the hopeless degeneracy of the life, which we find wherever man lives out of touch with Christianity! And what a sublime mission Christianity has to these immortal souls, with every capability of receiving and responding to the life-giving message from heaven! It is its peerless and sacred office to teach the truth about God; to give a spiritual conception of religion; to reveal the nature of sin; to proclaim the blessed tidings of the Incarnation and the atoning sacrifice; to show the only way of peace; to enforce the code of Christian ethics, not as a basis of merit, but as a glad and spontaneous expression of gratitude and a triumph of spiritual obedience; to cultivate the graces of devout piety; and to inspire a spirit of unselfish service. In the discharge of this manifold and magnificent mission Christianity must always, in the person of its missionaries and in the spirit of its teachings, reflect the divine patience and forbearance, and, while it gives no uncertain sound, it must ever speak the truth in love, and glorify the gentleness of the Gospel in its message to erring hearts. However vigorous and irreconcilable must be the antagonism between Christianity as a system of truth, and these great religions that have so blinded, deceived, and degraded the human mind, yet in the person of its messengers it must breathe the spirit of its Master, and seek to win by love, attract by persuasion, and subdue by conviction, rather than denounce, attack, and hold up to ridicule and contempt the religious faiths which it seeks to overthrow. It must rebuke, but let the rebuke be in love; it must challenge, but let the spirit of the challenge be free from bitterness and from all suspicion of spiritual pride and arrogance.

The controversy of Christianity with these great religions of the East is a much more serious matter in its purely intellectual aspects than many realize. It can be truly and properly said that were it not for the supernatural and spiritual intervention of God in the interests of the Christian religion, the difficulties would be disheartening and appalling. The fact that Christianity *is* winning its way, and scoring its victories to such a marvelous extent, is a manifest token of the divine blessing, and an unmistakable sign of the gracious operations of the Spirit in our foreign missionary fields. The Church of Christ hardly realizes the worth of these victories, hardly appreciates the sublime vindication of Christianity which they indicate, and the revelation of God's power and the Spirit's work which we have in them. It would not have been strange had God exacted a far larger measure of faith, a much longer trial of patience, a much more serious test to fortitude, and a much higher standard of sacrificial heroism, than He has been pleased thus far to require. The success of our foreign missionary work is wonderful, and unsurpassed by the triumphs of the Gospel even in the first century of the Christian era, yet the Church of Christ has but a feeble consciousness of these momentous signs of God's presence with her, and His work through her in the world.

I have said that the intellectual phases of the controversy of Christianity with false religions are attended with serious difficulties, and it is in contending with these hindrances in the realm of the reason that missionaries have been led to turn their attention so extensively to educational work among the young, as almost a necessary preliminary to any extended acceptance of Christianity among heathen nations. It is not only the renewal of the heart which is needed in foreign missionary fields, but also the restoration or reconstruction of the reason, that the mind may be prepared to receive the truths of Christianity, and grasp them with a discriminating recognition of the points of differentiation from corresponding and similar truths in the old religions.

The proclamation of Christianity among heathen nations is nothing less than the proclamation of another form of religion. It may be received either with contempt, or with some measure of curiosity, or with a spirit of intellectual inquiry. It has in itself, aside from any supernatural influence, considered simply as a system of religious truth, less to commend it to the blind devotees of Eastern religions than we who admire and love it so much would naturally suppose. We must bear in mind that its approach is from the outside, through feeble instrumentalities, with no glamour of spectacular effect or blare of trumpets, and that it comes to those who are already thoroughly possessed by some species of religious faith, whose lives have been spent in an environment of religious influences which has absorbed and captivated the spiritual nature, and placed it in an attitude of entire indifference to Christianity and independence of its teachings.

Now, let us suppose Christianity to address itself, as it must often do in the case of vast multitudes in heathen lands, to the reason or intelligence, without the living and transforming energies of the Holy Spirit carrying light and conviction with irresistible power to the mind. It is a new religion endeavoring to supplant other religions firmly established, and holding their place of supremacy by the power of immemorial tradition, and by virtue of what seems to their followers historic authenticity and sufficient authority. It is plain that the shadow of suspicion and the burden of proof would rest upon Christianity. It must therefore demonstrate its right to supplant, and make clear its claims to superiority. It must show that its origin is truly divine; nay, it must present some convincing evidence that there is a divine Power back of it. It must verify its alleged history; it must vindicate the incarnate glory of its central Personality. It must carry conviction with reference to its great central doctrines of the incarnation, of sin, atonement, regeneration, providence, resurrection, and conscious immortality. It must do all this in no spirit of amiable compromise or sentimental courtesy. It must sustain at once its supreme and exclusive claim, while it approaches gently, kindly, and graciously those who dispute that claim with passionate warmth and implacable bigotry. It is a conflict between an authentic revealed religion and a counterfeit manufactured imitation. Now, a manufactured religion is not necessarily in its original conception a deliberate and cunning scheme of imposture, nor is it a pure invention, nor is it invariably and altogether destitute of the elements of truth. On the contrary, its originator may be a man of genius, of high moral aims, of lofty aspirations, and of undoubted sincerity, with a measure of self-sacrifice and moral heroism in his career. He may stand as the human exemplar of the moral dignity of the reason in its search after something higher and better than is afforded by an unsatisfying religious environment. The elements of truth and moral aspiration which may be incorporated in the make-up of this manufactured article may be many of them borrowed and appropriated from a genuine source. We can imagine the possibility of a manufactured religion which has in combination nine tenths of the subject-matter of revelation, having omitted perhaps only some great essential truth, like the divinity of our Lord, and yet the manufactured character of the resultant can be discovered from the traces of human defects in the combination, and rationalistic blunders in the proportions and relations of the artificial product.

The ethnic religions of the world have fallen far short, however, of this high grade of artificial production. To an enlightened and discriminating Christian conscience their highest ideals, and much more their degenerate realities, are only shallow, pitiful, and bungling counterfeits of the unrivaled and unapproachable glories of our Christian faith; yet to those who have known only the spurious article of human manufacture, the genuine has become the mythical, and the counterfeit is to them the genuine. They are utterly unconscious that they are clinging to an unreality and putting their trust in a delusion.

Let us suppose that the light of Christian revelation had been utterly extinguished throughout our land, and we were dwelling in the spiritual ignorance and darkness of China and India five centuries before Christ, or in the gross idolatry and practical heathenism of Arabia in the seventh century of our era. It would not be long before we should have an American Confucius, a modern Gautama, a contemporary Mohammed, and human religious teachers and devotees by the hundreds, seeking to lead us into the light of some religious faith upon which we could stay our souls, and by which we could guide our religious instincts. If we were left for twenty centuries to the light of nature, the guidance of mere reason, the desolating sway of passion, and the degenerating effects of weakness, what do you think would be our moral condition and our spiritual need? The thought of twenty centuries is startling, but there are already more than two thousand years of dark, despairing, and pathetic history behind the thousand millions in the living heathenism of to-day, and even now Christianity is just awakening to a sense of its duty to these lost sheep of the race. The mission that it has to heathen souls is sublime in its dignity, beautiful in its graciousness, and imperative in its necessity. Christianity must expect to meet with apparently insuperable difficulties, but it must take no account of difficulties. It must expect to advance slowly, but it must take no account of time. It must expect to meet with fierce opposition, but it must be undaunted and unruffled by the violence of enemies. It must expect that infidelity and godlessness will dog its footsteps, and seek to hamper its work by the use of every facility which our modern age places at the disposal of the enemies of Christianity as well as its friends. It must expect that Theosophy and Esoteric Buddhism will pose even in Christendom, and that some one, sooner or later, will seek to introduce the tenets of Islam to the benighted minds of the West! It must expect that even its methods and instrumentalities will be imitated, as was the case within the past year when a Hindu conference assembled at Benares to organize a defensive campaign for the saving of the Hindu religion from the encroachments of Christianity. It must expect to meet the rivalry of reform movements within the lines of existing ethnic religion, which are intended to relieve the native mind from the pressure of Christianity's own influence, and make a new but still rationalistic and anti-Christian channel for the impetuous rush of thought toward something better, which its own influence has stimulated.

The Brahmo Somaj and the Arya Somaj in India are signs of the times with which Christianity will have to reckon more and more as its influence deepens; but in whatever way this restlessness within shall show itself, it is for Christianity with a wise and kindly dignity to recognize it as a sign of its own resistless influence, and to seek to guide and help those proud natures which are paying their unwilling tribute to its power into a better and more perfect way. Christianity must deliver its message, live its life, minister its consolation, organize its institutions, and go patiently, calmly, unflinchingly, and unremittingly forward in the discharge of its great commission to disciple all nations. It must neither modify nor transpose its spiritual formulæ, nor must it lower its moral standards, nor eliminate from its practical working organization any essential element placed there by God. If some features of revealed truth are more difficult than others, it must trust to the wisdom of God to vindicate in the end the value of a fully rounded Gospel and a complete biblical system of religious truth. If Christianity begins to compromise, the process of dismemberment will soon be completed. It must face alike the Jew, the apostate Christian, the Mohammedan, the Hindu, the Buddhist, the Confucianist, the Parsee, the Taoist, the Shintoist, the brute barbarian with his fetich, and every son of superstition, with the full light of the Bible, the undimmed glory of its message, and the inexorable righteousness of its moral requirements. Yet, while thus true to its sacred trust, and loyal to all the essentials of revealed religion, it must at the same time allow a large liberty in non-essentials, and draw no hard-and-fast lines in the realm of denominational differentia. It must minimize its differences, and bring into the presence of heathenism the spirit of unity and fraternity, as becometh the disciples of one Master and Lord.

Let us picture Christianity taking its stand in the midst of the reigning religions of the heathen world, unfolding its message, and pressing its claims. How incomparable are the lessons it teaches, yet how quickly they are challenged, and with what energy and zeal are even its choicest instructions repudiated and scorned. Its first lesson we may well imagine to be of God: His Eternal Being; His attributes; His relation to the creation as the Great First Cause, the Preserver and Governor of all things, upon Whom all creatures are depending, and to Whom all intelligent beings are accountable: yet this magnificent and lofty message of Christianity will no doubt be received with stolid immobility by the adherents of Eastern religions, as a truth which is neither new nor strange. It is something which the Oriental is already familiar with in the terms of his own religious faith, and, however polytheistic his religion may be, he still holds in some shadowy form or other the dim conception of a Supreme Being, and is more or less consciously under the influence of that deep undercurrent of monotheism which is characteristic of the early history of all ethnic religions, and which is so manifest in the earlier and purer literature of the East. Even the multiplicity of gods has not resulted in the entire obliteration of the monotheistic conception, since the supreme exaltation which is given for the time being to one god over another is an ever-recurring testimony to the underlying power of the monotheistic idea; and to express this thought of transient or individualized monotheism the term "henotheism" has been coined. To this marvelous message of Christianity concerning the One Supreme God, the ethnic religions will respond at once with characteristic complacency. "Agreed," say the adherents of the old Oriental Christian Churches, "we already believe that." "Look at our Brahm," says the Hindu. "There is no God but God," responds the Mohammedan. "Our Gautama is a sufficient revelation to us of God," says the Buddhist. "Our Supreme Spirit of heaven and earth," say the Confucianist and the Taoist, "is near enough to the Deity for us." "Our fetich, with its indwelling spirit, comes nearer to our consciousness," says the savage. "Our idols," exclaim the great majority in chorus, "are to us the pictorial and tangible representation of this mysterious divine Personality of which Christianity teaches."

Christianity speaks of its great mystery of the Trinity, although it is beyond its power fully to explain it. Islam at once repudiates the idea as speculative, inconceivable, and indeed blasphemous. The Hindu points to his Trimurti, the triple personification of Brahm the Creator, Vishnu the Preserver, and Siva the Destroyer. The Buddhist and the Confucianist receive the doctrine with incredulity, and see no shadow of reason for believing it.

Christianity teaches of an Almighty Creator. All assent that some system of cosmogony is essential. The point of dispute would be as to the nature or personality of the Creator. That somebody or something has existed from eternity is not denied. In place, however, of the simple Bible story of creation, we have myths and fables, or the gigantic philosophies of Pantheism.

Christianity advances its claim to a divine revelation. Lapsed Christianity replies with an indifferent assent, and turns to the visible Church as the source of present light and practical guidance. The Moslem replies, " Look at our Koran, which the Angel Gabriel brought us, and revealed to the last and greatest of the prophets. At the same time we do honor to the Old Testament, however much we may question the credibility of the New." The Hindu points to his Vedas, his Sastras, and his Puranas; the Parsee to his Zendavesta; the Buddhist to the sacred legend of the Buddha and the Wisdom Literature that has followed in its train. The Confucianist points with pride to the stupendous library of sacred literature which his great hero collated and transmitted from unknown antiquity, and which has grown with the ages. The Taoist boasts of the ancient philosophy of Lao-tse as all the revelation he needs.

Christianity announces its crowning central truth of the Incarnation. Islam replies: "We have all the prophets down to Mohammed, and he whom you call the Incarnate God is held in honor among us as a divinely commissioned messenger from heaven. Why should he be exalted into an incarnate deity?" The Hindu points to his Avatars, in which he finds not one but many incarnations of the gods for the benefit of humanity. The Buddhist is satisfied with the incarnate wisdom of the Buddha, and in his northern school of thought he has a present incarnation in the person of the pontifical Lama, who hides in the unapproachable mysteries of the sacred city of Thibet; while Confucius and Lao-tse, the incarnations of philosophy and wisdom, are all-satisfying to their followers; and to this entire doctrine of the incarnation lapsed Christianity renders a ready assent.

Christianity brings its doctrine of mediation through a divine Mediator, and this the Moslem denies, with scornful questionings as to either its necessity or its propriety. He is saved because he is a Moslem. His appeal is directly to God, without the intervention of any mediators, human or divine; and the whole system of Christian priesthood as it appears in the corrupt sacerdotalism of Oriental Christianity, he rejects with disgust and contempt. The Hindu, in his turn, points to the Brahmans, who serve as his mediators. Lapsed Christianity has robbed our Lord of His supreme function by its degradation and misuse of this sacred doctrine. The Buddhist points to his priests and idols, and the Confucianist to his exalted emperor—the "Son of Heaven"; while the truth about Hinduism, Buddhism, and Confucianism is that they teach a salvation by works, and pay only a shallow tribute to mediation.

Christianity teaches of sin and guilt, and to this the universal human heart responds, although with varied conceptions of what sin is, and what guilt implies.

Christianity proclaims the necessity of sacrifice, and announces that a divine provision has already been made. With this doctrine lapsed Christianity has no difficulty; although it denies the adequacy of the provision made, and demands a still further supplementary offering from its followers. The Moslem claims that it is needless, since God is merciful and is pledged to save a Moslem. The Hindu redeems himself through his forms and ceremonies, and so does the Buddhist; while the Confucianist looks to the "Son of Heaven" to sacrifice on his behalf, and diligently worships his ancestors.

Christianity teaches religious duties and the requirements of obedience. The Moslem bows himself in prayer, repeats his creed, gives his alms, keeps his fasts, and makes his pilgrimages, and in so doing has filled out the round of his religious duties. The lapsed Christian devotes himself to the ceremonial observances of his church. The Hindu plunges deeper into his idolatry, and gives himself more exclusively to the life of a devotee. The Buddhist pays his visits to his temples, and the Confucianist repeats the formulæ of his ancestral worship. Everywhere a supreme and elaborate legalism is the acme of a religious life.

Christianity names its prophets, apostles, pastors, and teachers, and there is not an Eastern religion among them all which cannot surpass

Christianity in its multitudinous array of prophets, priests, teachers, dignitaries, and exalted human functionaries.

Christianity teaches of judgment to come, and every false religion in some form echoes the teaching.

Christianity proclaims its heaven, its system of rewards and punishments, and its hope of immortality. The Moslem prefers his more congenial Paradise; the Hindu looks forward to a refuge from the weariness and spiritual unrest of this present existence in his absorption at last into Brahm; the Buddhist cherishes his mysterious and transcendent prospect of Nirvana, when he shall enjoy forever a rest from the harrowing round of transmigrations, and shall pass into that dreamy realm of blissful unconsciousness where the great woe of existence shall for him cease forever.

If Christianity finds that in these essential and transcendent doctrines its message has been already anticipated by the corruptions, caricatures, and blasphemous usurpations of these false faiths, can we not discover in all this an explanation of the intellectual difficulties which hinder the acceptance of Christian truth? Although Christianity presents these truths in their purity and sublimity, it is not, therefore, sure of acceptance. It must first convince the darkened reason of men that its own presentation of them is better than that which they have been familiar with before, and here it is involved in a most momentous, delicate, and solemn responsibility; one which calls for consummate wisdom, immense patience, exhaustless love, and, above all, for the divine power of that Almighty Spirit who alone can give light and life where both are irretrievably gone.

In a book which has just been issued, entitled "The Distinctive Messages of the Old Religions," the Rev. George Matheson, D.D., its accomplished author, has presented the spiritual contribution of ancient religions to the world's thought in a brilliant but somewhat misleading form. He has placed far too high an estimate upon the contribution of ethnic religions to the religious thought of the world, and has idealized their helpfulness to the souls of men. One feels in reading the book as if Christianity were regarded too much as simply a filling out of the imperfections of ethnic religions or merely an improvement upon them. The rich, subjective contributions of his own religious instinct have clothed the grim and unsightly realities of the old classical and the modern ethnic religions with a beauty and worth which is far beyond their deserts. His book is a poem on comparative religion, and he has not failed to avail himself of the privileges of poetic license. Christianity must be truer to itself, more conscious of its own inimitable individuality and unique supremacy, more loyal to the high meaning of its message, more painstaking and radical in its ministry to the sins, woes, and needs of heathenism than the spirit of this suggestive and stimulating but unreal book would secure. The truer method and, in the end, the more successful plan will be to insist upon its divine claims, and teach its whole message to those who are helpless and lost, and who need its instruction and its saving agencies as their only hope. The great conflict will inevitably be around the personality of the Incarnate Lord. Christianity may well make this the center of its teaching. It can afford for the present to give almost its entire strength to the vindication of the

Incarnation, the Atonement, and the mediatorial system. Christ Himself, once vindicated before the eyes of the heathen world, will make a breach in the massive walls of heathenism, through which the entire system of Christian truth will find an easy entrance. If we preach "Christ and Him crucified," we need have no fear of the issue.

Let us remember, moreover, while we are speaking of the intellectual difficulties which confront Christianity, that, so far as the merely human outlook and environment are concerned, it can make no appeal in the presence of the overshadowing supremacy of Eastern religions to any worldly éclat, nor to the promise of earthly gain, nor to higher antiquity, nor to a larger number of adherents, nor to the possession of great names and holy saints, nor to any exclusive historical basis for its teachings, nor to the fact that Christians alone are the true people of God. At all these claims the disciples of Asiatic religions would smile with incredulity. It is only as the darkened human mind is enlightened and taught of God, rescued from the fearful delusions of superstition, delivered from the crushing bondage of error, lifted above the glamour and worldly entanglements of former religious associations, and profoundly convinced of the folly and absurdity of the prevailing religious practices, that it can reach that vantage-ground of intellectual discrimination and spiritual vision where it can recognize and welcome the truth, and plant itself firmly upon a basis of unfaltering faith amidst the almost resistless currents that would bear it on with the multitude.

We have read recently in the newspapers of the proposal to establish an Islamic propaganda here in America, with the avowed purpose of converting Americans to Islam. We smiled at the folly of this proposal, and pronounced its author either a hopeless crank or a candidate for cheap notoriety; yet it seems to me that on the merely natural or human plane of approach there was hardly, at least in its initial efforts, any more hopeful opening for Christianity among the deluded, and yet conscientious, devotees of Eastern religions, than for Islam here in America. I am not referring, of course, to the inherent dignity and excellence and truth of Christianity, which in these respects stands peerless and alone among the religions of the earth, but my reference is rather to the atmosphere of its reception, and the attitude of those to whom it addresses itself, and the merely human facilities which would smooth the way for its success.

We can illustrate, perhaps, the difficulties which spring up in connection with the introduction of Christianity in heathen lands, by incidents which have occurred of late in connection with the recent cholera epidemic in northwestern Asia. In connection with the dangers of the contagion strenuous efforts were made on the part of the various governments to enforce scientific sanitary arrangements, and to provide the advantages of intelligent medical science for the suffering populace. It was apparent to every reader of the incidents connected with that effort that even government authority, with educated medical science at its service, working in the interest of the people and seeking their highest welfare in a time of manifest peril, could not overcome the prejudices, superstitions, and ignorant infatuation of the masses. The very effort to save them from their misery and danger, although backed by scientific credentials indorsed by the civilized world, only excited the most abject terror, the most unreasonable panic, and the most violent opposition. Ignorant and superstitious communities like these are even more hopelessly under the sway of passion and prejudice in all that relates to religious convictions and customs. Christianity, in its effort to enter, has the same hostile and fanatical spirit to contend with in even an intensified form, and although it comes from God, and is full of the loveliness and power of the truth, and brings the healing ministry of the Great Physician for the woes and sufferings of sin, and has to contend only with the most hideous and despicable spiritual quackery, yet such is the blindness and folly and wild unreasoning delusion of the devotees of false religions, that the very presence of the Great Physician, with His power to minister to the healing of the nations, is an occasion for the display of violent and fanatical opposition.

I have dwelt thus at length upon the darker and more discouraging aspects of these great controversies of Christianity with false religions that I might bring you somewhat into sympathetic touch with that great burden of disheartening experience which every missionary has to carry, with more or less consciousness of its weight, as he finds himself face to face with his tremendous task; and yet there is no good reason for us to lose heart. We should rather take courage, and glorify God, and behold in the progress of the missionary enterprise, and in the glorious record of the success of this first century of modern missions, the tokens of God's favor, and the promise of coming experiences which will both thrill and awe the world. Something sweeter and grander than we have ever dreamed of is coming in the approaching triumphs of Christianity. Another "fullness of time" is hastening on. The Incarnation lingered long, but it finally came. The glories of Christianity have been only as yet faintly revealed during these long and troubled centuries of conflict, corruption, manifold imperfections, and spiritual feebleness. There is much to be said in the interest of a pronounced and unfaltering optimism, even in the face of the most formidable present-day controversies that confront Christian truth in our mission fields. Christianity has, after all, a vantage-ground which will in the end secure to it a respectful and reverent hearing, and give a resistless power to its message. It is the voice of God, and must be heard. It is truth, and must prevail. It is light, and before it the darkness must vanish. Its message is divinely adapted to universal human need; it brings life, hope, solace, healing, and everlasting reconciliation. It is God Himself taking possession of the human heart, as Regenerator, Teacher, Deliverer, Comforter, and Almighty Friend.

Let us look at the message it brings to these deceived and bewildered and enthralled souls. The darkness of error is so deep and impenetrable that only flashes of its light have as. yet pierced the gloom, but the time is coming when it will banish the shadows with a brightness as pervading and resistless as the sunlight.

This wondrous message of Christianity is first of all a new and glorious revelation of the being and character of God. It teaches His personality, His gracious as well as almighty attributes, His universal Fatherhood, His overruling Providence, His fatherly chastisement and disciplinary training. It reveals the Deity in the personality of Christ, whose perfect character stands alone in human history, unrivaled in its beauty and unapproachable in its excellence. It teaches that in Christ God has come into visible relations and into personal contact with humanity, as a Mediator and Friend. It brings also its message of the Holy Spirit and His marvelous activities in the spiritual life of man, as the Regenerator, Inspirer, Guide, and Sanctifier. What a conception of God is this in contrast with the teachings of any human religion! What a startling transformation! What a majestic transfiguration of the whole conception of the Deity as found in the blank mysteries, the shadowy speculations, and the metaphysical monstrosities which have been substituted for God in Eastern religions!

Another important feature of this message which Christianity carries into the darkness of the Eastern world is the clear, bright, tender, and helpful teachings of Scripture. The Bible is the record of God's dealings with the race. It is in touch with all history and all life. It is luminous with instruction, bright with promise, warm with the glow of human feeling, uplifting in its moral inspiration, cheering in its solace, wise in its counsels, and unfailing in its guidance. It illumines the path of duty, and sheds a brightness even into the darkness of the grave. What a message is this for those who have sought for spiritual light in the sacred books of their heathen religions! It is as sure to supplant the cumbrous, obscure, foolish, and unhallowed travesties of revelation which characterize the sacred literature of the Orient, as the truth of God is sure to prevail over error.

In another respect the message of Christianity is a new and blessed one to the adherents of these colossal systems of meritorious legalism, in which every one must work out his own salvation by his own efforts. It brings the glad tidings of an all-sufficient and universally available remedy for sin and its penalty. It tells of a perfect sacrifice already offered and accepted, of a finished atonement forever complete and instantly available. It presents a Saviour who saves, not a mere exemplar who has left no word of hope and no assurance of help to his followers. What a message is this to the weary, struggling, and despairing soul which is striving by vain, fantastic, and cruel methods to propitiate a supreme power!

It bids him give up the struggle, and provides for him all the merit he needs. It tells him of One who has borne his burden, and paid that price which he seeks to offer, and secured that peace for which he is vainly searching. This message of Christianity, when once received and understood, is indeed " glad tidings of great joy " to Eastern hearts, and when it becomes more fully known it is sure to banish self-righteousness and overthrow the childish and disgusting ceremonialism of Eastern religions.

This message of Christianity is a grand one to the East in another aspect. It gives such a new and splendid meaning to life. It so hallows it, and dignifies it, and lifts it up, and makes it in such an inspiring sense a nobler thing to live. The ethics of Christianity fairly transfigure the whole of life when compared with the outlook from the standpoint of Oriental religions. The supreme aspiration of millions in the East is to escape from existence, to be lost in nothingness, to find a refuge in extinction from the dreary and endless transmigrations of being. The whole outlook at its very best is one of sad and dreary pessimism. To such as these Christianity comes with its message of a new life and a regenerate nature. It teaches of an indwelling Spirit who enters into communion with the soul now in this present life, with the avowed purpose of inspiring and invigorating the individual character without destroying the personality. That personality it proposes to transform into the likeness of God, and assures to it a life of conscious fellowship with Him. What a magnificent destiny in contrast with the dismal prospect of absorption into nothingness! It is simply the transfiguration of the individuality as contrasted with its extinction, and it is God Himself who is the agent in accomplishing and perfecting this marvelous change. The whole ethical outlook of life is glorified, the fetters of legalism are loosed, and the soul moves in the free air of grace, and has the exhilarating consciousness of spontaneous obedience, with a holy character as its goal. The whole ethical atmosphere becomes charged with the spiritual ozone of optimism. What a message is this to souls who have hitherto looked upon life as merely a weary struggle, which could only end in nothingness!

Still another feature of Christianity's message is full of marvelous inspiration and hope to the

Orient. It is the remedy it brings for the social wrongs of the Eastern world. In the train of Eastern religions have followed the gigantic social miseries of the Orient—the practical annihilation of the home, the disintegration of the family, the degradation of woman, the sufferings of child-life, the extinction of the larger spirit of brotherhood, the system of caste, the reigning superstitions, such as the Chinese slavery to Fungshui, and the colossal cruelties of heathenism, happily now to some extent abolished. Christianity's mission is to regenerate the social life of the East, and to introduce the spirit of unselfish love, kindly service, and genial brotherhood into the social system. It seeks to establish the organized Christian Church as the center of social religious worship, the rallying-point of Christian fellowship, and the starting-point of missionary service, and to teach the duties that should govern all the relations of the family and of society. Had Christianity no other mission than simply to deliver Eastern nations from their social wrongs and rescue humanity from the cruelties and miseries that afflict society, it would still be a high and sacred duty to establish our missions.

It is a hopeful feature of the outlook also that Christianity is identified in the eyes of the Eastern world with every uplifting and ameliorating agency which has come to them from the realms of Western civilization. Education, in the true and helpful sense of the word, has been the gift of Christianity, and so has philanthropy; and to a certain extent this is true of more secular civilization, although Christianity has, alas! in this respect been sadly handicapped by phases of so-called civilization which have been a discredit and a blemish to the fair fame of Christian purity and honor.

There is much also to inspire hope in the fact that Christianity has entered the East after the prevailing religions have had a long and undisturbed opportunity to work out their natural results and demonstrate what they could accomplish for mankind, and have only succeeded in making their own failure everywhere more conspicuous. They have been tried and found wanting, and the best that they could do for humanity is in frightful contrast with the fruits of Christianity, wherever it has been accepted and practiced. As the old classical world was ripe for the coming of Christ by reason of the moral collapse and hopelessness of paganism, so the Oriental world of to-day is ripe for the mission of Christianity, in view of the manifest and colossal failure of every human system of religion to satisfy the wants of humanity and rescue society from its hopelessness, its degradation, and its manifold miseries.

There is another bright and glowing element of hopefulness in the present relations of Christianity to the false religions of the East. It is the fact that in the case of multitudes of native converts its power to produce its spiritual fruit and accomplish its transforming work in the character, has been abundantly demonstrated. Christianity is already bringing forward its own living witnesses among heathen people. It is becoming better known by its fruit in many lands and among many peoples. It is yielding more and more its own evidence and demonstrating its own divine excellence in the hearts and lives of the constantly increasing number who have accepted it, and who are ordering their lives in accordance with its instruction. It is a touching and suggestive fact that some of the most marvelous transformations and the most brilliant triumphs of missionary history have been in connection with the introduction of the Gospel among the lowest and most degraded populations. Some of those Isles of the Pacific are like jewels in Christianity's crown, and among the wretched Pariahs of India, the submerged low-caste, lower even than the ordinary depths of Indian heathenism, there are signs which point to a large and magnificent fruitage of Christian effort.

Amidst the turmoil of discussion and the clash of contention over the philosophical mysteries of Christian truth, let us never forget the inherent beauty, the incomparable sublimity, and the unapproachable worth of the simple Gospel. Let us never for an instant be betrayed into unconsciousness of the duty of disseminating it. Let us believe in it, and in it only, as the hope of the world. Let us cherish renewed confidence in its power, and give ourselves with fresh enthusiasm and devout zeal to the great and hopeful task of discipling all nations in the name of our Master.

LECTURE VI.

THE PRESENT-DAY SUMMARY OF SUCCESS.

"What hinders the immediate effort to plant the Gospel in every nation and island and home in all the earth within the next decade? Nothing but the faltering zeal and purpose of the mass of Christian believers now on the earth. That precisely is the critical question. Are we, the Christians of to-day, awake to these facts, and responsive to the claims of this glorious work? Do we understand that this vast responsibility rests upon us; that it is possible now, as never before in the world's history, to preach the Gospel to all the nations? And do we mean, God helping, that this work shall be done ere we die? This is the deep significance of the hour to this generation."—REV. JUDSON SMITH, D.D.

"The connection between prayer and missions has been traced thus over the whole field of missionary conditions, simply to show that every element in the missionary problem of to-day depends for its solution chiefly upon prayer. The assertion has been frequently made in past years, that with 20,000 men, properly qualified and distributed, the world could be evangelized in thirty years. And actually there is need of an immediate, undaunted effort to secure 20,000 men. Neither, perhaps, can the world be evangelized without them, nor can they be secured without effort. But it is hopeless to endeavor to obtain them, and they will be worthless if obtained, unless the whole effort be inspired and permeated with prayer. 'Thrust Thou forth Thy laborers into the harvest.' . . . The evangelization of the world in this generation depends, first of all, upon a revival of prayer. Deeper than the need for men; aye, deep down at the bottom of our spiritless life is the need for the forgotten secret of prevailing, world-wide prayer."

ROBERT E. SPEER.

VI.

THE PRESENT-DAY SUMMARY OF SUCCESS.

WE have considered the present status of the foreign missionary enterprise from various points of view, and with a desire to form a comprehensive estimate of its significance and importance, and of the difficulties which it encounters. We have considered its message to the churches, its demand for recognition and support, its conflicts, its problems, and its controversies, and we purpose now to inquire as to the measure of success which it has achieved. We use the word success advisedly, yet it is desirable to explain in this connection what is meant by success. In all great moral movements—in fact, wherever spiritual forces are in the field—success is not usually a matter of mathematical demonstration. It cannot be expressed in exact terms, or collected into statistical tables, or brought to the notice as a visible product. There is an element of intangibility about it which places it beyond the reach of material tests. It hides in the realm of the spiritual, and cannot be fully reached except by the aid of the spiritual faculties. We can only grasp it by a process of faith. It can be felt where it cannot be expressed; it can be recognized where it cannot be demonstrated; it can be a matter of assurance where it cannot be clearly proven.

The estimate of success in missions must be therefore a variable quantity. It may be overestimated, or, on the other hand, it may be wholly underestimated. It should be formed by a sober judgment in a conservative spirit, and yet with full appreciation of all the elements and actors involved, and with a reasonable and justifiable faith in the underlying spiritual forces which are necessarily implied in the idea of Christian missions. The judgment which will be formed as to the measure of success attained will therefore depend largely upon the point of view from which we regard the enterprise, upon our faith in its resources, and our capacity to discover and appreciate the signs of progress which it gives.

A glance over the Old Testament history will convince us of the difficulty of gauging the progress of a great spiritual purpose as it is slowly evolved through a long period of development. It is still a matter of profound investigation, requiring a deep and sympathetic spiritual insight into the undercurrents of religious history, to trace out the progress of the Messianic idea in the Old Testament dispensation. Even in such a material business as war, involving to such an extent forces which can be gauged and estimated by physical tests, it is difficult to form an accurate estimate of the progress of a contest, or to pronounce a verdict as to the success attained at any single point of progress. There are hidden forces involved, and there are undiscoverable contingencies in reserve. There are the elements of enthusiasm, patriotism, moral heroism, fortitude, endurance, the assurance which comes from the consciousness of right and justice, and the inspiration which is quickened by the love of liberty and unfaltering devotion to duty. Considerations like these will turn the scale of judgment in favor of success when all else looks dark and threatening.

In our recent presidential election we had an illustration of the impossibility of judging of success where even political issues are involved, except as we are able to search that hidden realm in which the intangible forces of influence move. The estimate of success for weeks and even months before the election varied in accordance with the point of view of the observer, and his faith in the principles which he advocated. Even a single day before the election the result was entirely beyond the ken of human intelligence, because of that unknown element of moral conviction and political impulse which was secretly controlling the issues of the campaign.

A true estimate of missionary success must therefore take cognizance of many things besides mere visible results. It must take a wider survey, and have a deeper insight than can be obtained from a mere study of statistical tables. It must consider the substantial basis which there is for faith in missions, in view of the divine purpose to redeem the world. It must take into account the coöperation of God in the enterprise, and must calmly weigh the power of those resistless spiritual forces which have been instituted by

God for the very purpose of pulling down strongholds. It must not forget our Saviour's parable of the leaven; it must measure the reserve force which there is in the encouragement and practical support of Christendom, the growth of the missionary spirit in the churches, and the increasing sense of obligation which is beginning to have such a manifest grip upon the Christian conscience. It must mark the rapid growth of the missionary plant in foreign lands, and the growing power of native converts themselves to push on the work. It must take into consideration the astonishing progress which the missionary enterprise has already made, although conducted with an utterly inadequate force, with only a moderate measure of Christian public sentiment in its favor even at home, with formidable and multiplying difficulties to contend with abroad, where Christianity is in conflict with the misguided and hardened conscience, national pride, antagonistic public sentiment, and fanatical religious opposition. It must not fail to note that the missionary himself has been much of the time in the attitude of a despised foreigner, with civilization itself frequently placing him at a still greater disadvantage by its discreditable failure to coöperate in any sense with him and his work. It must bear in mind that the element of time is to be considered, not from a human standpoint, but rather with reference to the divine outlook upon history, and that human haste is not a characteristic of the divine method. It must take due note of the fact that God does not work with any view to spectacular effect, and that His kingdom cometh without observation, and that it is in fact His glory to conceal a thing. It must remember that God makes use of human instrumentalities, and that there is a certain relation, which, though mysterious, is nevertheless real, between the fidelity, earnestness, devotion, and prayerful zeal of the instrument and the results attained. It must remember that apparent failure is often the herald of success, and that long delay in the harvest may mean nothing more than that the natural processes of seed-sowing and growth toward ripened maturity are allowed to go on, according to the laws and processes of the spiritual kingdom. A generation without a convert has been shown by experience to be no sufficient cause for discouragement or abandonment of hope.

These, then, are some of the side lights upon this question of missionary success. It is not simply a question of individual conversions, and growing church rolls, and tabulated statistics, although in respect to these tests foreign missionary success will bear favorable comparison with the average results of aggressive Christian work in Christendom.

It is now a century, dating back from October, 1892, since the formation at Kettering, England, under the impulse of Carey's famous sermon at Nottingham in the previous month of May, of the first of the organized missionary societies that have multiplied so wonderfully during the past hundred years. It is a century, dating back from June, 1893, since Carey and his companion Thomas sailed for India. These incidents should not be regarded as by any means the first efforts at missions, or be exalted into such prominence as would dim the noble and glorious record of the Moravian pioneers, or the missionary heroes of the three previous centuries, conspicuous among whom stand the honored names of Eliot, Heyling, Von Welz, Von Westen, Ziegenbalg, Schwartz, Hans Egede, Zinzendorf, and Brainerd —men who gave themselves to missions with an exalted enthusiasm, and a depth of self-sacrificing consecration that have not been surpassed in the history of the Church. We must not be unmindful of those who prayed and toiled for missions in mediæval times, when the Church itself was dark and cold, and was sunk in superstition and ignorance and worldliness—such men as Columba, Aiden, Columbanus, Clement, Boniface, Anskar, Raymond Lull, Francis of Assisi, the Nestorian pioneers in China, and the Syrian messengers to Malabar. As our thoughts still run back to the early days of Christian history, we come into the light of a missionary era which was full of the freshness and power of a living Christianity.

It remains true, however, that our modern era of missionary progress may very properly be dated from those magnetic words of Carey: "Expect great things from God; attempt great things for God." The "consecrated cobbler," as Sydney Smith called him, was God's chosen instrument for giving a living impulse to this sacred cause. He has become a glorified leader in the grandest movement of modern history. His "dreams of a dreamer who dreams that he has been dreaming" were rather the visions of a seer who thinks the thoughts of God. Those humble tools of iron with which he worked upon leather and last at Paulerspury have been transfigured into spiritual instruments with which he has shod the feet of the century with the preparation of the Gospel of Peace.

If we undertake now to review the progress of the past hundred years from a standpoint which insures us a comprehensive survey of all the essential features of missionary success, we will find that the record is both brilliant and inspiring. Let us endeavor to summarize the leading features of progress along these main lines of advance to which we have referred.

I. We shall note first of all the success which is indicated in the manifest tokens of God's favor, and the signs of His providential coöperation for the advancement of missions. Long before the century began we can discover now, in the light of subsequent events, the meaning of those magnificent spiritual and intellectual movements, which were so full of the very breath of life to the world. With the revival of letters in the fifteenth century came that right arm of the quickened intellect, the printing-press, and then came the era of discovery, and the grand spiritual and intellectual uprising of the Reformation, with its opening of the Word of God to the eyes of men, and the dissemination of its quickening truth throughout Europe. There was a gathering significance in all this, and the unfolding of a steady purpose to prepare the world for its larger life and grander progress, and the Church of Christ for her sacred mission among the nations. We are living in an era of cumulative resources and mighty consummations. Rich, full currents of history have been converging upon our century, and have lifted us as upon a flood-tide of material prosperity, intellectual culture, and spiritual power. At the same time our age is marked by providential facilities and openings, which reveal the presence of God in the molding of history as clearly as any events since Calvary and Pentecost.

The marvelous changes, to which previous reference has been made, were, however, only preliminary to the subsequent widening and expansion of Christendom, and the training of the Church for her missionary function. The foundation of the Baptist Missionary Society in 1792 was followed by that of the London Missionary Society in 1795, the Scottish Missionary Society in 1796, the Netherland Society in 1797, what is now known as the Church Missionary Society in 1799, the British and Foreign Bible Society in 1804, and the American Board of Commissioners for Foreign Missions in 1810. But these signs of a quickened missionary conviction in the hearts of Christians at home were as yet unattended by any manifest intervention on the part of divine Providence for the purpose of opening the heathen world then so tightly closed to the entrance of missions. It was with difficulty that Carey and Marshman and Judson and Ward gained a footing in India. The opposition of the East India Company, which at that time had the monopoly of trade and government in India, was both violent and implacable; yet it shows the rush of events that the very company which scoffed at the coming of a missionary, and forbade him to touch the soil of India, lowered its flags to half-mast when Carey died, after a residence of forty years in the country, as a token of respect to his memory.

The special Providence of God in the interests of missions during the past century has been revealed chiefly in five ways: (1) He has opened the world to the entrance of the missionary. (2) He has not only opened the world to the entrance of missions, but He has sheltered and supported them by the great colonization movements of the century. (3) He has not only bid them enter, and provided them with a sufficient escort, but He has surrounded them with a wonderful environment of unprecedented facilities. (4) He has not only introduced them, and supported them, and given them facilities, but He has called the attention of modern scholarship to the fields of literary, historical, philosophical, archæological, and religious research into which they have entered. (5) He has not only unsealed closed doors, and subsidized government ambitions, and cast up modern highways, and kindled the spirit of scholarly research, but He has secured the removal of hindrances, and put a restraint upon human violence and opposition.

If we turn now to look a little more closely at the marvelous openings which God has made for the entrance of Christian missions, we are met by the fact that at the beginning of the century almost the entire world outside of Christendom was closed to mission effort. It was inaccessible. No Christian missionary could name the name of Christ among the heathen nations. It is difficult for us at the present time to realize what was implied in this fact. We have become so accustomed to an opened world that the solemn and awful meaning of a closed world is lost upon us. We have, however, still before us two illustrations of these closed doors, in the country of Thibet and the city of Mecca. No Christian missionary could penetrate to the sacred city of L'hassa in the interior of Thibet, or to the Moslem stronghold of Mecca, in southwestern Arabia, without exposing himself to a violent death upon the very threshold of the undertaking, and should any attempt be made to force an entrance for missionary purposes it would no doubt precipitate a frightful war.

At the beginning of the century this condition of things was practically world wide. At least a thousand millions of souls were, with scattered exceptions, inaccessible to the Christian missionary. The Islands of the Pacific were known only through the discoveries of adventurous navigators, and so barbarous and cruel were the inhabitants that it was death to land upon their shores, and, moreover, there were practically no facilities for reaching them. Now twenty-seven of the more prominent groups have come under the protection of Christian powers, while missionary work is conducted in the great majority of them, and the Gospel has triumphed in those dark regions as in no other part of the heathen world. Japan had banished Roman Catholic Missions in 1614, and closed its doors to the entrance of foreigners, but on July 4, 1859, they were thrown open, and before January 1, 1860, three missions, the American Reformed, Episcopal, and Presbyterian, had entered and established themselves. Korea, the "Hermit Nation," remained long hidden from the outer world, but in 1884, less than ten years ago, it was opened, and our Presbyterian Church entered with a mission, and already five other societies have followed, and the whole country is at last accessible both to the traveler and the missionary. China, with its vast dependencies, except where a foreign nation had secured a foothold, as at Hong-Kong, was closed until in 1842 five ports were opened, and in 1860 the Treaty of Tientsin threw the whole empire open to the world, and missionaries at the present moment are occupying every great province, with two exceptions, where itinerating work is done. The same story practically is true of Siam and Burma, both of which have become accessible within the century. In Siam our missions have been received with royal favor, and treated with distinguished courtesy by the government. The struggle of Carey and his companions to secure an entrance into India has been referred to. As early as 1813 liberty of evangelization had been conceded by the East India Company, a stipulation which was secured at the time of the renewal of its charter. The country is at present occupied by fifty-three missionary societies and twelve independent missions. The third Decennial Conference of these societies has recently been held at Bombay, January, 1893. Madagascar was entered in 1818, the Turkish Empire in 1820, and Persia in 1834.

As we touch the shores of Africa, we have reached the scene of perhaps the most remarkable providential developments of the century. When most of us were born the great interior regions of Africa were unexplored and unknown. To-day they are the scene of the political, commercial, and missionary activities of all the great nations of Christendom. Modern steamers are navigating the interior lakes and rivers, and railway trains will soon be rushing up and down the great Valley of the Congo, and both the East and West Coasts of the continent are connected by cable with the European telegraphic system. At this moment the fate of Uganda, which represents the latest movement toward a Christian protectorate in the depths of the continent, seems to be virtually decided. A royal commissioner from the English government has been sent there, and the world receives with keen interest the report of his mission, and the assurance that an English protectorate has been declared. At the present time European governments have assumed a certain measure of control over 9,950,000 square miles, which is slightly over four fifths of the area of the continent. Out of a total population of

160,000,000 there are 110,000,000 who are already, to a greater or less extent, under European control and influence, and at the present moment there are fifteen exploring expeditions busily at work unsealing the yet undisclosed secrets of the continent. It is only a question of time when the continent of Africa shall be penetrated and absorbed by European control. Those northern borderlands along the Mediterranean that have been for a thousand years under the control of the Moslem shall revert again to the Christian. The present English occupation of Egypt is a typical and prophetic incident. The lesson of toleration and religious freedom is yet to be learned even in some sections of modern Europe and western Asia. There are great convulsions which must come ere long in both the European and the Oriental worlds, and He who rules the nations will reveal His power to guide and control the changes of history in the interest of His spiritual and eternal kingdom on the earth. Everywhere in the world His strong hand has been busy during this past century in preparing for it a highway among the nations of the earth.

Let us note also the introduction during the past century of the era of colonization, and the immense expansion of Christendom along the lines of colonial enterprise. The Dutch were here early in the field, and were colonizers even before the century began, but during the century England has taken the lead, and has extended her political supremacy in every direction throughout the world. France, Italy, Portugal, and Germany have followed. In the recent rush into Africa there has been a perfect scramble and frolic of colonization throughout that vast continent. The result has been that in the interior of Africa the Congo Free State, under the protection of the European powers, has sprung into being as if by political magic, and a modern map of the African continent is freshly partitioned into vast patches of color, which indicate the varied spheres of European possession and influence. The result of all this has been a marvelous extension of the English language throughout the world, and the establishment of a measure of political and civic order over vast regions of the earth where hitherto irresponsible power has held undisputed sway.

Let us note how the modern facilities of the

century have to a wonderful extent entered these open doors among the nations. There are 18,000 miles of railway in India and 1500 miles in Japan, and even in China some 150 miles of railway have cut a passage through the rocky barriers of Chinese conservatism within the past five years. Projected lines are planned for in the Turkish Empire, and it is a matter of expectancy that the exigencies of European occupation in various sections of the continent will soon require that Africa shall exchange her slow-winding caravans for the swift rush of the "iron horse." A railway from the East Coast to the Victoria Nyanza is already in sight as the result of the British protectorate of Uganda. The whole Oriental world is now accessible by sea in magnificent modern steamers; banking facilities have been established; protection has been widely secured; the printing-press has been quickly adopted and put to service in many languages; the highest achievements of the century are hastening to render service to missions, not of course with any conscious design, but with that unconscious coöperation which the providence of God quietly exacts.

Once more, the scholarship of the century has followed hard upon the track of missions, and has found in the researches of missionaries its highest stimulus and its freshest available material. No one can trace the recent progress in Oriental study without being impressed with the rich mines of philology, archæology, ethnology, folk-lore, ancient philosophy, and comparative religion which have been opened up to the investigations of Oriental scholars. The sacred books of the East have been opened and read to the world; the philosophical content and the practical outcome of the great ethnic religions of antiquity have been laid bare. The real condition of a hitherto unknown world has been exposed to view. The spiritual and practical failure of human religions has been demonstrated anew. The world is learning more than it knew before of the tendencies of Christless history. The Church is appreciating more and more the magnitude of her task, and is learning to prize with new veneration and assurance the priceless message of the Christianity which she is commissioned to disseminate among men.

We have still another example of God's providential intervention in lifting out of the way the barriers that have confronted the pathway of missions, in restraining the barbarities which have threatened them, in subduing the fierce spirit of fanaticism, and in putting an end to some of the great and cruel wrongs that have flourished in the dark days of undisputed heathen supremacy.

II. We note another element in the missionary successes of the century in the rapid multiplication of missionary agencies. A marked change of sentiment and an astonishing expansion of effort is noticeable in this connection. At the beginning of the century the organization of a missionary society for the avowed purpose of sending the Gospel to the heathen world was a matter of considerable difficulty. The proposals of Carey were received with ridicule by the world and with coldness by the Church, although the devoted Moravians had been laboring for over fifty years at that time, and other forerunners of Carey had made earnest but comparatively fruitless appeals to the Christian Church to consider this neglected duty. Two typical incidents will illustrate public sentiment at the two extremes of the century. In 1796 the subject of foreign missions was introduced and debated in the Scottish General Assembly, and was regarded at that time by that representative body as hardly worthy of serious consideration, and the proposal was characterized as both absurd and revolutionary. At the gathering of the Free Church division of this same body in 1886, the Moderator, the venerable Dr. Somerville, as he took the chair announced that he had brought with him a new prayer-book which he intended to introduce and make use of during the sessions of the Assembly. At the same time he lifted before the eyes of the audience one of Keith Johnston's pocket atlases, and as he offered prayer session after session he literally prayed through that pocket atlas, naming in succession the countries and peoples of the earth. The impression of this detailed and specific prayer for the nations of the earth by name was profound and suggestive, and in harmony with the developed missionary spirit of our age.

When the American Board of Missions was incorporated the proposal excited considerable opposition in the Massachusetts Legislature, upon the plea that America had no religion to spare. The London *Times*, until quite recently, has spoken in terms of disparagement and mild contempt of the missionary enterprise, but now its tone has changed, and in the weekly edition for January 27, 1893, I find a long and cordial notice of the Decennial Missionary Conference which had just been held at Bombay, in which the missionary work in India is referred to in terms of high respect and appreciation. That sign which used to be placed over the doors of Christian churches in Cape Colony, South Africa, announcing that "Dogs and Hottentots" were not admitted, has long ago been discarded. Monuments to missionary pioneers are beginning to appear. There is one of Livingstone, with Bible and ax in hand, in Edinburgh, and another to him in Westminster Abbey, where he is buried. There is a Memorial Church to Judson in Washington Square, New York.

In connection with this marked change in public sentiment, we can trace all through the century a chain of great missionary societies which have been organized, and have developed rapidly in numbers and resources and in the expansion of their operations. For the sake of limiting our survey to the progress of the past century, we will consider only the development of missionary agencies as dated from the time of Carey. Counting, then, from the organization of the Baptist Missionary Society of England in 1792, we have at that date one society, which in 1842 (fifty years) had increased to 27; in 1867 (seventy-five years later) to 58; and in 1892, at the end of the century, to 280. In 1792 the income of that one society was $415; in 1842 $3,000,000, were given to the different societies; in 1867 the united income had reached $5,100,000; while in 1892 the total income of all the societies had become $14,588,354. Three of these agencies—the Church Missionary Society of England, the Methodist Episcopal and Presbyterian of the United States—have passed the million-dollar line of annual income. The first Bible Society, the British and Foreign, was formed in 1804, and the American Bible Society in 1816. In 1892 there were 80 Bible Societies in the world. In the year 1800 the Bible translations in existence were 47. They now number

90 entire versions and 230 partial, making a total of 320, while the total circulation of the Scriptures during the century amounts to 350,000,000 copies, and the Word of God is at present within sight and in possible touch with the hearts of at least 500,000,000 of our race, who were practically unconscious of its existence at the beginning of the century.

The growth of Woman's Foreign Missionary Societies is also a striking feature in the advance of the century. Although there is a woman's society in Great Britain which dates back to 1834, the first organization of the kind in the United States was in 1861, where at present they number 33. If we add 9 in Canada and 30 in Great Britain and the continent of Europe, we have a total of 72 in Europe and America. There are still a few others in various parts of the world which are not included in the above enumeration. Other missionary societies are springing up in connection with the Students' Volunteer Movement, the Young Men's Christian Associations, and the Young People's Societies of Christian Endeavor. The International Missionary Union is already a power, and although its aim is rather in the line of the discussion of missionary themes, its field of influence is unique, and its promise of usefulness is most encouraging. Its annual symposiums deserve to be published as a permanent contribution to missionary literature.

The Inter-Seminary Missionary Alliances have a noble field for their activities. A distinctive feature in connection with the Columbian Exposition is to be the consideration of the religious state of the world and the advance of Christian Missions.

The missionary literature of the century has grown to remarkable proportions, and every year of the last decade has brought us a rich additional contribution upon this subject. Much valuable experience has been gained as to the methods of a wise missionary policy. Mistakes have been discovered and rectified. Problems have been discussed, and partially, if not fully, solved. The entrance of a new century finds the missionary operations of the Christian Church under the control of trained and experienced organizations, which are prepared to press on under the impulse of hopeful courage, and under the guidance of mature experience. We must not forget to note also the rise and growth of missionary societies in lands which were themselves heathen countries at the beginning of the century. There are already partially organized efforts of this character in Japan, China, India, and at many points in the Pacific Islands.

Let us not forget, however, that although there is much to record in this connection which is inspiring and encouraging, yet there are some features which indicate that the missionary earnestness of the century has developed slowly, and that the resources of Christendom have as yet been hardly touched in the interests of missions. The estimate is not far from the truth which credits nine tenths of what is given for missions to about one tenth of the Christian membership of our churches, and there is good reason to fear that at least one half of our church-membership give nothing for the support of missions. If every Protestant church-member in the United States (estimating the number at 14,000,000) gave even one cent a Sunday to foreign missions, the result would be an income of $7,280,000 instead of $5,000,000. If the church-membership of Protestant Christendom on both sides of the Atlantic (estimating it at 40,000,000) should give the same amount, the income would be $20,800,000 instead of $14,588,354. If the Protestant church-membership of the United States should give a nickle a Sunday to this cause, it would result in an income of $36,400,000. If they should become what the Bible calls "hilarious givers," as President Merrill Gates aptly characterizes the full significance of the expression which is translated "cheerful giver," and should revel in the gift of ten cents a Sabbath for the redemption of the world, our resources for foreign missions would reach the astonishing figure of $72,800,000. It is apparent that there are still undeveloped resources in the Christian Church which are yet to be consecrated to missions, and the coming century will no doubt witness substantial progress in this respect, while the development of the missionary possibilities of the foreign fields themselves is still a reserved force of as yet unknown proportions.

III. We have another important and promising factor in the successes of the century in the establishment of the mission plant in foreign lands. We shall deal here with statistics which speak for themselves, without any attempt to demonstrate their success.

There are at the present time 3388 principal stations where missionaries reside, and from which mission work is conducted in outlying regions containing numerous substations. These outstations, in addition to the centers already named, number 13,432, making a total of 16,820 localities where mission work is planted. There are 7800 organized churches in the foreign mission fields, and 4500 ordained native preachers, and, in addition, 40,032 native lay-helpers. There are about 7000 Sabbath-schools with 1,006,768 scholars. In this summary of evangelistic agencies we must not forget to notice the special work in the zenana and in the home, which has been so recently and rapidly organized, and so successfully conducted by devoted women who have made it their specialty. It is only since 1851 that this work was begun in India, and this "storming of the zenana," which is a stronghold of Hindu and Mohammedan jealousy and superstition, by the missionary heroines of India, with their weapons of love, tact, and sympathy, is one of those silent conquests by spiritual forces which resembles the victory of the sunlight as it melts the mighty masses of snow and ice which would be immovable by any other force.

The educational plant is scarcely less remarkable than the evangelistic. There are colleges, higher educational institutions, theological seminaries, and common schools; and in these institutions there are gathered 678,370 of the young of both sexes receiving the inestimable advantages of a Christian education. What this one fact means to the world in the coming generation is beyond all computation. He who came as the Light of the World is the real Founder of these agencies of instruction, and it is under the guidance of His Spirit that the instruction given through these educational channels is so full of spiritual illumination and religious edification. The significance of the educational aspect of foreign missionary work appears further in the fact that the whole educational impulse in lands where missions have entered can be traced largely to the influence of missionary example and suggestion. The governmental system of education in India is due to the energy and wisdom of Dr. Duff, and in Japan, where such wonders have been accomplished in this line, it is fair to say that the educational plans of missionaries have led the way to the present large and generous scheme of the Japanese government.

Evangelistic and educational agencies are nobly supplemented by literary achievements. The mastering of languages, their reduction to writing, and the construction of a workable grammatical system, so that they are ready for literary use, both in the hands of the author and the printer, has been one of the most brilliant intellectual triumphs of missions. During the century many languages that were hitherto beyond the reach of pen or type have been brought into literary being, and the first, as also the most sacred, use to which these linguistic creations have been put is to make them the medium of transmitting the thoughts of God to the minds and hearts of His children. But aside from the languages which have been born again to this high service, the great existing languages of the earth have been made the medium of a choice and affluent contribution of religious and educational literature to nations that were almost utterly destitute of the literary riches of the Gospel or the higher moral instruction of Christianity. At the beginning of the century—a fact which will bear repetition—the Bible translations numbered 47; at the present time the entire Bible is found in 90 languages, and the New Testament, or portions of the Bible, are found in 230 additional languages, making a total of 320 full or partial translations of the Scriptures at present in existence. In connection with foreign missions there are many presses, or publication houses, issuing at the present date hundreds of thousands of volumes annually, representing an annual total of many millions of pages printed. Newspapers, periodicals, and tracts are issued under mission auspices in every language through which mission work is conducted.

The first printing-press in India was established at Serampore in 1800, for which Carey supplied the brains and Ward the hands, and they were soon working in thirteen different languages, and in 1812 they were actually printing the Bible in eight different languages, with three other translations ready for the press. At the present time the Bible is printed entire in thirteen of the principal languages of India, and portions of it in over thirty of the less important ones.

The literary invasion of China began with the first attempt at a printing establishment, in 1833, by Dr. S. Wells Williams, and at the present time our Presbyterian Mission Press at Shanghai alone has over seven hundred publications in the native language upon its catalogue, and the issue for 1891 amounted to 615,450 volumes, representing a total of over 41,000,000 pages. In addition to this there are four other evangelical publication agencies in China, doing a work of incalculable value in distributing the leaven of the truth throughout the empire. One tract alone, from the pen of Dr. Griffith John, issued by the Central China Religious Tract Society at Hangkow, has reached a circulation of 224,000. Another, upon "The Great Themes of the Gospel," has attained a circulation of 223,000, and still another of 68,000. The total sales of this one tract society up to 1891 are reported as

5,879,984 volumes. China boasts of its literature both old and new, but a literary force is now at work in the empire which will ere long rob the vast treasures of ancient heathen literature of their glory.

A work of similar character has been going on through the agency of the Arabic, the sacred language of the Mohammedan world, designed in the providence of God to be the literary medium of approach to Moslems. The Arabic Bible translated by Drs. Eli Smith and C. V. A. Van Dyck is one of the noblest literary monuments of this age. Our Presbyterian Mission Press at Beirut has 483 volumes upon its catalogue, and prints about 25,000,000 pages annually. At the present time the whole New Testament in the languages of New Guinea and Uganda is being printed by the British and Foreign Bible Society in England, and the Bible newly translated in six languages of foreign mission fields is going through the press of our American Bible Society.

The medical plant is full of power, and is charged with a gracious and blessed ministry in the mission fields. The Edinburgh Medical Missionary Society, founded in 1841, was the first to organize, and there are now five societies established exclusively for the conduct of medical missions, while all missionary societies to a greater or less extent include medical work in their operations. In 1849 there were 12 medical missionaries in the non-Christian world. They have now increased to 359, of whom 74 are women. It is said of Dr. Parker, the first medical missionary to China, in 1834, who was afterward instrumental in founding the Edinburgh Medical Missionary Society, that "he opened China at the point of the lancet." Medical work is now carried on through medical schools for the training of native physicians, prominent among which are the Medical Department of the Syrian Protestant College at Beirut, and the Dufferin Training Schools in India.

The personal services of medical missionaries are given in connection with hospitals and dispensaries, and by itinerant visitation through destitute regions. The highest type of medical heroism has been illustrated in the devotion, fearlessness, and self-sacrificing toils of these missionary physicians. They fight every species of fearful and loathsome disease. They stand face to face with frightful epidemics, and lay their healing hands on helpless human sufferers in places where there is no ear to hear, and no arm to save but theirs. The medical missionary work in China is a magnificent triumph. To quote the London *Times:* "China had no efficient hospitals or medical attendance until the missionaries established them, and in truth she has no other now, and when her great men, such as Li Hung Chang and Prince Chun, are in serious danger they have to go to the despised missionary doctor for that efficient aid which no Chinaman can give them."

Still another department of the mission plant, and one which is coming into greater prominence year by year in certain sections of the world, is the industrial. The name industrial does not imply that this department of work is without educational and evangelistic features. In many so-called industrial schools the work of Christian instruction is simply combined with industrial training, with singularly happy and useful results. The mission fields which are opening up in Africa seem to call for industrial training as a most valuable feature of missionary effort. A new and promising field is also in view in connection with mission work among women in India and elsewhere. A conspicuous example of success in the sphere of industrial effort is the Lovedale Institute, in Cape Colony, South Africa, under the auspices of the Free Church of Scotland. The Jubilee of this institute was celebrated in July, 1891. It began with 20 pupils; it has now 660. Over two thousand graduates of the school are now engaged in useful occupations, and have received the spiritual benefits of their training there. The school is rapidly becoming self-supporting, as only twenty-five per cent. of the annual expenditure is now drawn from home sources. Sir Langham Dale, superintendent-general of education in Cape Colony, gives it as his testimony that "undoubtedly Lovedale is one of the noblest and most successful missionary agencies founded and supported in Cape Colony by British philanthropy." The Rev. Dr. James Stewart, the present principal of Lovedale, has now gone into British East Africa, at the request of friends in Scotland, to establish a similar institution, to be named "New Lovedale." Its location has already been selected, about eighteen days' journey into the interior from Mombasa, on the regular caravan route to Uganda. A situation has been found three thousand feet above the level of the sea, and the necessary buildings are now approaching completion. Industrial training is also a special feature of Bishop Taylor's self-supporting missions in Africa. This department is regarded with marked favor by the Lutheran Church and the Basle Missionary Society, and institutions have already been established for Mohammedan women in India.

The number of these industrial schools is increasing, and their practical usefulness is becoming more and more manifest. Among the branches of industry in which instruction is given may be named wagon-building, blacksmithing, printing, bookbinding, telegraphing, tailoring, tanning, shoemaking, weaving, baking, and tile-making, and many departments of agricultural production. In some cases the higher arts, as civil and mechanical engineering, the manufacture of industrial implements, and the making of locks and watches, are taught. To women instruction has been given in embroidery, sewing, in the use of the sewing-machine, in nursing, pharmacy, domestic service, and housekeeping. In India a woman graduate of one of these schools has been appointed to the charge of the post-office at Mandapasalai. This method of combining a training which opens the door for a self-supporting and self-respecting future with the spiritual instruction of Christian missions is one which promises to be specially fruitful among uncivilized and barbarous races. It opens to them a new world, which is doubly blessed with spiritual guidance and industrial occupation, so that the exit from barbarism has not only a promise for the life to come, but a prospect for the life that now is.

IV. The fourth element in the successes of the century is the introduction of the Gospel leaven throughout the heathen world. The success here cometh in a large measure without observation, but no believer who has studied the significance of our Saviour's parable can doubt that a wonderful and mysterious force is active in our mission fields. Wherever mission work has been inaugurated and the Bible introduced among a people, mighty changes are silently progressing, the significance and power of which are known only to God. The wealth of Christian leaven which this century has introduced among heathen nations is something which cannot be known, nor can its silent and mighty transformations be estimated or demonstrated.

V. Still another force which must be brought into line in estimating the mission successes of the past hundred years, is the growing coöperation of native agencies, and the growth of spontaneity in the mission churches. The native converts are coming to the front. They are already rallying by tens of thousands to the service of the kingdom in mission lands. There are already over 44,000 native laborers upon mission fields. Some of the most prominent positions—as, for example, the presidency of the Meiji Gakuin at Tokyo, Japan, and of the Doshisha at Kyoto—and chairs of instruction in colleges, as well as prominent pastorates, are now occupied by natives. In many of the South Sea Islands, in New Guinea, Burma, India, China, Japan, Madagascar, the Turkish Empire, and Persia, the work of the native preachers and evangelists is giving a magnificent impulse to the whole missionary movement. There are missionary societies in the Sandwich Islands, in Madagascar, in India, in Japan, in the South Sea Islands, and in Turkey. Some of the native churches of India are sending their missionaries into regions where no foreign missionary can enter, as Independent Bhutan, and Thibet. A work similar to that of George Müller has been undertaken by a native of Japan, who has his orphanage in that country. Mr. L. D. Wishard reports since his recent missionary tour around the world the existence of 185 associations of native young men in foreign mission fields who are banded together under the auspices of Young Men's Christian Associations. Of this number 45 bands are student organizations in connection with colleges. The missionary spirit in these associations is active and aggressive. The service of Christian natives finds also an extensive and important field in journalism, in translation, and in original contributions to Christian literature. The contribution of native churches to the treasuries of our home missionary societies has grown to be of most encouraging proportions; especially is this true of the London

Missionary Society, which in its annual report for 1892 acknowledges from that source an income of $110,720, and the Church Missionary Society of $65,865, and the Wesleyan Missionary Society of $21,360. What this coöperation of native churches will expand to in the coming century no one can foresee. "The fruit thereof may shake like Lebanon" throughout all the heathen world.

VI. We have come now to what might be considered by many as the most conspicuous and convincing evidence of success that the century affords—the actual conversions that have resulted from mission work. The record is indeed a cheering and inspiring one. The present statistics of mission churches report about 900,000 living church-members. If we added to this those church-members who have died in the faith within the century, we may with all assurance increase the number by 200,000 more, making a round 1,100,000. If we add still an unknown quantity, namely, those who have found Christ, and whose names to-day, whether they be living or dead, are on the rolls of the Church Invisible, we may count with assurance upon 500,000 more. We have been speaking of souls brought into saving contact and spiritual union with Christ. There is a still larger environment of Christian adherents, or those who have been brought within the circle of Christian missionary organizations, and are publicly known as adherents of the Christian religion, in distinction from those who are identified with other religious faiths. The number of these we have no hesitation in reckoning as at least 3,000,000, making a total of adherents and communicants of nearly 4,000,000.

In the Almanac of the American Board for 1893, carefully prepared statistics indicate the number of communicants added last year in the foreign missions under the care of American societies alone as over 50,000. If we add to these those received by the societies of Great Britain and the continent of Europe, we shall have without a doubt 50,000 more—in all, 100,000 converts in the past year. It is nearly 2000 per week. Let us imagine ourselves, upon the first Sabbath morning of 1892, seated in the gallery of some large American church which would seat a round thousand on the ground-floor, and looking down, with moistened eyes and swelling heart, upon a reverent assembly of a thousand souls literally from all nations and kindreds and tribes and tongues and peoples of heathen lands, with every specimen of strange physiognomy and every variety of curious costume, gathered together for the first time, with tender hearts and beaming faces, to partake of the communion at our Lord's table. Let us imagine ourselves duplicating this same experience upon the afternoon of the same Sabbath, in the same church, with another and entirely different audience, of very much the same character, met together for the same purpose, and let us imagine ourselves thus engaged morning and afternoon during every Sabbath of the past year, through winter's cold and summer's heat, in sunshine and in storm, without a single omission; as we came to the last Sabbath of the year, would we believe in foreign missions or not? If the Christian Church could have one year of visible evidence such as this, we should have no occasion to plead or beg for the support of foreign missions. It would seem like a veritable sabbatical year of Christian jubilee, and yet it would be only the visible exemplification of sober actual fact.

Bishop Thoburn, of the Methodist Episcopal Church, missionary bishop of India and Malaysia, has recently visited America upon a brief vacation from his laborious duties. He has just returned to India, and in a letter written soon after his landing he mentions the fact that during his absence in America he finds that 15,000 souls have been admitted to the communion in his diocese. Fifteen thousand conversions during a missionary vacation shows us at once the impulse and the headway which the work has gained, and the way in which God can carry it on, even though the one whom he has placed at the head as its leader and chief counselor is resting apart for a while.

The startling rapidity with which changes are taking place and the astonishing percentage of growth in missionary progress should both cheer and encourage us. That mighty system of caste in India, which hitherto has been the very symbol of inflexible tenacity and inexorable fixedness, is already tumbling into chaos. Men who were born without one word of Scripture in their native language at the time of their birth, are already reading the Word of God in their own tongue. In the English political papers at the present time there are solid columns of matter about Uganda and the political bearings of the problem concerning it which has so suddenly sprung into prominence, but in an unnoticed corner in some obscure missionary periodical we will perhaps find the mention of a fact which has in it more of significance, more of hope, more of latent energy, and more of the magnificent plans of God, than all the political changes and upheavals that are just now stirring that little kingdom in the depths of Africa. It is the fact that the New Testament is ready for Uganda. Listen to the description of its reception on the ground, penned by a missionary of the Church Missionary Society, the 22d of June last. "Talk about sieges," he writes, "if ever there was a siege it was yesterday, and this morning it seems likely to be renewed tenfold. I mentioned that our canoes had come, and I gave out on Sunday that the Gospel of St. Matthew would be sold Monday morning. I was aroused up before it was light by the roar of voices, and after dressing hurriedly, sallied out to the—I had almost said fight. Close to my house is a slight shed, used for the cows to stand in in the heat of the day. This we barricaded, keeping the people outside; but barricades were useless. In came the door, and we thought the whole place would have fallen. In ten minutes all the hundred Gospels were sold." Bishop Tucker writes of preaching to an audience of five thousand at Mengo, the capital of Uganda, upon Christmas Day, 1892, which was a Sabbath. He reports the desire for the purchase of Scriptures as so great that it has been decided to offer each invoice for sale simultaneously at several designated localities. Twenty-five years ago the first Christian building was erected in Tokyo, Japan; now there are ninety-two Christian churches and chapels. In the New Hebrides, within the lifetime of the venerable Dr. Paton, whom many of us have seen and heard, twenty-three islands of the New Hebrides have been occupied. The Bible, in whole or in part, has been translated into fourteen different languages, and fourteen thousand native converts have been gathered in. The merest mention of startling and significant facts in the history of missions indicating the rapidity with which changes are taking place, and the headway which this work is gathering, would more than occupy the solid hour of a lecture.

We have no time left to speak of the indirect results of mission work, so interesting and suggestive, the intellectual, scientific, and commercial stimulus they have given to the world, the place they occupy as a factor in the world's progress, the modifications they are introducing into the manners and customs of heathen nations, the way in which they are helping to stamp out barbarism and cruelty and wrong, the aspirations they are kindling in the religious thought of our times, the checks that they are putting upon superstition, the restraints which they are placing upon the irresponsible tyranny of hierarchical religions, and the training they are giving to native races in the direction of better government, freer life, and higher self-control.

We must omit also all but the most cursory reference to these indirect results as revealed in the reflex influence of missions upon the spirit and tone of the Christianity of our home churches. What a lesson have they given us in the beauty and value of an aggressive union of Christian forces for the upbuilding of Christ's kingdom! What riches they have brought to the Church of Christ even in the present generation! How they have actually lifted Christianity to a height of aspiration and a breadth of purpose and a plane of action far higher than it occupied at the beginning of the century! What a heritage of heroism they have left us! Would the Church of Christ for any amount of yellow gold sell the honor of this century's record of missionary heroism? Is it little to the Church in this age of the world that she can point to her Livingstone dying upon his knees in the jungles of Africa, or unfold that rough mat in which her Patteson was shrouded as his martyred body was brought back to the ship, and point to *his* five wounds, no more, no less? Is it little to her that so many have died for Christ and truth upon mission fields, and that the tramp of the noble army of martyrs still rings through the golden streets? Is it little to her that she has upon her roll that faithful band of missionary workers who have represented her in many lands? Is it little to her that she can point to her trophies and victories which have grown in number and significance as the century has advanced? Is it little to her that she can refer to those Pentecostal seasons in the Pacific Islands and in India, to that first Sabbath in July, 1838, when 1705 souls were baptized in the Sandwich Islands, and that first Sabbath in July, 1878, when 2222 were baptized in the Telugu Mission in India? Is it little to her that she has such tokens of her Lord's presence, such assurances of His benediction, and such promise of immortal glory through the advancement and triumphs of His kingdom? Oh, let the Church follow hard after this sublime victory, and press on prayerfully and eagerly toward this hallowed goal.

APPENDIX.

A SELECT BIBLIOGRAPHY OF RECENT LITERATURE ON MISSIONS.

(VOLUMES PUBLISHED SINCE 1890.)

(A full bibliography of mission literature will be found in the Encyclopedia of Missions, published by Funk & Wagnalls, as an appendix to Volume I, compiled by Rev. Samuel Macauley Jackson, LL. D., assisted by Rev. G. W. Gilmore, and bringing the subject down to the close of 1890. A similar list, although less complete, by the same author, will be found at the conclusion of Volume I of the Report of the London Missionary Conference of 1888, published by Fleming H. Revell Company. To these valuable sources of information the student is referred, as the list here given is intended to include, with a few exceptions, only books which have been published since the above lists were compiled. This will account for the omission of many works of standard value.)

CONTRACTIONS.

L. = London.
N. Y. = New York.
P. = Philadelphia.
C. = Chicago.
B. = Boston.
T. = Toronto.

I. HISTORICAL, PHILOSOPHICAL, AND GENERAL.

ATLAS, THE CHURCH MISSIONARY. In three parts. Part I, Africa; Part II, India; Part III, Ceylon, Mauritius, China, Japan, N. W. America, and North Pacific Missions. L.: Church Mission House, 1892. 5s. each part.

CAREY, WILLIAM. An Enquiry into the Obligations of Christians to use Means for the Conversion of the Heathens. Reprinted in facsimile. L.: Hodder & Stoughton, 1891. 10s. 6d.

CUST, R. N. Linguistic and Oriental Essays. L.: Kegan Paul, Trench, Trübner & Co., 1892. 21s.

CUST, R. N. Normal Addresses on Bible Diffusion. L.: Elliot Stock, 1893.

DENNIS, REV. JAMES S. Native Agents and Their Training. N. Y.: Christian Literature Co., 13 Astor Place, 1892. Paper, pp. 37, 25 cts.

DENNIS, REV. JAMES S. Foreign Missions after a Century: Lectures on Missions, delivered at Princeton Theological Seminary, 1893. N. Y., C., & T.: Fleming H. Revell Co., 1893. 12mo, pp. 368. $1.50.

GORDON, REV. A. J. The Holy Spirit in Missions. N. Y., C., & T.: Fleming H. Revell Co., 1893. 12mo, pp. 233, $1.25.

GRACEY, LILLY RYDER. Gist. N. Y.: Hunt & Eaton, 1893.

GREEN, REV. ASHBEL. Presbyterian Missions from 1741-1838. With Supplemental Notes by Rev. John C. Lowrie. N. Y.: A. D. F. Randolph & Co., 1893. $2.00 net.

HEADLAND, EMILY. Brief Sketches of C. M. S. Missions. In three parts.

Part I, Africa; Part II, India; Part III, Ceylon, China, Japan, N. W. America, etc. L.: James Nisbet & Co., 1890. In one vol., 3s. 6d.

HISTORICAL SKETCHES. Missions of the Presbyterian Church (North). P.: W. F. M. S. of Pres. Ch., 1334 Chestnut St., 1891. $1.00.

HODDER, E. Conquests of the Cross. A Record of Missionary Work Throughout the World. 2 vols. L.: Cassell, 1890. 9s.

HORSBURGH, J. HEYWOOD. Do Not Say; or, The Church's Excuses for Neglecting the Heathen. N. Y., C., & T.: Fleming H. Revell Co., 1892. Paper, 10 cts.

JOHNSTON, REV. JAMES. A Century of Christian Progress. 2d edition. N. Y., C., &. T.: Fleming H. Revell Co., 1890. 50 cts.

JOHNSTON, REV. JAMES. Missionary Points and Pictures. L.: Religious Tract Society, 1892. 8vo, 1s. F. H. Revell Co., N. Y. 12mo, 50 cts.

JUBILEE MEMORIAL. Edinburgh Medical Mission. Edinburgh: Scott & Ferguson, 1892.

LAMB, REV. M. T. The Great Commission. Davenport, Iowa: Mossmann & Vollmer, 1893. 40 cts.

LEAVENS, REV. PHILO F. The Planting of the Kingdom. N. Y.: A. D. F. Randolph, 1891. Pp. 48, 12mo, 40 cts.

LIGGINS, REV. JOHN. The Great Value and Success of Foreign Missions. N. Y.: Baker & Taylor Co., 1890. Pp. 232, 35 cts.

LOWE, JOHN, F. R. C. S. E. Medical Missions; Their Place and Power. N. Y., C., & T.: Fleming H. Revell Co. (3d ed.), 1891. 12mo, pp. 308, $1.50.

MISSIONARY EXERCISES. No. 3, for the use of Sabbath-schools, Mission Bands, and Christian Endeavor Societies. P.: Pres. Board of Pub., 1893. Pp. 192, 30 cts.

MUDGE, REV. JAMES. The Pastor's Missionary Manual. N. Y.: Miss. Soc. M. E. Church, 150 Fifth Ave., 1891. 25 cts.

MYERS. REV. JOHN BROWN. Centenary Volume of the Baptist Missionary Society. J B. Myers, editor, with seven special contributors. L.: Bapt. Miss. Soc., 21 Furnival St., 1892.

PATERSON, REV. S. R. Gospel Ethnology. N. Y., C., & T.: Fleming H. Revell Co., 1891. $1.00.

PIERSON, REV. ARTHUR T. The Divine Enterprise of Missions. N. Y.: Baker & Taylor Co., 1891. 12mo, $1.25.

PIERSON, REV. ARTHUR T. The Greatest Work in the World. N. Y., C., & T.: Fleming H. Revell Co., 1891. 35 cts.

PIERSON, REV. ARTHUR T. The Crisis of Missions. (New ed.) N. Y., C., &. T.: Fleming H. Revell Co., 1891. $1.25.

PIERSON, REV. ARTHUR T. The Miracles of Missions. N. Y.: Funk & Wagnalls, 1891. 35 cts.

RANKIN, WILLIAM. Handbook and Incidents of Foreign Missions of the Presbyterian Church, U. S. A. Newark, N. J.: W. H. Shurts, 1892.

SCOTT, REV. T. J. Sparks from the Anvil of a Busy Missionary. N. Y.: Methodist Mission House, 150 Fifth Avenue, 1891. 25 cts.

SMITH, GEORGE. Short History of Christian Missions. New and Revised Edition; Handbook for Bible Classes. Edinburgh: T. & T. Clark, 1890. 2s. 6d.

SOMERVILLE, REV. A. N. Precious Seed Sown in Many Lands. L.: Hodder & Stoughton, 1890. Pp. 332, 8vo, 5s.

STRONG, REV. JOSIAH. The New Era; or, The Coming Kingdom. N. Y.: Baker & Taylor Co., 1893. Cloth, 75 cts.

TITTERINGTON, MRS. S. B. A Century of Baptist Missions. P.: American Baptist Publishing Society, 1420 Chestnut St., 1892.

TODD, REV. ELBERT S. Christian Missions in the Nineteenth Century. N. Y.: Hunt & Eaton, 1890. Pp. 171, 12mo, 75 cts.

WARNECK, DR. GUSTAV. Evangelische Missionslehre; Ein Missionstheoretischer Versuch. 1te Abth. Gotha: Fr. Andr. Perthes, 1892.

YOUNG, ROBERT. The Success of Christian Missions: Testimonies to their Beneficent Results. L.: Hodder & Stoughton, 1890. 8vo, pp. 270, 5s.

II. BIOGRAPHICAL.

BRYSON, MRS. MARY I. John Kenneth Mackenzie, Medical Missionary to China. N. Y., C., & T.: Fleming H. Revell Co., 1891. 8vo, pp. 412, $1.50.

GILMOUR, JAMES, of Mongolia: His Diaries, Letters, and Reports. Edited by Richard Lovett, M.A. N. Y., C., & T.: Fleming H. Revell Co., 1892. $1.75.

HAMLIN, REV. CYRUS. My Life and Times. B.: Congregational Pub. Society, 1893. (In press.)

HARDY, ARTHUR SHERBURNE. The Life and Letters of Joseph Hardy Neesima. B. & N. Y.: Houghton, Mifflin & Co., 1891. $2.00.

HAYDN, REV. H. C. American Heroes on Mission Fields. (1st series.) Brief Missionary Biographies. N. Y.: American Tract Society, 1890. $1.25. (2d series in press.)

KENNEDY, JAMES. Biography of Margaret Stephen Kennedy. L.: James Nisbet & Co., 1892. 8vo, 6s.

LAPSLEY, REV. S. N. Memoir of the late Mr. S. N. Lapsley, American Presbyterian Missionary in the Congo Valley. Richmond, Va.: Whittet & Shepperson, 1893.

LAURIE, REV. THOS. Woman and the Gospel in Persia. Memoirs of Miss F. Fiske. N. Y., C., & T.: F. H. Revell Co., 1892. Pp. 100, 30 cts.

MACKAY. Pioneer Missionary of the Church to Uganda. By his sister. L.: Hodder & Stoughton, 1890. Pp. 450, 8vo, 7s. 6d. N. Y.: A. C. Armstrong & Son. $1.50.

MACKAY OF UGANDA, The Story of the Life of. Told for Boys. By his Sister. L.: Hodder & Stoughton, 1892. 8vo, 5s. N. Y.: A C. Armstrong & Son. $1.50.

MISSIONARY ANNALS. A series published by the Woman's Presbyterian Board of Missions of the Northwest.
C.: Room 48, McCormick Block, 1892. Cloth, per vol. 30 cts. N. Y., C., & T.: Fleming H. Revell Co.

MISSIONARY HEROES. A series published by the Woman's Board of Foreign Missions. N. Y.: 53 Fifth Ave. 1892.

PATON, JOHN G. Missionary to the New Hebrides. 2 vols., illustrated. N. Y., C., & T.: Fleming H. Revell Co., 1892. 12mo, $2.00 net.

PATON, REV. JAMES. The Story of John G. Paton. Told for Young Folks. L.: Hodder & Stoughton, 1892. 8vo, 5s. N. Y.: A. C. Armstrong & Son. $1.50.

POPULAR MISSIONARY BIOGRAPHIES. (A series.) N. Y., C., & T.: Fleming H. Revell Co., 1891-93. 12mo, pp. 160, 75 cts.

PORTER, ELIZA CHAPPELL. A Memoir. By Mary H. Porter. N. Y., C., & T.: Fleming H. Revell Co. $1.75 net.

RANNEY, MISS RUTH W. Lives and Missionary Labors of Rev. and Mrs. Cephas Bennett. B., N. Y., & C.: Silver, Burdett & Co., 1892. $1.00.

ROBERTSON, REV. WILLIAM. The Martyrs of Blantyre—Henry Henderson, Dr. John Bowie, Robert Cleland. 2d edition. L.: James Nisbet & Co., 1892. 8vo, 2s. 6d.

ROWE, REV. G. STRINGER. James Calvert of Fiji. L.: C. H. Kelly, 1893. 3s. 6d.

SMITH, MRS. AMANDA. An Autobiography and Account of Her Work as an Independent Missionary. Introduction by Bishop Thoburn of India. C.: Myer & Bro., 1892.

SMITH, GEORGE. Henry Martyn, Saint and Scholar. N. Y., C., & T.: Fleming H. Revell Co., 1892. $3.00.

VERMILYEA, ELIZABETH B. The Life of Alexander Duff. Woman's Pres. Board Missions of the Northwest. C.: 1891. Pp. 123, 8vo, 30 cts.

III. LITERATURE ON SPECIAL FIELDS.

(Some of the volumes inserted in this list refer only casually to Missions, but give instructive and vivid descriptions of Mission fields.)

AFRICA.

ARNOT, F. S. Bihé and Garenganze. L.: J. E. Hawkins & Co., 1893. N. Y., C., & T.: Fleming H. Revell Co. 70 cts.

CAMPBELL, BELLE MCPHERSON. Madagascar. C.: Woman's Presbyterian Board of Missions of the Northwest, Room 48, McCormick Block. 30 cts.

CUST, ROBERT NEEDHAM. Africa Rediviva; or, The Occupation of Africa by Christian Missionaries of Europe and North America. L.: Elliot Stock, 189'.

DRUMMOND, H. Tropical Africa. With introduction replying to Mr. Stanley. N. Y.: Scribners, 1891. 12mo, $1.00.

EASTERN EQUATORIAL AFRICA MISSION of the Church Missionary Society. 1837-1891. L.: Church Mission House, Salisbury Sq. 6d.

GUINNESS, MRS. H. G. On the Congo. L.: Hodder & Stoughton, 1890. N. Y., C., & T.: Fleming H. Revell Co. 50 cts.

HORE, CAPT. E. C. Tanganyika. L.: Stanford, 1892. 8vo, 7s. 6d.

HUGHES, REV. W. Dark Africa and the Way Out. L.: Sampson Low, Marston & Co. 1893.

JOHNSTON, REV JAMES. Missionary Landscapes in the Dark Continent. N. Y.: Randolph & Co., 1892. 12mo, pp. 264.

KELTIE, J. SCOTT. The Partition of Africa. L.: Edward Stanford, 26 and 27 Cockspur St., Charing Cross, S. W., 1893.

LIVINGSTONIA MISSION of the Free Church of Scotland in Nyassa-land. Glasgow, 1891. 8vo, pp. 36.

MACDONALD, REV. JAMES. Light in Africa. L.: Hodder & Stoughton, 1890. Pp. 264, 8vo, 6s.

MOIR, JANE F. A Lady's Letters from Central Africa. With an introduction by Rev. T. M. Lindsay, D.D. N. Y.: Macmillan & Co., 1891. 12mo, pp. 91.

PETERS, DR. CARL. New Light upon Dark Africa. L.: Ward & Lock, 1891. 8vo, pp. 600. 16s.

PICTORIAL AFRICA. Its Heroes, Missionaries, and Martyrs. N. Y., C., & T.: Fleming H. Revell Co., 1890. $2.50.

PINNOCK, REV. SAMUEL G., Baptist Missionary in Western Africa. The Yoruba Country: Its People, Customs, and Missions. L.: JOYFUL NEWS Book Depot, 152 Fleet St., 1893. 6d.

PRUEN, S. T. The Arab and the African: Experiences in East Equatorial Africa During a Residence of Three Years. L.: Seeley, 1891. Pp. 320, 8vo, 6s.

SMITH, REV. G. FURNESS. Uganda: Its Story and Its Claim. L.: Church Mission House, 1891.

STANLEY, HENRY M. Slavery and the Slave Trade in Africa. N. Y.: Harper Bros., 1893. Pp. 86, 32mo, 50 cts.

STOCK, SARAH GERALDINE. The Story of Uganda. N. Y., C., & T.: Fleming H. Revell Co., 1892. $1.25.

TOWNSEND, WILLIAM J. Madagascar: Its Missionaries and Martyrs. N. Y., C., & T.: Fleming H. Revell Co. 12mo, 75 cts.

TUCKER, BISHOP. Uganda and the Way Thither. L.: Church Mission House, 1892. 2s.

TYLER, REV. JOSIAH. Forty Years Among the Zulus. B. & C.: Congregational Publishing Society, 1891.

WHITE, A. S. The Development of Africa. L.: Philip & Son, 1891. 8vo.

WINGATE, MAJOR F. R. Ten Years' Captivity in the Mahdi's Camp. L.: Sampson Low, Marston & Co., 1892. 8vo, pp. 450.

YOUNG, ROBERT. Trophies from African Heathenism. L.: Hodder & Stoughton, 1893.

CHINA.

FIELDE, ADELE M. Pagoda Shadows. L.: T. Ogilvie Smith, 1891.

GILMOUR, JAMES. More About the Mongols. L.: Religious Tract Society, 1893. 5s. N. Y., C., & T.: Fleming H. Revell Co. $1.75.

GUINNESS, GERALDINE. In the Far East. Letters from China. N. Y., C., & T.: Fleming H. Revell Co., 1891. Quarto, pp. 191, $1.50.

GUINNESS, GERALDINE. The Story of the China Inland Mission. L.: Morgan & Scott, 1893.

MORRIS, REV. T. M. A Winter in North China. N. Y., C., & T.: Fleming H. Revell Co., 1892. $1.50.

MOULE, ARCHDEACON A. E. New China and Old. L.: Seeley, 1891. 8vo, pp. 310, 7s. 6d.

MOULE, ARCHDEACON A. E. The Glorious Land. L.: Church Mission House, 1891. 1s

NEVIUS, REV. J. L. Demon Possession To-day, and Kindred Phenomena. N. Y., C., & T.: Fleming H. Revell Co., 1893. 12mo, $1.50.

REID, REV. GILBERT. Glances at China. N. Y., C., & T.: Fleming H. Revell Co., 1892. 80 cts.

SMITH, REV. ARTHUR H. Chinese Characteristics. Third edition, revised, with illustrations. N. Y., C., & T.: Fleming H. Revell Co., 1895. 8vo, cloth, $2.00.

INDIA.

BAILEY, WELLESLEY C. The Lepers of our Indian Empire. L.: John F. Shaw & Co., 1892.

BARRETT, REV. R. N. The Child of the Ganges. A Tale of the Judson Mission. N. Y., C., & T.: Fleming H. Revell Co., 1892. 12mo, pp. 254, $1.25.

DICKEN, REV. W. H. JACKSON. The Story of Muttalakshmi. L.: Charles H. Kelly, 1893.

DOWNIE, REV. DAVID. The History of the Telugu Mission. P.: American Bap. Pub. Soc., 1420 Chestnut St., 1893.

DROESE, MISS. Indian Gems for the Master's Crown. L.: Religious Tract Society, 1893. N. Y., C., & T.: F. H. Revell Co. 80 cts.

EVEN, REV. J. India: Sketches and Stories of Native Life. L.: Elliot Stock, 1892.

FALLON, MISS. Premi: The Story of a Hindu Girl. With introduction by Sir M. Monier-Williams. L.: J. Nisbet & Co., 1892. 16mo, 1s.

GORDON-CUMMING, MISS C. F. Two Happy Years in Ceylon. 2 vols. L.: William Blackwood & Sons, 1892. 8vo, 30s.

HUNTER, SIR W. W. Brief History of the Indian Peoples. Oxford: The Clarendon Press, 1892. N. Y.: Macmillan & Co.

HURST, BISHOP J. F. Indika. N.Y.: Harper Bros., 1891. $3.75.

KNOX, REV. M. V. B. A Winter in India and Malaysia Among the Methodist Missions. N. Y.: Hunt & Eaton, 1891. Pp. 308, $1.20.

MAXWELL, MRS. ELLEN BLACKMAR. The Bishop's Conversion. N. Y.: Hunt & Eaton, 1892. $1.50.

MÜLLER, F. MAX. India: What Can It Teach Us? Lectures before the University of Cambridge. N. Y.: Longmans, Green & Co., 1892. $1.25.

MURRAY, J. ROSS. Hindu Pastors. L.: John Heywood, 1893.

PADMANJI, BABA. Once Hindu—Now Christian L.: J. Nisbet & Co., 1891. N. Y., C., & T.: F. H. Revell Co. 75 cts.

SERAMPORE LETTERS. Correspondence of William Carey and others with John Williams. N. Y. & L.: G. P. Putnam's Sons, 1892. Pp. 150.

SMALL, A. W. Light and Shade in Zenana Missionary Life. Paisley: Parlane, 1891. 16mo, 1s.

THOBURN, BISHOP J. M. India and Malaysia. N. Y.: Hunt & Eaton, 1892. $2.00.

WHYMPER, F. Every-day Life in South India; or, The Story of Coopooswamey. N Y., C., & T.: Fleming H. Revell Co., 1891. Pp. 256, 12mo, $1.00.

WILKINS, W. J. Breaking His Fetters. L.: Religious Tract Society, 1893. N. Y., C., & T.: Fleming H. Revell Co. $1.25.

JAPAN.

BATCHELOR, REV. JOHN. The Ainu of Japan. N. Y., C., & T.: Fleming H. Revell Co., 1892. $1.50.

BICKERSTETH, MISS M. Japan As We Saw It. L.: Longmans, Green & Co., 1893. 21s.

CHAMBERLAIN, BASIL HALL, and W. A. MASON. Handbook for Japan. L.: John Murray (third edition), 1891.

DE FOREST, REV. J. H. A Brief Survey of Christian Work in Japan, 1892. Yokohama, Japan: F. Staniland, 70 Main St., 1893.

GORDON. REV. M. L. An American Missionary in Japan. B. & N. Y.: Houghton, Mifflin & Co., 1892. $1.25.

GRIFFIS, WILLIAM ELLIOT. Japan: In History, Folk-lore, and Art. B. & N. Y.: Houghton, Mifflin & Co., 1892. 16mo, 75 cts.

STOCK, EUGENE. Japan and the Japan Mission. L.: Church Mission House, 1891. 3s. 6d.

VARIOUS OTHER FIELDS.

BISHOP, MRS. (Isabella L. Bird.) Journeys in Persia and Kurdistan. 2 vols. N. Y. & L.: G. P. Putnam's Sons, 1891. $6.50.

BUTLER, REV. WILLIAM. Mexico in Transition. N. Y.: Hunt & Eaton, 1892.

CHAPMAN, REV. M. B. Lands of the Orient.

COBB, REV. HENRY N. Far Hence. A Budget of Letters from our

Mission Fields in Asia. N. Y.: W. B. F. M. Ref. Ch., 25 East 22d street.

COUSINS, GEORGE. From Island to Island in the South Seas. L.: Lond. Miss. Soc., 14 Blomfield St., 1893.

CURZON, GEORGE N. Persia and the Persian Question, 2 vols. L. & N. Y.: Longmans, Green & Co., 1891. 8vo, $12.00.

GILMORE, REV. GEORGE W. Korea from Its Capital. P.: Presbyterian Board Publication, 1334 Chestnut St., 1892. $1.25.

GRUBB, G. C. What Hath God Wrought? An Account of a Mission Tour in Ceylon, South India, Australia, New Zealand, and Cape Colony. L.: Marlborough, 1891. Pp. 390, 8vo, 4s.

HALLETT, HOLT S. A Thousand Miles on an Elephant in the Shan States. L.: Blackwood & Sons, 1890.

MABIE, REV. HENRY C. In Brightest Asia. 4th edition. B.: W. G. Corthell, 1892.

MACLEAN, ARTHUR JOHN and WILLIAM HENRY BROWNE. The Catholicos of the East and His People. L.: S. P. C. K. 5s. N. Y.: E. & J. B. Young & Co., 1892.

MARCH, REV. DANIEL. Morning Light in Many Lands. B. & C.: Congregational S. S. and Pub. Soc., 1891.

MICHELSEN, O. Cannibals Won for Christ. A Story of Missionary Perils and Triumphs in Tongoa, New Hebrides. L.: Morgan & Scott, 1893. Pp. 200, 8vo, 2s. 6d.

MUTCHMORE, REV. S. A. The Moghul, Mongol, Mikado, and Missionary. N. Y.: Ward & Drummond, 1891. 2 vols., pp. 553, pp. 325, 12mo, $2.50.

OUTLINE MISSIONARY SERIES. A series of sixpenny manuals on the various Mission Fields of the world, prepared by authors thoroughly conversant with their respective subjects, and embracing the missions of all denominations. L.: John Snow & Co., 2 Ivy Lane, Paternoster Row. N. Y., C., & T.: Fleming H. Revell Co. Each 20 cts.

The following are ready:

MADAGASCAR. Country, People, Missions (with Map). By Rev. J. Sibree.

INDIAN ZENANA MISSIONS. Their Origin, Agents, Modes of Working, and Results. By Mrs. E. R. Pitman, author of "Heroines of the Mission Field."

CHINA. Country, People, Religious Systems, Christian Missions (with Map). By Rev. J. T. Gracey.

POLYNESIA. Islands, Races, Missions (with Map). By Rev. S. J. Whitmee.

SOUTH AFRICA. Country, People, European Colonization, Christian Missions (with Map). By Rev. J. Sibree.

FEMALE MISSIONS IN EASTERN LANDS. Fields of Labor, Mission Work, Agencies. By Mrs. E. R. Pitman.

INDIA. (In two parts.) Country, People, History, Manners, and Customs; Hinduism; History of Christianity, Obstacles, and Hindrances: Forms of Labor, Results. By Rev. E. Storrow.

THE WEST INDIES. Islands, Aborigines, and European Colonization; Negro Life, Slavery, and Emancipation; Christian Missions. By Mrs. E. R. Pitman.

MEDICAL MISSIONS. By Rev. John Lowe.

OUTLINE MISSIONARY SERIES. By Rev. J. T. Gracey. Rochester, N.Y.: Scranton, Wetmore & Co. N. Y., C., & T.: Fleming H. Revell Co. (India, pp. 212, 50 cts.; China, pp. 64, 15 cts.; Open Doors, pp. 64, 15 cts.)

ROCKHILL, W. W. The Land of the Lamas. Notes of a Journey Through China, Mongolia, and Thibet. L. & N. Y.: Longmans, Green & Co., 1892.

SCHNEIDER, H. G. Working and Waiting for Thibet. L.: Morgan & Scott, 1891.

THWING, REV. EDWARD P. Ex Oriente: Studies of Oriental Life and Thought. L.: S. W. Partridge & Co., 1892.

WINSTON, W. R. Four Years in Upper Burma. L.: C. H. Kelly, 1892.

IV. LITERATURE OF COMPARATIVE RELIGION.

BETTANY, G. T. Mohammedanism and Other Religions of Mediterranean Countries. L. & N. Y.: Ward, Lock, Bowden & Co., 1892. $1.00.

BETTANY, G. T. The Great Indian Religions. L. & N. Y.: Ward, Lock, Bowden & Co., 1892. $1.00.

BETTANY, G. T. The World's Religions. N. Y.: Christian Literature Co., 13 Astor Place, 1891. Pp. 896, 8vo, $5.00.

BROWNE, EDWARD G. A Traveler's Narrative Written to Illustrate the Episode of the Báb. 2 vols. Cambridge, Eng.: University Press, 1891.

CODRINGTON, REV. R. H. The Melanesians: Studies of their Anthropology and Folk-lore. Oxford: Clarendon Press, 1891. N. Y.: Macmillan & Co. $4.00.

COPLESTON, REV. R. S. Buddhism, Primitive and Present, in Magadha and Ceylon. L. & N. Y.: Longmans, Green & Co., 1892. $5.00.

DE LA SAUSSAYE, P. D. CHANTEPIE. Manual of the Science of Religion. L. & N. Y.: Longmans, Green & Co., 1891. $3.50.

DODS, REV. MARCUS. Mohammed, Buddha, and Christ. 7th edition. L.: Hodder & Stoughton, 1893. N. Y.: Thomas Whittaker. $1.50.

EDKINS, REV. JOSEPH. The Early Spread of Religious Ideas, Especially in the Far East. L.: Relig. Tract Soc. N. Y. & C.: Fleming H. Revell Co., 1893. $1.20.

ELLINWOOD, REV. F. F. Oriental Religions and Christianity. N. Y.: Chas. Scribner's Sons, 1892. $1.75.

JESSUP, REV. HENRY H. The Greek Church and Protestant Missions; or, Missions to the Oriental Churches. N. Y.: Christian Literature Co., 13 Astor Place, 1891. Paper, pp. 40, 25 cts.

KELLOGG, REV. S. H. The Genesis and Growth of Religion. L. & N. Y.: Macmillan & Co., 1892. $1.50.

LANE, REV. EDWARD W. Selections from the Koran. L.: Kegan Paul, Trench, Trübner & Co., 1890. 8vo, 9s.

LANE-POOLE, STANLEY. Studies in a Mosque. L. and Sydney: Eden, Remington & Co., 1893.

LYALL, SIR ALFRED. Natural Religion in India. The Reed Lectures, 1891. Cambridge, Eng.: University Press, 1891. N. Y.: Macmillan & Co. 75 cts.

MACDONALD, REV. JAMES. Religion and Myth. N. Y.: Chas. Scribner's Sons, 1893. $2.25.

MATHESON, REV. GEORGE. The Distinctive Messages of the Old Religions. N. Y.: A. D. F. Randolph & Co., 1892.

MUIR, SIR WILLIAM. The Caliphate: Its Rise, Decline, and Fall. L.: Religious Tract Society, 1891. N. Y., C., & T.: Fleming H. Revell Co. $4.20.

MÜLLER, F. MAX. Anthropological Religion. Gifford Lectures before University of Glasgow in 1891. L. & N. Y.: Longmans, Green & Co., 1892. 8vo, $3.00.

NÖLDEKE, THEODOR. Sketches from Eastern History. L. and Edinburgh: Adam & Charles Black, 1892.

NON-BIBLICAL SYSTEMS OF RELIGION. A symposium by Farrar, Rawlinson, Wright, and others. Cincinnati: Cranston & Curts, 1893. Cl., 90 cts.

NON-CHRISTIAN RELIGIONS OF THE WORLD. Special Volume of Present-Day Tracts. N. Y., C., & T.: Fleming H. Revell Co., 1891. 1 vol., $1.00. Rise and Decline of Islam. By Sir William Muir. Christianity and Confucianism Compared in their Teaching of the Whole Duty of Man. By Prof. James Legge. The Zend-Avesta and the Religion of the Parsis. By Rev. J. Murray Mitchell. The Hindu Religion. By Rev. J. Murray Mitchell. Buddhism: A Comparison and a Contrast Between Buddhism and Christianity. By Rev. Henry Robert Reynolds. Christianity and Ancient Paganism. By Rev. J. Murray Mitchell.

POOL, JOHN J. Studies in Mohammedanism. L.: Archibald Constable & Co., 1892.

RAE, GEORGE MILNE. The Syrian Church in India. L.: William Blackwood & Sons, 1891. 8vo, 10s. 6d.

RELIGIOUS SYSTEMS OF THE WORLD. A contribution to the study of comparative religion. Addresses by representative scholars. N. Y.: Macmillan & Co., 1891. 8vo, $4.50.

ROBSON, REV. JOHN. Hinduism and Christianity. Edinburgh and L.: Oliphant Anderson & Ferrier, 1893.

SCOTT, REV. ARCHIBALD. Buddhism and Christianity: A Parallel and a Contrast. The Croall Lectures for 1889-90. L.: Simpkin, 1891. 7s. 6d.

SWEET FIRST-FRUITS. A Tale of the Nineteenth Century on the Truth and Virtue of the Christian Religion. (Translated from the Arabic by Sir Wm. Muir.) L.: Religious Tract Society, 1893. N. Y., C., & T.: Fleming H. Revell Co. $1.00.

WILLIAMS, SIR M. MONIER. Indian Wisdom. (New ed.) L.: Luzac & Co., 1893. 21s.

V. PERIODICAL LITERATURE.

(The missionary periodicals have increased rapidly in number and volume. They contain a large amount of fresh and valuable matter, including direct correspondence from the fields, recent incidents and statistics, and also many able and timely discussions of living questions. The following is a representative list of the more important issues.)

THE MISSIONARY REVIEW OF THE WORLD. N. Y.: Funk & Wagnalls, 18 & 20 Astor Place.

THE CHURCH AT HOME AND ABROAD (Pres. Ch. in U. S. A.). P.: 1334 Chestnut street.

WOMAN'S WORK FOR WOMAN (Pres. Ch. in U. S. A.). N. Y.: 53 Fifth Avenue.

THE MISSIONARY (Pres. Ch., South). Nashville, Tenn.

HERALD OF MISSION NEWS (Ref. Pres. Ch. in N. A.—Covenanter). N. Y.: 325 West 56th street.

MISSIONARY RECORD (Cumb. Pres. Ch.). St. Louis, Missouri: 904 Olive street.

MISSIONARY REPORTS (U. P. Ch. in U. S.). P.: 136 N. 18th street.

MISSION FIELD (Ref. [Dutch] Ch. in America). N. Y.: 25 East 22d street.

MISSION GLEANER (Woman's Board Ref. [Dutch] Ch. in America). N. Y.: 25 East 22d street.

THE MISSIONARY HERALD (A. B. C. F. M.). B.: Congregational House, 1 Somerset street.

LIFE AND LIGHT (Woman's Board of Cong. Ch.). B.: No. 1 Cong. House.

THE GOSPEL IN ALL LANDS (M. E. Ch.). N. Y.: Hunt & Eaton.

WORLD-WIDE MISSIONS (M. E. Church). N. Y.: Methodist Mission Rooms, 150 Fifth Avenue.

HEATHEN WOMAN'S FRIEND (Woman's For. Miss. Soc. M. E. Ch.). B.: 36 Bromfield street.

MISSIONARY REPORTER (M. E. Ch., South). Nashville, Tenn.

THE BAPTIST MISSIONARY MAGAZINE (Amer. Bapt. Miss. Union). B.: 2A Beacon street.

HELPING HAND (Woman's Bapt. For. Miss. Soc., North). B.: 2A Beacon street.

SPIRIT OF MISSIONS (P. E. Ch. in U. S.). N. Y.: Fourth Ave. & 22d St.

THE MISSIONARY JOURNAL (Gen. Synod Evan. Luth. Ch. in U. S. A.). Baltimore, Md.: 1005 W. Lanvale street.

THE MISSIONARY MESSENGER (Gen. Council Evan. Luth. Ch.). P.: 1009 S. Fourth street.

THE MISSIONARY LINK (Woman's Union Miss. Soc. of America). N. Y.: 41 Bible House.

THE STUDENT VOLUNTEER. C.: 80 Institute Place.

LIBERIA (Amer. Col. Soc.). Washington, D. C.: Colonization Building, 450 Penn. Avenue.

THE AFRICAN NEWS. N. Y: 150 5th Avenue.

BIBLE SOCIETY RECORD. N. Y.: Bible House.

THE INDEPENDENT (Monthly Letters from the Mission Field). N. Y.: 130 Fulton street.

THE MEDICAL MISSIONARY RECORD. N. Y.: 118 East 45th street.

THE PRESBYTERIAN RECORD (Pres. Ch in Canada) Montreal, Canada.

THE CANADIAN MISSIONARY LINK (Bapt. Ch. of Canada). Toronto, Canada.

METHODIST MAGAZINE (Meth. Ch. in Canada). Toronto, Canada: Methodist Pub. House.

THE CHURCH MISSIONARY INTELLIGENCER (Ch. Miss. Soc.). L.: Salisbury Square, E. C.
THE CHRONICLE (London Miss. Soc.). L.: 14 Blomfield street.
THE MONTHLY MESSENGER AND GOSPEL IN CHINA (Pres. Ch. of England). L.: 14 Paternoster Square.
BAPTIST MAGAZINE AND MISSIONARY HERALD (Bapt. Miss. Soc.). L.: Alexander & Shepheard, 21 Furnival street.
THE EVANGELICAL MAGAZINE (Organ of Cong. Ch., with Missionary Supplement). L.: Elliot Stock, 62 Paternoster Row, E. C.
WORK AND WORKERS IN THE MISSION FIELD (Wesleyan Miss. Soc.). L.: 17 Bishopsgate Street Within.
WESLEYAN MISSIONARY NOTICES. L.: Wesleyan Mission House, 17 Bishopsgate Street Within.
UNITED METHODIST FREE CHURCH MAGAZINE (U. M. F. Ch.). L.: A. Crombie, 119 Salisbury Square, E. C.
GLEANINGS IN HARVEST FIELDS (Meth. New. Con.). L.: 30 Furnival St., Holborn.
CHINA'S MILLIONS (China Inland Miss.). L.: 4 Pyrland Road, Mildmay.
CENTRAL AFRICA (Universities' Miss. to Cent. Africa). L.: 14 Delahay street, Westminster, S. W.
REGIONS BEYOND (East London Institute). L.: S. W. Partridge & Co., 9 Paternoster Row, E. C. N. Y., C. & T.: Fleming H Revell Co.
SOUTH AMERICAN MISSIONARY MAGAZINE (S. A. Miss. Soc.) L.: Seeley & Co., Essex street.
EVANGELICAL CHRISTENDOM (Evangelical Alliance). L.: J. S. Phillips, 121 Fleet street.
THE REVIEW OF THE CHURCHES. L.: Sampson Low, Marston & Co.
BIBLE SOCIETY MONTHLY REPORTER. L.: 146 Queen Victoria street.
MORAVIAN MISSIONARY REPORTER. L.: 32 Fetter Lane.
NORTH AFRICA (N. A. Miss.). L.:
S. W. Partridge & Co., 9 Paternoster Row.
MISSION FIELD (S. P. G.). L.: 19 Delahay street, Westminster.
ANTI-OPIUM NEWS. L.: Rose Street Corner, Paternoster Square.
THE ZENANA; OR, WOMAN'S WORK IN INDIA (Zenana Bible and Medical Mission). L.: James Nisbet & Co.
INDIA'S WOMEN (Ch. of Eng. Zenana Miss. Soc.). L.: James Nisbet & Co.
MEDICAL MISSIONS AT HOME AND ABROAD. L.: John F. Shaw.
THE FREE CHURCH OF SCOTLAND MONTHLY. L. & N. Y.: T. Nelson & Sons.
THE CHURCH OF SCOTLAND HOME AND FOREIGN MISSION RECORD. Edinburgh: 42 Hanover street.
THE MISSIONARY RECORD OF THE UNITED PRES. CH. Edinburgh: United Presbyterian College Buildings.
THE MISSIONARY HERALD (Irish Pres. Ch.). Belfast, Ireland: 12 May street.
JOURNAL DES MISSIONS EVANGELIQUES. Paris: 102 Boulevard Arago.
ALLGEMEINE MISSIONS-ZEITSCHRIFT. Ed. Warneck. Gütersloh, Germany.
INDIAN EVANGELICAL REVIEW. Calcutta: Traill & Co., 20 British Indian street.
YOUNG MEN OF INDIA. Madras: Young Men's Christian Association.
HARVEST FIELD. Madras: Meth. Epis. Publishing House.
THE CHINESE RECORDER. Shanghai, China: Amer. Pres. Mission Press.
CHINA MEDICAL MISS. JOURNAL (Quarterly). Shanghai, China: Amer. Pres. Miss. Press.
MESSENGER (Chinese Missions). Shanghai, China: Amer. Pres. Miss. Press.
MISSIONARY TIDINGS (Mission Work in Japan). Yokohama, Japan: F. Staniland, 70 Main street.
THE IMPERIAL AND ASIATIC QUARTERLY REVIEW. Oriental University Institute, Woking, Surrey, England.

VI. ENCYCLOPEDIAS AND REPORTS.

THE ENCYCLOPEDIA OF MISSIONS. 2 vols. Edited by Rev. E. M. Bliss. N. Y.: Funk & Wagnalls, 1891. $12.00.
REPORT OF THE LONDON MISSIONARY CONFERENCE (1888). 2 vols. Edited by Rev. James Johnston. N. Y., C., & T.: Fleming H. Revell Co. $2.00 net.
RECORDS OF THE GENERAL CON-

ference of the Protestant Missionaries of China, held at Shanghai, May 7 to 20, 1890. Shanghai: American Mission Press, 1890. $4.00.

Classified Digest of the Records of the Society for the Propagation of the Gospel in Foreign Parts. 1701-1892. L.: S. P. G. Office, 1893.

Proceedings of the Ninth Continental Missionary Conference, held in Bremen in May, 1893.

Fifth General Council Pres. Alliance, Toronto, 1892. Edited by Rev. G. D. Matthews. T.: Hart & Riddell.

Proceedings of Decennial Conference at Bombay, Jan., 1893.

A Manual of Modern Missions. Rev. J. T. Gracey. N. Y., C., & T.: Fleming H. Revell Co., 1893. $1.25.

ANNUAL REPORTS.

(The Annual Reports of the various Missionary Societies and Boards afford the most recent and reliable sources of current information. The following list is a partial one, but the reports mentioned may be considered as essential in any comprehensive survey of Mission progress.)

American Board, 1 Somerset St., B.
Presbyterian Ch. (North) in U. S. A., 53 Fifth Ave., N. Y.
Presbyterian Ch. (South) in the U. S., Nashville, Tenn.
Reformed (Dutch) Ch. in America, 25 E. 22d St., N. Y.
United Pres. Ch. of N. A., 136 N. 18th St., P.
Cumberland Pres. Ch., 904 Olive St., St. Louis, Mo.
Ref. Pres. Ch. (Covenanter) in N. A., 325 West 56th Street, N. Y.
Ref. Pres. General Synod, 2102 Spring Garden St., P.
Baptist Missionary Union, 2A Beacon St., B.
Baptist Southern Convention, Rev. R. J. Willingham, Sec., Richmond, Va.
Meth. Epis. Ch. (North), 150 Fifth Ave., N. Y.
Bishop Taylor's African Mission, 150 Fifth Ave., N. Y.
Meth. Epis. Ch. (South), Nashville, Tenn.
Prot. Epis. For. Miss. Soc., Fourth Ave. and 22d St., N. Y.
Evangelical Luth. Gen. Synod, 1005 W. Lanvale St., Baltimore, Md.
Evangelical Luth. Gen. Council, 4784 Germantown Ave., P.
Arabian Mission, Prof. J. G. Lansing, Treas., New Brunswick, N. J.
American Bible Society, Bible House, N. Y.
American Board Almanac, 1 Somerset St., B.
Pres. Ch. in Canada, Toronto, Canada.
Canada Meth. Miss. Soc., Toronto, Canada.
Canada Bap. Miss. Soc., Woodstock, Ontario, Canada.
Church Missionary Society, Salisbury Square, E. C., L.
London Missionary Society, 14 Blomfield St., L.
Pres. Church of England, 14 Paternoster Square, L.
Baptist Missionary Society, 21 Furnival St., L.
Wesleyan Missionary Society, 17 Bishopsgate Street Within, L.
United Meth. Free Ch., 119 Salisbury Square, L.
Methodist New Connexion, 4 London House-Yard, St. Paul's, L.
Primitive Methodist, 71 Freegrove Road, Holloway, L.
Universities' Mission to Central Africa, 14 Delahay St., Westminster, S. W., L.
China Inland Mission, 4 Pyrland Road, Mildmay, L.
Moravian Missionary Society, 32 Fetter Lane, L.
Archibishop's Mission to Assyrian Christians, 7 Dean's Yard, Westminster Abbey, L.
Soc. for the Prop. of the Gospel, 19 Delahay St., Westminster, L.
Welsh Calvinistic Methodists, 28 Breckfield Road, South Liverpool, Eng.
Friends' For. Miss. Association, Hitchin, Eng.
United Pres. Ch. of Scotland, United Pres. College Buildings, Edinburgh.
Church of Scotland, 42 Hanover St., Edinburgh.
Free Church of Scotland, 15 North Bank St., Edinburgh.

APPENDIX.

PRES. CHURCH OF IRELAND, 12 May St., Belfast, Ireland.

PARIS EVANGELICAL SOCIETY, 102 Boulevard Arago, Paris.

BASEL EVANGELICAL MISSION SOCIETY, Basel, Switzerland.

BERLIN EVANGELICAL MISSIONARY SOCIETY, Berlin, Germany.

RHENISH MISSION, Barmen, Germany.

GOSSNER MISSION, 31 Potsdamer Strasse, Berlin, Germany.

EVANGELICAL LUTHERAN, Leipzig, Germany.

HERMANNSBURG EVANGELICAL LUTHERAN MISSION, Hermannsburg, Germany.

CHURCH OF CHRIST IN JAPAN, F. Staniland, 70 Main St., Yokohama, Japan.

INDEX.

ADHERENTS, native, of Christianity in foreign fields, 35, 338.

Africa: Macedonian appeal of, 105-119; area, 105; population, 106; exploration, 107, 108; present exploration of, 108; languages of, 109; Bible translations, 109; religions of, 110; number of Christians in, 111; modern partition of, 112; area under control of various governments, 112; the Congo Free State, 113; chronological survey of missions, 113-115; various societies conducting work, 114; missionary statistics, 117; slave-trade and rum traffic, 116, 170, 177; trophies of the Gospel, 117; number of converts on the roll of prominent societies, 117; statistics of Presbytery of Corisco for 1891, 46; of Batanga Church for 1892, 46; the influence of Islam, 110, 117; the modern discovery of, 118; the present need of, 118.

Allen, Dr. H. N., first missionary in Korea, 74.

American Board, enters Africa, 114; number of its converts in Africa, 117; enters Turkey, 120; enters Persia, 129; when founded, 307.

Aneityum, memorial tablet to Geddie at, 92.

Archbishop's Mission to Assyrian Christians, when founded, 129; its object, 129; spirit of its work, 162.

Arya Somaj, in India, 104; membership of, 185, 268.

Assam, statistics of missions in, 94.

BAPTIST MISSIONARY SOCIETY (of England), enters Africa, 114; when founded, 307.

Baptist Missionary Union (of America), missions of in Burma, 94; enters Africa, 114.

Basle Missionary Society, enters Africa, 114; enters Persia, 129; missionaries expelled, 129.

Batanga, statistics of Church for 1892, 46.

Beirut, activity of mission press at, 330; medical school at, 331.

Belgium, connection with the Congo Free State, 113.

Berlin Missionary Society, enters Africa, 114; converts in Africa, 117.

Bible, circulation of, in Japan, 71.

Bible translations, number of, 34; Japanese translation, 71; Korean, 75; Chinese, 84; Polynesian, 90; Siamese, 95; Burmese, 94, 95; Karen, 95; African, 109; in Turkish Empire, 125; Persian, 128; Syriac, 130; total circulation of Scriptures during the century, 321.

"Blue Books," Chinese, statements of, 166.

Bradford, Dr. Mary, her medical services in Persia during cholera epidemic, 131.

Brahmo Somaj, in India, 104; description of, 185, 268.

British and Foreign Bible Society, when founded, 307.

Bruce, James, first African explorer, 107.

Buddhism, in Japan, 66; introduced in Korea, 73; in China, 81; in India, 101; special phases of controversy with Christianity, 272-277.

Burma: the Macedonian appeal from, 93-95; absence of caste in, 93; interior tribes of, 94; entrance of Christian missions, 94; statistics of mission work, 94; translation of Bible, 94, 95; native evangelists among the Karens, 94; introduction of opium, 174.

CAREY, WILLIAM, his arrival in India, 101; his instrumentality in forming Baptist Missionary Society, 303; his leadership in modern missions, 304; establishment of his press at Serampore, 328.

Caroline Islands, Church of Rome in, 161; government outrages in, 183.

Central America, state of missions in, 140.

Ceylon, Christians in, 101.

China: Macedonian appeal of, 76-85; population of, 76; population of Chinese Empire, 76; density of population, 76; striking facts about, 77, 78; divisions of language, 84; opening of, 78, 82; references to Christianity in treaties with, 78; status of foreigners in, 79; religions of, 80-82; history of evangelical missions in, 82; mission progress in, 82, 83; missionary statistics of, 82, 83; statistics of Shantung Presbytery for 1891, 44; Dr. Mitchell on the needs of, 54; famines in, 83; translation of Bible in, 84; Romanism in, 161; opium traffic in, 169-171; cultivation of poppy in, 175; enmity to missionaries in, 180; miles of railway in, 315; circulation of mission literature in, 329.

China Inland Mission, statistics of, 84.

Chinese Exclusion Bills, 78, 79.

Churches, number of organized in foreign field, 325.

Church Missionary Society, enters India, 102; early explorations in Africa, 108; establishment in Africa, 114; occupies Uganda, 114; converts in Africa, 117; undertakes mission work in Persia, 129; when founded, 307; contribution acknowledged from mission churches, 338.

Church of Christ in Japan, 69; seeks admission to Presbyterian Alliance, 224.

Clark, Rev. Francis E., quoted, 196.

Coan, Titus, number of converts baptized by, 92.

Colonial expansion, its relation to missions, 314.

Comity, missionary, importance of, 223.

INDEX.

Conflicts of missions, 151–193; with a self-centered Christianity, 153; with rival and intrusive missions, 159; with misrepresentations, 163; with dangerous climates, 166; with political and commercial hindrances, 168; with vice and greed, 178; with governments and hierarchies, 178; with heathenism aroused to self-defense, 184; with religious instincts and training of the native mind, 187; with the powers of evil, 191.

Confucianism, as a religious system, 80; special phases of controversy with Christianity, 272–277.

Confucius, 80.

Congo Free State, liquor traffic in, 170, 177.

Controversies of Christianity with opposing religions, 245–293; intellectual difficulties of, 262; special features of, 270–277; the victory of Christianity anticipated, 284, 285.

Conversions, total number of during 1892 in foreign mission fields, 43, 339.

Converts in foreign mission fields, number of, 35, 338; number of in Japan, 70; in Korea, 74; in China, 83; in Polynesia, 90; in Burma, 94; in Assam, 94; in India, 103; in Africa, 115; in Persia, 132; in South America, 141; difficulties of in embracing Christianity, 187–190.

Coöperation of missionary agencies, 222–228; examples of in China, 223; in Korea and China, 225; recent conference on, 227.

Coptic Church, animosity of, 162.

Corisco Presbytery, statistics of for 1891, 46.

Critics of missions, their frequent misrepresentations, 163; notable answers to, 164.

Cust, Dr. R. M., his researches into the languages of Africa, 109.

DOSHISHA UNIVERSITY, presidents of, 69; its location and number of students, 70.

Duff, Alexander, his work in India, 102; leader of educational movement in India, 327.

Dufferin Training Schools in India, 331.

EAST INDIA COMPANY, its early attitude to missions, 307; lowered its flag to half-mast when Carey died, 308; liberty of evangelization granted by, 311.

Education, place of, in missions, 230–233.

Evangelism, its relation to other missionary agencies, 223–236.

FAIRBAIRN, DR. A. M., quotation from, 10.

Fetichism in Africa, 110.

Fiji, the Training Institution, 91; laws regarding the liquor traffic, 171.

Finances of missions, 218–222; the proper administration of, 219; giving to missions a Christian duty, 220; economy of administration demanded, 221; coöperation desirable, 222.

Free Church of Scotland, 114.

French Evangelical Society (*see* Paris).

Fusan, a treaty port of Korea, 74; occupation of, 75.

GARDINER, ALLEN, his missionary work in South America, 135.
Geary Act, 78, 79.
Geddie, memorial tablet to, at Aneityum, 92.
Gensan, a treaty port of Korea, 74.
Gordon Memorial Institute, 117.
Gospel, the, needed by all men, 201-214; a divine provision, 213.

HAAS, REV. F., begins mission work at Tabriz, 129.
Hawaiian Islands (*see* Sandwich Islands).
Heathen, the, salvability of, 191; their need of Gospel, 192, 202-214; is there hope for? 207-212.
Heishiro, assassination of, in Kyoto, 70.
Hinduism, its religious character and extent, 100, 101; special phases of controversy with Christianity, 272-276.
Hopkins, President Mark, quoted, 196.
Huguenot Seminary, 117.
Hunan, province of, its anti-foreign sentiment, 79.

IBUKA, REV. K., president of Meiji Gakuin, 69.
Income, of missionary societies, 320; possible advance if all church-members contributed, 323, 324; unreached resources in the Church, 324.
India: the Macedonian appeal of, 96-105; area and population of, 96, 97; results of recent census, 97; political history of, 98; establishment of British rule in, 98; material progress in, 99; government system of education, 100; religions of, 100, 101;
entrance of Protestant missions, 101; missionary statistics of, 102, 103; progress of zenana missions, 103; educational and medical statistics, 103; religious changes in, 104; new openings among the lower castes, 104; work of native missionaries, 105; ravages of disease in, 167; opium traffic, 169; liquor traffic, 170; Presbyterian Union in, 224; number of missionary societies in, 311; Third Decennial Conference on Missions, 311; miles of railway in, 315.
Industrial schools, as a missionary agency, 234; usefulness of, 332-335.
International Missionary Union, 321, 322.
Inter-Seminary Missionary Alliances, 322.

JAPAN: a Macedonian telegram from, and its purport, 63-72; political history of, 64; establishment of constitutional government in, 64; population of, 65; geographical extent of, 65; physical features of, 65; arts and sciences in, 66; religions of, 66; Papal Christianity in, 66; opened to intercourse with foreign nations, 66; phenomenal changes in, 66; newspaper press of, 66; elementary education in, 67; entrance of evangelical Christianity, 67; intellectual conflicts in, 68; best educational facilities called for in, 68; ecclesiastical organization in, 69; Church of Christ in, 69, 224; history of Christian missions in, 70; missionary statistics of, 70; translation of Bible in, 71; religious prospects of, 71; its inviting character as a mission field, 71; Romanism in, 160; government hostility to propagation of Gospel, 183; miles of railway in, 315.

Japanese, personal characteristics of, 65; ability of native, 69.

Java, oppressive policy of Dutch in, 170.

Jesuits, their opposition to evangelical missions, 159; political agents in foreign fields, 160; intrigues of in Syria, 161.

John, Dr. Griffith, large circulation of his Chinese tracts, 329.

Judson, Rev. Dr. Adoniram, his arrival in Burma, 94; his translation of Bible into Burmese, 94; his arrival in India, 102.

KANAKA TRAFFIC in Polynesia, 169.

Karens, success of Gospel among, 95; first convert among, 95; jubilee of missions among, 95.

Korea: Macedonian message from, 72-76; area and population of, 72; government of, 72, 73; ethnic peculiarities of, 72; physical features of, 72; foreign relations of, 73; Buddhism introduced into, 73; supplanted by Confucianism, 73; introduction of Roman Catholicism, 73; persecutions in, 73; Papal adherents in, 74; opening of treaty ports in, 74; status of foreigners in, 74; entrance of Gospel into, 74; mission statistics in, 74; missionary societies in, 75; number of missionaries, 75; attitude of government to Christianity, 75; anti-foreign spirit, 183.

Ko-Tha-byu, first Karen convert, 95.

Kozeki, Rev. H., president of Doshisha University, 69.

Kyoto, location of Doshisha in, 70.

LABAREE, REV. DR. BENJAMIN, his revision of Syriac Bible, 130.

Ladd, Prof., visit of, to Japan, 68.

Laos, statistics of Laos Presbytery for 1891 and 1892, 45; the banner presbytery of the Church, 45.

Liquor traffic, in India, 170; in Africa, 170, 177.

Literature, Christian, as a missionary agency, 233; value of, in missions, 328

Livingstone, David, explorations in Africa, 108; his death, 108; tablet of Royal Geographical Society, 108; monuments in Edinburgh and Westminster Abbey, 319.

London Missionary Society, its first missions in the South Seas, 88; enters India, 102; enters Africa, 114; number of converts in Africa, 117; when founded, 307; contribution acknowledged from foreign mission churches, 338.

Lovedale Institute, 117; a prominent example of an industrial school, 333; foundation of similar institution in British East Africa, 333, 334.

Lowell, James Russell, quoted, 39.

MACEDONIAN VISION, present-day meaning of, 55-147; its typical significance, 55-58; a call to foreign missions, 55; its counterpart in present experience of Church, 58; present-day phases of stated, 60–147; the Macedonian call of Japan, 63; of Korea, 72; of China, 76; of the Pacific Islands, 85; of Siam and Burma, 93; of India, 96; of Africa, 105; of the Turkish Empire, 119; of Persia, 127; of South America, 132; of Central America, 139; of Mexico, 140; Macedonian calls still unvoiced, 142; the present urgency of these calls, 143–147.

Malua, Samoan Missionary Seminary at, 91.

Martyn, Henry, his arrival in India, 102; his work in Persia, 128; translation of New Testament into Persian, 128; his death, 129.

Martyrs, missionary, in the South Sea Islands, 92.

Matheson, Rev. George, critical remarks on his "Distinctive Messages of the Old Religions," 278, 279.

Mecca closed to missions, 309.

Medical Missionary Societies, when founded, 330; number of, 331; number of medical missionaries in the world, 331; heroic character of their work, 331, 332.

Meiji Gakuin, native president of, 69.

Methodist missions in India, statistics of 1892, 104.

Methods, missionary, 228–236; analysis of, 228; comparison of, 230–236.

Mexico: Macedonian appeal of, 139–142; establishment of Protestant missions, 140; statistics of mission work, 141; attitude of the government, 141; material progress of, 141; Romanism in, 161.

Micronesia (*see* Pacific, Islands of the).

Mirza Ibrahim, his martyrdom in Persia, 130.

Missionaries, number of, in the world, 35; in Japan, 70; in Korea, 75; in China, 82; in Burma, 94; in India, 102; in Africa, 115; in South America, 138; in Mexico, 141.

Missions, the true theory of, 199–214; motive in, 201; object of, 201; necessity of, 202; result desired, 214; aim of, not merely to bear witness to the truth, 215; their larger purpose, 215; the witness in its fullness, 217; the special message which they bring to the heathen world, 285–290; indirect results of, 344, 345.

Mitchell, Rev. Dr. Arthur, quoted, 54.

Mohammedanism, in India, 101; in Africa, 110, 117; opposition of to Christian missions in Turkey, 180; special phases of controversy with Christianity, 272–277; recent effort to introduce in America, 281.

Monier-Williams, Sir M., quoted, 244.

Moravian Missionary Society, early entrance into Africa, 113; enters South America, 135; pioneers in missions, 303.

NATIVE AGENCY, its importance in missions, 236–242; the problems involved in, 238; Church organization as a feature of, 239; its growing power as an evidence of mission success, 336; extensive coöperation of,

336; founding missionary societies, 337; contribution of native churches, 338.
Natives, number of engaged in mission work, 35, 336; prominent positions occupied by, 336.
Neesima, Joseph Hardy, 69.
Nestorian Church, Archbishop's Mission to, 129.
Netherland Society, when founded, 307.
New Guinea, native missionary service in, 91.
New Hebrides, trade in intoxicants and firearms in, 170; restrictive legislation toward, 170; statistics of mission work in, 343.
New Lovedale, its foundation, 333, 334.
Norfolk Island, St. Barnabas College, 91.

OCEANIA (*see* Pacific, Islands of the).
Opium traffic, 169-176; in China, 171; protest of British Parliament against, 172; in India, 173; in Upper Burma, 174; arguments of those who favor, 175; its evil effects, 172-176.

PACIFIC, ISLANDS OF THE: Macedonian appeal of, 85-93; geographical divisions of, 86; entrance of evangelical missions, 87, 88; number of islands and population, 89; extension of missions among, 89; missionary statistics, 90; groups practically Christianized, 90; prominent missionary training-schools in, 90; activity of native missionaries, 91; native contributions, 91; missionary martyrs of, 92; islands still to be evangelized, 92; labor traffic in, 169; great ingathering in Sandwich Islands in 1838, 346.
Paris Evangelical Missionary Society, enters Africa, 114; converts in Africa, 117.
Park, Mungo, his explorations in Africa, 107.
Parker, Dr., first medical missionary to China, 331.
Parsees in India, 101.
Paton, Dr. J. G., his testimony to mission progress in the New Hebrides, 343.
Patteson, Bishop, his martyrdom, 345.
Perry, Commodore, expedition of, to open Japan, 66.
Persia: Macedonian appeal of, 127-132; area and population, 127; prominent races, 127; religions, 128; translation of New Testament by Martyn, 128; various missions in, 129; persecutions, 130; martyrdom of Mirza Ibrahim, 130; Syriac translation, 130; ravages of cholera in 1892, 131; mission statistics, 132; Archbishop's Mission in, 129, 162; persecution in, 183.
Pfander, Rev. C. G., missionary in Persia, 129.
Plutschau, a pioneer missionary in India, 101.
Plymouth Brethren, their relation to evangelical missions, 162, 163.
Polynesia (*see* Pacific, Islands of the).
Ponape, Roman Catholics in, 161.
Presbyterian churches, number of non-contributing, 156.
Presbyterian Church (North), first missions in India, 102; converts in Africa, 117; Persian mission transferred to, 129.

Presbyterian Church of Scotland, first missions to India, 102.
Presbyterian Union, in Japan, 69, 224; in India, 224; in Korea, 225; in China, 225.
Press, Mission, issues of at Shanghai, 329; at Beirut, 330.
Problems of missions, 197-242; problem of theory, 199; of finance, 218; of coöperation, 222; of method, 228; of native development, 236.
Providence of God favors missions, 305, 306; by opening the world to the entrance of the missionary, 308-313; by developing colonial enterprise, 314; by affording them every facility, 315; by the advancement of Oriental scholarship, 316; by removing hindrances, 317.
Punjab, Church of Rome in, 161.

RELIGION, definition of, 247, 248.
Religions, false, 248-254; genesis and development of, 248, 249; historic relation of to revealed truth, 250, 251; traces of original truth in, 253; idealized representations of, 256, 257; characteristics of, 258, 259; mission of Christianity to, 259; spirit of Christianity toward, 260; serious nature of conflict with, 262; Christianity must never compromise with, 264; special message of Christianity to, and various replies of, 270-277; power of, illustrated, 282; message of Christianity to, indicated in detail, 285-293; failure of, conspicuous, 291.
Rhenish Missionary Society enters India, 114.
Roman Catholic Missions, opposition of, 159; status of, in Japan, 160; in China, 161; in the Caroline Islands, 161; in the Punjab, 161; in Syria, 161; in Mexico, 161; in Uganda, 162.
Ross, Rev. John, his missionary work in Korea, 74; his translation of New Testament into Korean language, 74.

SAMOAN ISLANDS, the contribution of natives to London Missionary Society in 1890, 91.
Sanatoria, missionary, 168.
Sandwich Islands, Pentecostal ingathering at, 346.
Scholars, in higher educational institutions, 35; in village mission schools, 35; in mission Sabbath-schools, 325; total of pupils in mission institutions, 326.
Schools, mission, their importance and proper function, 228-236.
Scottish Mission Society, when founded, 307.
Seoul, mission churches in, 74; a treaty port, 74; baptism of first convert, 74.
Shanghai, the conference of 1890, 84, 85; action of conference with reference to Bible translations, 84; call for 1000 missionaries, 85; activity of Mission Press at, 329.
Shantung Presbytery, statistics of for 1891, 44.
Shintoism, 66.
Siam: Macedonian appeal from, 93-96; religions of, 93; progress of Gospel in, 95; missionary statistics of Laos field, 45; attitude of Siamese government toward missions, 95; Siamese translation of Bible, 95.
Singapore, Chinese coolies at, 169.

Slave-trade in Africa, duty of civilized governments with reference to, 170.
Smith, Dr. Eli, his work in translation of Arabic Bible, 330.
Smith, Dr. Judson, quoted, 296.
Societies, missionary, number of, in the world, 35; in Japan, 70; in Korea, 75; in China, 82; in Burma, 94; in India, 102; when founded, 307; growth of, 317; rate of increase, 320; advances in income, 320; those having annual income of over a million, 320; growth and number of woman's societies, 321; growth of native, 337.
Somerville, Dr., his use of Pocket Atlas as Prayer-book, 318.
South America: Macedonian appeal of, 132–139; area and population, 133; various races, 133; political divisions, 133; natural features, 133; religious history, 134; spirit of Papal Church, 134; missionary societies, 135; religious needs of, 137; dearth of missionaries in various states, 137; statistics of mission work, 138.
Southey, quoted, 211.
South Sea Islands (*see* Pacific, Islands of the).
Speer, Robert E., quoted, 296.
Stations, mission, number of in the world, 325.
Statistics, of foreign mission work in the world, 35, 320; of mission converts in 1892, 43, 339; of missions in Japan, 70; in Korea, 75; in China, 82, 83; in Polynesia, 90, 91; in Siam and Burma, 94; in India, 102; in Africa, 115, 117; in the Turkish Empire, 125; in Persia, 132; in South America, 138; in Mexico, 141; of mission stations in the world, 325; of native churches and helpers, 325; of Sabbath-schools in foreign fields, 325.
Stewart, Rev. Dr. James, his work at Lovedale and as founder of New Lovedale, 333, 334.
Storrs, Rev. Richard S., quoted, 150.
Students' Volunteer Movement, 321.
Stundists, persecution of, 183.
Success of Foreign Missions, 297–346; how estimated, 298; characteristics of, 299; indicated by providential coöperation, 305, 306; by multiplication of missionary agencies, 317; by establishment of the mission plant in foreign lands, 325; by introduction of Gospel leaven throughout the heathen world, 335; by coöperation of native agencies and growth of spontaneity in the mission churches, 336; by actual conversions, 338, 339; indirect results of, 344; great ingatherings, 346.
Syria, statistics of Tripoli field for 1891, 43; Jesuit intrigue in, 161.
Syrian Protestant College, medical department of, 331.

Taoism, 81.
Taylor, Dr. J. Hudson, his statement in regard to opium in China, 172.
Telugu Mission, large number baptized on first Sabbath of July, 1878, 346.
Testimony of eminent men as to the value of missions, 164.
Theory of missions, the true, 200.

Thibet, still inaccessible to missionaries, 309.

Thoburn, Bishop J. M., quoted, 10, 30; his report of progress in India, 341.

Tokyo, newspaper press of, 66; missionary statistics of, 70; number of students in, 71.

Treaty rights of missionaries, 180.

Tripoli, mission statistics of, for year 1891, 44.

Turkish Empire: Macedonian appeal of, 119-127; political history, 119; condition of Christian races, 119, 120; perils of Moslem converts to Christianity, 120; entrance of Protestant missions, 120; progress of the Christian races, 121; spirit of Islam, 121; obstructive policy of Turkish government, 121, 122; the coming conflict between Islam and Christianity, 122; struggle for religious liberty, 123; Bible translations in, 125; statistics of missions, 125; American colleges, 125; progress of evangelical literature, 125; relations of the American churches to missionary enterprise, 126; anti-missionary spirit manifested, 180; power of ecclesiastics in, 184.

UGANDA, occupied by Church Missionary Society, 114; martyrs of, 117; Romanism in, 162; British protectorate declared, 312; reception of New Testament in, 342, 343; Bishop Tucker preaches to an audience of 5000, 343.

Underwood, Dr. H. G., his baptism of first convert in Korea, 74; his Korean Dictionary, 75.

United Presbyterian Church (American), 114; converts in Africa, 117.

United Presbyterian Church (Scotch), 114.

Universities' Mission, 114.

VAN DYCK, DR. C. V. A., his work in translation of Arabic Bible, 330.

WESLEYAN MISSIONARY SOCIETY, entrance into India, 102; converts in Africa, 117.

Williams, Dr. S. Wells, founder of mission literature in China, 329.

Wishard, Mr. L. D., his report of Y. M. C. A. in foreign fields, 337.

Witness-bearing to the truth, the true meaning of, as an aim of missions, 214-217.

XAVIER, FRANCIS, in Japan, 66.

YOUNG MEN'S CHRISTIAN ASSOCIATIONS, 321; in foreign fields, 337.

ZENANA MISSIONS, their progress in India, 103; importance of, 325, 326.

Ziegenbalg, a pioneer missionary in India, 101.

www.ingramcontent.com/pod-product-compliance
Lightning Source LLC
Chambersburg PA
CBHW020316240426
43673CB00039B/825